A

VIEW OF CONGREGATIONALISM,

ITS

PRINCIPLES AND DOCTRINES;

THE

TESTIMONY OF ECCLESIASTICAL HISTORY IN ITS FAVOR, ITS PRACTICE, AND ITS ADVANTAGES.

BY

GEO. PUNCHARD.

WITH AN INTRODUCTORY ESSAY,

BY R. S. STORRS, D.D.

THIRD EDITION, REVISED AND ENLARGED.

BOSTON:
CONGREGATIONAL BOARD OF PUBLICATION,
16 TREMONT TEMPLE.
1856.

CAMBRIDGE:
ALLEN AND FARNHAM, STEREOTYPERS AND PRINTERS.

TO

JOHN PUNCHARD, ESQ.,

SALEM, MASS.,

MY AGED AND REVERED PARENT,

WHOSE INSTRUCTIONS AND EXAMPLE FIRST TAUGHT ME THE VALUE OF THE SYSTEM HERE ADVOCATED — THESE PAGES ARE RESPECTFULLY AND AFFECTIONATELY

DEDICATED.

PREFACE

TO THE FIRST EDITION.

THIS work is designed to answer the inquiry, WHAT IS CONGREGATIONALISM — IN THEORY AND IN PRACTICE?

It accordingly contains an exposition and discussion of the fundamental PRINCIPLES of the system; a statement and defence of its more important DOCTRINES respecting church order and discipline; the testimony of ECCLESIASTICAL HISTORY, that such for substance was the polity of the Primitive Churches; an enumeration and explanation of the ecclesiastical PRACTICES of Congregationalists; and a development of some of the prominent ADVANTAGES of this system over all others.

No one can be more sensible of the difficulty of executing such a plan, than the writer now is; had he been equally so before he undertook the task, it probably would have saved him the trouble of this preface.

An apology for the work may perhaps be found in its history. About three years since, the writer was appointed by the Clerical Association of which he is a member, to prepare a dissertation upon Congregationalism. This he was requested to publish; but, though the result of considerable reading and reflection, it was regarded by him as too immature to be offered to the public. A renewal of the request of the Association at their next meeting, induced the author to re-write the essay and to preach the substance of it to the people of his charge. The unsolicited opinion of intelligent parishioners, who were ignorant of the doings of the Association, led to the belief that the substance of the discourses might prove acceptable to the denomination generally. A revision was accordingly begun. This revision led to a further examination of authorities, a multiplication of topics, a more extended range of discussion, and ultimately, to the decision to submit this volume to the judgment of the public.

The work has been written, not for the wise, nor for those exactly who are simple; but, mainly, for that large class of persons who occupy the intermediate space between the learned and the ignorant.

The English reader will occasionally find a word or phrase in Latin or Greek; but rarely unaccompanied by a translation, and never, it is believed, in such a position as to break the sense of the sentence.

It is no part of the author's plan to make war on other denominations: yet, he has felt constrained to speak freely, though it is hoped kindly, of those from whom he differs.

That he has fallen into no errors, in a work so abounding in distinct and controverted topics, is, perhaps, more than can be reasonably expected; but, he has certainly used his utmost care to avoid mistakes. The opinions expressed in these pages may possibly be somewhat modified by further investigation and reflection; but as they now appear, they are not the offspring of haste, nor, it is confidently believed, of mere prejudice.

The Appendix contains numerous articles of considerable importance to the illustration of the general subject of Congregationalism.

Adopting the language of the learned and excellent Samuel Mather, in his "Apology for the Liberties of the Churches in New England," the author commends his labors to the favor of the churches and to the blessing of God: — "I am far from assuming any thing of authority to myself in the following sheets. If I have collected the sense of others right, and well epitomized their thoughts, which are variously dispersed, and reduced them to a clear and natural order, I shall think it sufficient."

PLYMOUTH, N. H., July, 1840.

PREFACE

TO THE SECOND EDITION.

In publishing a second edition of this little work, the author would first express his grateful acknowledgments for the unexpected kindness and favor with which the first edition was received. And as the best return that he can make for this, he has endeavored to render the present edition more deserving of public confidence and regard. To this end, it has been thoroughly revised, and large portions of it entirely re-written; the range of discussion has been considerably extended, and the number of distinct topics multiplied; the usages of our churches have been more particularly detailed; a number of new forms of letters missive, etc., have been inserted, and the most approved modes of transacting ecclesiastical business more distinctly described. The whole amount of new matter which has been thus added, is equal to about one third of the entire volume.

It is hoped that the book will now be found a guide, both safe and complete, however humble, to all that pertains to the principles, doctrines, and practice of the Congregational denomination.

That the blessing of the great Head of the Church may attend this, and every effort to awaken and enlighten the public mind respecting the nature and design of a christian church — is the heart's desire and prayer to God of the author.

November 3, 1843.

PREFACE

TO THE THIRD EDITION.

At the request of the Congregational Board of Publication, the author has carefully revised this work; re-written portions of it; and he thinks, somewhat increased its value as a book of reference on the subject of church polity.

Boston, July 22, 1856.

CONTENTS.

APPENDIX.

INDEX.

INTRODUCTORY NOTICE.

It is a matter of devout congratulation, that, among the friends of Congregationalism, the scriptural polity of the church is now becoming the subject of more serious and thorough investigation, than for many bygone years. Unhappily, it has been too long regarded as a matter of insufficient importance to engage the earnest attention of the churches, if not also as positively interfering with the prosperity of religion; nor is it too much to affirm, that an overweening confidence has been reposed in the common-sense, the sound judgment, and sterling piety of the Congregational churches, as insuring to them, in perpetuity, a system of government, so strongly recommended by the purity of its principles, the clearness of its doctrines, the simplicity of its rules, and the consonance of its spirit with the meek breathings of the gospel. But the day of slumber is passing away. Our invaluable religious immunities are coming again to be rightly appreciated. The spirit of Puritanic times is reviving. The labors accomplished, and the sufferings endured by our fathers in defence of a scriptural organization and discipline of the churches, are remembered with increasing veneration and gratitude; and the solemn question, 'What will the Lord have us to do,' for the maintenance of the primitive "order of the gospel,' is agitated with an earnestness, and to an extent, that has called forth prompt and able responses from several of the watchmen on the walls of Zion. UPHAM and POND, BACON and MITCHELL — not to mention others — have successfully devoted a portion of their strength to the enlightenment of the public mind, and the revival of the better days of New England Congregationalism, when the Mathers, and Cottons, and Wises, stood forth as its expounders and defenders. But there remaineth much land yet to be possessed. Ignorance, fanaticism, and superstition, are not yet driven from the field. Other leaders of the "sacramental host" are called for by the exigencies of the times. They can hardly be multiplied too much. The energies of the churches need to be aroused and judiciously directed, if the hopes of the fathers and the aims of their most enlightened sons are ever to be accomplished. The appearance of every new and skilful champion in this cause, will therefore be hailed with pleasure. The field before him is wide. To retain what has been already gained, demands great firmness and prudence. To make further conquests, and secure them against future intrusion, requires high resolve and heroic courage. Antagonistical principles are everywhere to be met and combated; and their defenders, relying on that love of variety and change which is wrought so deeply into the constitution of man, press onward with bold hearts, and confident expectation of establishing themselves in possession of the same ground once covered exclusively with the trophies of Congregational and evangelical achievement. Their efforts are commensurate with their hopes. Their pulpits abound with earnest discussions — their presses teem with elaborate arguments — their measures are all conceived and carried out with an address that indicates a determination to put to flight the imperfectly organized, and unmarshalled hosts of Congregationalism. Nor are they to be blamed for their conscientious adherence to principles they believe to be scriptural, nor for any honorable efforts they make to extend those principles. Their consistency is worthy of honor — and more than that — of imitation. Would that the friends of Congregationalism might emulate their zeal, and furnish to the world equally bright examples of devotedness, in defence of their distinguishing views of church polity. But how rarely, in point of fact, is "the order, the discipline, and the worship of the church," discussed in a Congregational pulpit! How long the term of years, in which no volume came from the press, explaining and vindicating the principles, doctrines, and usages of our churches! How few, jejune, and powerless are the measures that have been adopted to secure the influence of those principles over any portion of the public mind! There is a reason assigned for this; but is it defensible? If the weightier matters of the law may not be omitted, are we justified in neglecting to pay our tithes of the mint, anise, and cummin? If the great doctrines and duties of vital godliness are of paramount importance, are the doctrines and duties involved in the scriptural regulation of the churches of no importance at all? Let every thing have its appropriate place in the church of the living God! True — it will not be inquired in the day of judgment — 'belonged you to this denomination or that — were you an Episcopalian, a Presbyterian, or a Congregationalist?' but will not the amount of individual spirituality, and usefulness, be inquired after? and is there no intimate connection between the improvement of the heart, and the observance of the most scriptural form of church government and discipline? It is the firm conviction of many, that the symmetry and perfection of the Christian's character depend in no slight degree, on his acquaintance with the teachings of the Holy Spirit on "the order of God's house," and his obedience thereto. And it is under this conviction, that I cheerfully venture a compliance with the suggestion of the beloved and respected author of the following pages, to associate my own name with his, by this brief introductory notice, in an earnest enforcement of the claims of this subject, on the renewed and prayerful attention of the whole body of Congregational ministers and churches. The volume has evidently been prepared with great care and labor. It embodies in a succinct form, and in regular order, the distinguishing features of Congregationalism, as hitherto received by the great body of our denomination, whether in our own or other lands; and discriminates fairly between this and other systems of ecclesiastical government, that claim, like it, the Holy Scriptures as their basis. It is a work well adapted to the existing wants of the Congregational community, and conducted throughout in a spirit of candor and faithfulness that all must admire, whether or not they approve of the conclusions at which it arrives. Its highly popular form of discussion, its simple yet elegant style, together with its studied brevity and fulness, recommend it strongly to the widest circulation.

Finally, if Congregationalism finds much to commend it, in its consonance with the genius of Christianity, and with the design of Revelation to place all men on an equality of rights and privileges before God, and lead them to look beyond all forms, and penetrate the mysteries of godliness — it finds not a little additional commendation to US, in the fact that it stood approved to the judgment of the Fathers of New England, men of whom the old world was not worthy, and of whom the new world thinks not highly enough — men of learning, zeal, and self-sacrificing devotion — men who boldly threw off from them the manacles of religious despotism, and every shred of the false faith protected by it, pushing to the utmost their researches into the oracles of God, and receiving his testimony without equivocation or demur, even at the cost of expatriation and the loss of all the pleasures of kindred and home. We honor their memory, we hold fast to the inheritance they bequeathed us, and sell not our birthright for the "mess of pottage."

RICHARD S. STORRS.

BRAINTREE, July 20, 1840.

CONGREGATIONALISM.

PRELIMINARY REMARKS.

God has always had in this apostate world "a seed" to serve him. This seed has been variously called — "the Sons of God" — "the People of God" — "the Church of God" — "the Church, or the body of Christ." In order to serve God more efficiently, his people have always had some visible organization, and have been subjected to some rules of order, discipline, and worship, varying with the different circumstances and necessities of the Church and the world. To these rules we give the general name of Church Polity.

The polity of the Patriarchal Churches partook of the simplicity of that age, and was adapted to the migratory habits of those pious nomades. The family of each believing patriarch was a sort of congregational church. The head of the family was its prophet and priest: he announced the revealed purposes of heaven, he gave religious instruction, exercised godly discipline — commanding his children and his household to keep the way of the Lord, and to do justice and judgment — and officiated at the family altar, presenting sacrifices, and offering prayers to the Most High God.* Such appears to have been the Patriarchal Polity: and but for the growing wickedness of man, it might, for aught that we can see, have continued for substance to the present day.†

In the days of Enos there may have been some modification of this family-church order. We are told that "then began men to call upon the name of the Lord," — Gen. 4: 26; or, as the margin reads, "then began men *to be called by the name of the Lord.*" At this period of the world, family religion may have so far degenerated, as to have made it necessary for the pious members of different households to separate themselves from their irreligious kindred and to meet together in order to worship God. But, notwithstanding this attempt to revive religion, iniquity continued to abound, until the "holy seed" was found only in the family of Noah — perhaps in Noah alone. After the Flood, the Church of God was reduced to the family order again; and the world began anew. But human nature remained unaltered: and, for the greater security of the "godly seed," God chose the family of Abram; called them from their native land and their idolatrous kindred; made a covenant with them; and instituted the rite of circumcision. This

---

* Compare Gen. 4: 3–5. 8: 20–22. 12: 7, 8. 13: 3–5. 14: 14, 18–20. 15: 17: 18: 19. 20: 7. 26: 24, 25. 27: 26–40. 35: 1–15. 49: 1–28. Job 1: 1–5.

† See Rom. 16: 5. Col. 4: 15. Philemon 2.

family-church was thus strongly guarded against the corrupting influences of the age, and its continuance as a pure church of God rendered more secure. The households of Abraham, of Isaac, and of Jacob all appear in sacred history as religious communities — churches — assembling together and worshipping God under the direction of their respective heads, and in conformity with the established rites and order of the Abrahamic Church.

It had long been the revealed purpose of God, to set apart from all the nations of the earth the descendants of Abraham, Isaac, and Jacob, as the depositaries of his truth — as his visible Church in the world. When the time for the accomplishment of this purpose had arrived, and Jehovah was about to remove his chosen people to the promised land, there to be settled compactly as an agricultural people, he saw fit to re-organize his Church, and to adapt it to its new position. To prevent his people from amalgamating with the surrounding nations, and to accomplish his purposes of truth and mercy in and through them, he gave the Israelites "ordinances of divine service," as remarkable for their number and minuteness as the previous ordinances had been for their extreme simplicity.*

These ordinances had their designed effect, in making the Israelites a separate and peculiar people. But, as the nation degenerated in its religious character, these outward rites and ceremonies were perverted from their intended use, and came at length

* See Exodus, Chaps. xxv–xxx. Lev. Chaps. i–vii. xxi–xxvii. 1 Chron. xxii–2 Chron. vii.

to be regarded as constituting the very substance of true religion, instead of being but "a shadow of good things to come, and not the very image of the things." Thus it was when Christ appeared in the world: the professed people of God had wellnigh lost all the power of religion in their devotion to its forms.

There seems to have been, however, a prevailing belief, that the Messiah might introduce some changes into the existing institutions and ordinances of religion. Accordingly, upon the introduction of Christianity, men were taught that the old dispensation was but a type and shadow of the new; that its significant rites and ceremonies were intended to point the mind towards a dispensation in which the shadow should be exchanged for the substance, the type for the anti-type. It was announced by the Divine Author of Christianity, that the hour was coming, yea and then was, when, neither in the mountain of Samaria, nor in Jerusalem alone, should men worship the Father acceptably: or, in other words, that the true worshippers of God were no longer to be confined to any of the existing forms and rites of religious service; the grand desideratum of acceptable worship being spirituality and truth. — See John 4: 23–26. In accordance with this doctrine, the private house, the open field, the lake shore, were all made places of public worship by Christ and his apostles, with religious forms remarkable chiefly for their entire simplicity.

The order and discipline of the first Christian Church were extremely simple. The same is true of all those churches which were erected by the apostles and their fellow laborers. They were all copies of the Divine original at Jerusalem. But, when the fervency of their first love had subsided, and outward peace and prosperity had softened and ungirt the spirits of Christians, then worldliness and ambition rapidly undermined the apostolic polity of the churches, and erelong built upon the ruins thereof a splendid hierarchy, of materials partly Jewish and partly Pagan. Doctrinal errors and unchristian practices followed in the train and paved the way for "the Man of Sin."

The establishment of the tyrannous polity of Rome was succeeded by a dreary night of a thousand years.

At the dawn of the Lutheran Reformation, the constitution of the church attracted much less attention than the gross religious errors, and the infamous superstitions of Romanism. And so engrossed were the Reformers in purifying the church of these evils, that they overlooked for a time, the sources through which many of these evils had entered the church. If the connection between a pure and simple church order and a sound religious faith and practice occurred to them, they acted upon the common principle, of reforming the greatest abuses first; leaving the lesser ones for after consideration. An apology for their course was found in the ignorance and prejudices of the common people, and the fear of fanatical excesses.*

---

* See Luther's Tract on the regulation of the external matters of the churches. — *Milner*, Century 16th, ch. 8.

The regulations respecting the constitution, government, form

There was, perhaps, another more serious impediment to a thorough reform: I refer to the connection of the Church with the State. The Reformers were more or less dependent on the princes and nobles of this world; and these are generally the last men to desire simplicity in the order and worship of the church. Whether, indeed, those princes who favored the Reformation would have countenanced a reform in doctrine and morals even, had this been connected with a thorough reformation in church polity, is very doubtful. Wickliffe, the pioneer of the Reformation, seems to have lost the support of his prince and of the nobility when he started sentiments which countenanced such a reformation. And whether Luther would have succeeded in his labors without the protection of Frederic, the Elector of Saxony; whether the Reformation in England could have been carried so far, without the concurrence of Henry VIII. and Edward VI.; whether what was done could have been accomplished except by the coöperation of these princes, without an entire overturn of their respective governments, is very improbable. However this may be, one thing seems evident, that while these princes supported the Reformers in their partial labors, they held them back from a thorough and radical reform of the Church — from reinstating it in its primitive simplicity, and independency of the State.

---

and mode of public worship in the Lutheran Church were not drawn up until 1527. — *Mosheim*, Vol. III. p. 39, 40, Harper's Edition.

The Reformation may be said to have commenced as early as 1517. The German Liturgy was not, however, completed until 1543. — *Mackenzie's Life of Calvin*, p. 77.

In republican Switzerland, however, the Reformation was more of a popular movement: the people were consulted, and they acted; and their ecclesiastical rights were more fully restored, and the reformation of the church was more thorough than in Germany or in England.*

It was not generally until men began to experience the extreme difficulty of preserving purity of doctrine and practice under worldly and unscriptural establishments, that their thoughts were turned earnestly towards a reformation in the general polity of the church. The philosophy of the connection between church order and church purity seems not to have attracted much attention prior to the latter part of the sixteenth century. Yet this is remarkable, since all previous history had shown, that a simple form of ecclesiastical government and purity of religious faith and practice had ever been intimately associated.

The English Puritans, if not the discoverers of this connection, were the men who acted most fully upon the discovery. The religious ancestors of the Congregationalists of New England, of all men who ever lived, had, perhaps, most occasion to study church polity in all its connections and bearings. Thrown out of the church which they regarded as

---

* D'Aubigne, in his elegant History of the Reformation, says: "Luther had restored the Bible to the Christian community — Zwingle went further — he restored their *rights*. This is a characteristic feature of the Reformation in Switzerland. The maintenance of sound doctrine was intrusted, under God, *to the people*; and recent events have shown that the people can discharge that trust better than the priests or the pontiffs." — Vol. III. p. 251.

the mother of them all; driven to a land of strangers; left to begin the world anew, and to decide what form of ecclesiastical government they would adopt; being men of piety, and learning, and experience; familiar with the Scriptures, and well read in the history of the world; conversant with the treasures of antiquity — with the writings of the Fathers and with classic authors; having had great experience of the workings of an ecclesiastical establishment in their native land, and having, while in Holland, opportunities to examine the polity of the Reformed Churches on the Continent; and feeling the deep responsibility of laying aright the religious foundations of a new world: — under such circumstances it was natural, it was unavoidable, that the constitution, discipline, and worship of the church should arrest, and fix, and for a time all but absorb their attention. If men in their circumstances could not and did not study to advantage this great subject, then may we well despair of ever having it thoroughly and impartially investigated. Our fathers did study the science of church polity as no other men ever did; and the fruits of their study New England and the world at large have long been gathering. For many years after the settlement of New England, the subject of church order and government received much attention; some have thought too much. But he who has well weighed the bearings of this question upon the interests of pure religion, will be of a different opinion.

DECLINE OF CONGREGATIONALISM — CAUSES.

However it may have been in the days of our fathers, certain it is that for many years past this subject has excited comparatively little interest among the Congregational descendants of the Puritans. Various causes have contributed to this state of things. Among the more prominent, perhaps, may be named:

1. The anxiety of Congregationalists to unite different denominations in benevolent, religious associations.

To accomplish this, there has been a readiness on their part to keep out of sight, and even to sacrifice, their denominational peculiarities. However benevolent the design of these Unions, the influence of them has been injurious to Congregationalism. Other denominations, while acting to a limited extent with us in these Associations, have kept up their separate and denominational organizations. But we have had nothing of this sort by which to propagate our peculiar views. And though Congregationalists have furnished a large proportion of the funds of these Unions, yet, as a denomination, they have derived probably the least benefit from them. They have even in some instances, with an unauthorized generosity, yielded the entire advantage to other denominations.

"What then," it may be asked, "shall we give up all united attempts to save men, through fear of injuring Congregationalism?" If the question were — Shall we save men *or* promote the interests of Congregationalism? it would be easy to answer. This, however, is not the question. It is — Shall we, *in connection with* our efforts to save and benefit men, endeavor to promote the interests of our most scriptural and excellent system of church government; or shall we utterly disregard this?

Our denomination have contributed largely of money and of mind to erect and sustain churches at the West; yet scarce one in fifty of these is upon the Congregational Platform.* Scores of young men, professedly Congregationalists, have gone out from our Theological Seminaries, educated by the aid of Congregational funds, and thrown themselves into the bosom of the Presbyterian Church. And why have they done this? — "To do good!" But could they not have done good and yet have retained their Puritan principles? Have these principles made New England an intellectual and moral gar-

---

* "It is computed that 400 churches, or more, have been gathered in the West, for the Presbyterian Church, by the benevolence of Connecticut alone. And I have seen it stated by high Presbyterian authority, that not less than 1500 of their churches are essentially Congregational in their origin and habits." —*Mitchell's Guide to the Principles and Practice of the New England Churches*, p. 71, note.

It must be borne in mind that these Preliminary Remarks were written in 1840 and revised in 1843, since which time there has been more attention given to Congregationalism as a simple, scriptural, and beautiful system of church polity than for a long period prior to those dates. But, as most of the causes here assigned for the decline of Congregationalism, still continue to operate, though some of them with much less force than formerly, and as a matter of historical record, I have retained the chapter nearly as originally written.

den! and yet shall we be told, that "they will not answer for the South and West?" Had New England men and money carried New England principles of church government wherever they went, and boldly and faithfully sustained them, other sections of our country would now, it is verily believed, more nearly resemble the land of the Pilgrims.

2. Another cause of this state of things may be, the operation of the principle on which some or all of our Theological Seminaries in New England have been conducted. Though endowed and sustained by Congregationalists, these seminaries have been equally accessible to Protestants of all denominations. To this, as a general principle, there certainly can be no objection, if evidence of piety be made an essential requisite for admission. But if, in connection with this admission of different denominations, there must be any hesitation on the part of the teachers to advocate openly, thoroughly, and earnestly, Congregational Principles of Church Government, the influence of this policy cannot be otherwise than injurious to our own denomination. If young men of other denominations please to avail themselves of the advantages of our institutions, they should be welcomed, and kindly treated; but should hear all the doctrines of the Puritan Congregationalists of New England faithfully and earnestly advocated. But if the Professors of any of our Theological Seminaries are even *apparently* indifferent to our church polity, we need not be surprised to find their pupils *really* so.

3. Another cause of the apathy of our churches on this subject, may be found in the impression that

no efforts are required to protect and promote our excellent system of church government. It has perhaps been thought, that intelligent New England men must, of course, prefer, to every other system, that to which they have been accustomed from their childhood; especially, as it has so many incontrovertible arguments to support it, and is so perfectly in accordance with the spirit of our free institutions. That, however, must be a good cause indeed which will take care of itself; a better cause than this world has yet known. The truth is, while Congregationalists have been sleeping in their fancied security, other denominations have not been idle. Other systems of church order have been advocated and urged with a zeal and confidence which, contrasted with our own apathy, have been as arguments for them and against us.

4. Another cause of the state of things of which we complain, is found in the neglect of our pastors to preach upon this subject, and in the dearth of modern books upon Congregationalism.

The fathers of New England felt the importance of keeping the community awake to this subject. They therefore frequently proclaimed from the pulpit and published from the press the principles of Congregationalism. They demonstrated the consistency of these with the light of Nature, the teachings of God's Word, and the testimony of Ecclesiastical History. But, how rarely have such discussions been heard of late—unless it be very lately—from the sacred desk, or read from the press!

Within a few years, it is true, several valuable works relating to this subject, have been published;

among which may be named: Dr. Hawes' "Tribute to the Pilgrims," — Dr. Bacon's "Church Manual," — Prof. Pond's work, "The Church," — Mr. Mitchell's "Guide," — Prof. Upham's "Ratio Disciplinæ," — and Cummings' "Dictionary of Congregational Usages and Principles." These have found many readers, and have done much to awaken an interest in our excellent system of church government. Yet only one of these, Prof. Upham's, professes to give more than a summary account of our church polity: and even this, though a work of great value, is chiefly devoted to our church usages, rather than our principles. The things of which I speak, while they illustrate the apathy of Congregationalists, suggest also one of the causes of the declension of Congregationalism.

5. Once more. A prevalent impression, that Congregationalists have no well-defined and settled principles of church polity, has operated injuriously upon our denominational interests. From whatever source this impression may have come, I must regard it as alike erroneous and injurious. We have not, it is true,—and I rejoice in the truth — any authoritative church canons, of human origin, to which pastors and churches must bow, under pains and penalties; but we have general principles of church order and discipline, as well defined, and as effective in the government of our churches as their highest interests require.

If, through ignorance or disregard of these principles, any of our churches have failed to be well governed, the fault is in the churches, and not in the system which they have professedly embraced.

2

If it be asked, Where are these principles to be found? and who has defined and explained them? The answer is — They are found in the New Testament: and their expounders are all the standard writers of the denomination; such as Johnson, Ainsworth, Robinson, Jacob, Thomas Hooker, John Cotton, John Owen, the Mathers, the authors of the Cambridge Platform, etc. I might go even further back — to Penry, and Greenwood, and Barrowe, who suffered martyrdom for these very principles of church order now called Congregational.* After a somewhat careful examination of the writings of all these worthy men — our ecclesiastical ancestors — I feel justified in saying, that although they differ among themselves, and from modern Congregationalists on some minor points, yet, in regard to all the essentials of our church polity, there is a most remarkable agreement among them, and with modern authorities, as to what is Congregationalism.

---

* See some account of these good men, in the "History of Congregationalism;" and of Penry, particularly, in Waddington's Life of "John Penry, the Pilgrim Martyr," London: 1854, and republished by the Congregational Board of Publication, Boston. In Hanbury's "Historical Memorials relating to the Independents, or Congregationalists, from their Rise to the Restoration of the Monarchy, A. D. 1660," the student will find notices of all the distinguished writers of our denomination, together with very full analyses of their writings on church order and government. It is a work of great value to the Congregationalist student, and indeed, to every one who would fully understand the religious history of England during the 16th and 17th centuries. For a vindication of Barrowe, Greenwood, and Penry, see Bradford's Dialogue, in New England's Memorial, new edition published by the Cong. Board, p. 327–356.

If the above suggestions respecting the causes of the decline of Congregationalism be in accordance with truth, they furnish an obvious answer to the question: How shall the evil be remedied?

This little volume has been prepared with the hope of contributing something towards awakening an interest in Congregationalism, and affording instruction relative to the principles and usages of this most APOSTOLIC SYSTEM OF CHURCH ORDER AND GOVERNMENT.

PART I.

PRINCIPLES OF CONGREGATIONALISM.

In pursuance of the plan which has been adopted, our attention is to be directed, first, to the Principles of Congregationalism.

By the *principles* of Congregationalism, I mean the most essential, fundamental truths of the system. What, then, are the principles of this system? Or, in other words: —

WHAT IS CONGREGATIONALISM?

Congregationalism is that system of church government in which the Scriptures are recognized as the only infallible guide respecting church order and discipline; — and which maintains, that according to the Scriptures, a Church is a company or congregation of professed Christians, who, having voluntarily covenanted and associated together to worship God and to celebrate religious ordinances, are authorized to elect necessary officers, to discipline offending members, and to act authoritatively and conclusively on all appropriate business, independently of the control of any person or persons whatsoever.

This definition is believed to embrace the fundamental, distinctive principles of Congregationalism. Some of these principles it holds in common with other systems of church government; others of them are peculiar to itself; but all are essential to sound Congregationalism. And who will deny that a system based on principles like these, has, independently of any direct proof, much to commend it to our confidence:—its Protestantism, in taking the Bible for its only infallible guide; its recognition of the inalienable rights of man, in giving to the church the power to choose its own officers and to administer its own affairs; its provision for securing the purity of the churches, by giving the power of discipline to those most interested in the maintenance of that purity; and its care for the rights and privileges of every church, however small, manifested by its recognition of the independency of each:*—these, and such like considerations, might be urged as *a priori* arguments for the Congregational System. But I shall waive, for the present, all particular consideration of these topics, and proceed at once to discuss the principles which have been brought to view in the definition of Congregationalism. And in this discussion the Scriptures will be appealed to as the infallible standard of truth.

What, then, say the Scriptures? Are the princi-

---

* The terms "independency" and "independent," as applied to Congregational churches, are never used in these pages as synonymous with *unaccountability* and *unaccountable*, but to denote *completeness* of church powers and privileges.

ples of Congregationalism recognized and authorized by the Word of God?

I. It is a principle of Congregationalism, that *the Scriptures are the only infallible guide in matters of church order and discipline.**

By this is meant, that the injunctions of Christ and his apostles, and the authorized practice of the apostolic churches as exhibited in the New Testament, are a sufficient guide, *in all ages*, to the order and discipline of the churches of Christ. Or, in other words, that the churches founded by the apostles are the models, after which, "for substance," all Christian Churches should be formed.

If the Scriptures furnish not an infallible directory to what is essential to the constitution of a christian church, we certainly have no such directory; and if we have not, how are we to know that any such thing as a church of Christ now exists? The very idea of a christian church, necessarily presupposes a knowledge of what constitutes such a church: but,

---

* To show on what authority these assertions are made, a number of references will be given under each head, to approved Congregational authors. These references will show whether or not our denomination have any fixed principles.

This first principle may be found in the Creed of John Robinson and the Leyden Church. — See Prince's New Eng. Chronology, Part II. sec. 1, p. 176, ed. of 1826; Thomas Hooker's Survey of Chh. Discipline, ch. 1, Definition, and p. 5, 6; Cotton Mather's Ratio Disciplinæ, Intr. p. 9; Samuel Mather's Apology for N. E. Chhs. p. 2, and App. Part IV. Nos. 1, 2; Cambridge Platform, ch. 1, § 3; Cummings' Congregational Dictionary, Art. "Scriptures a sufficient Guide to Order." See also History of Congregationalism, *passim*.

if the Scriptures do not furnish this knowledge, then they do not furnish us with the means of forming any distinct notion of what is meant by a church of Christ. And if they fail in this particular, on what authority are any existing organizations called churches of Christ? And by what authority can any person be required to unite with one of these organizations? *

* Dr. George Campbell, though unwilling to admit that any particular form of church government is binding upon all Christians, yet allows: . . . "That a certain external model of government must have been originally adopted [that is, by Christ and his apostles, as I understand him] for the more effectual preservation of the evangelical institution [the church] in its native purity, and for the careful transmission of it to after ages." — *Lectures on Ecc. Hist.*, Lect. iv. p. 47, Phil. ed. 1807.

As I shall have occasion frequently to refer to the works of this learned and impartial writer, it may be well to state, for the information of any who may be unacquainted with his writings, that Dr. Campbell was a distinguished scholar, Principal of Marischal College, Aberdeen, Scotland. He is the author of a standard work on the Four Gospels, and of a celebrated answer to Hume's work on Miracles. Dr. C. was a Presbyterian by profession; yet, he seems not to have regarded any particular church organization as essential, — "it affects not the essence of religion in the least," he says. He supposed that one form of church government might be more convenient in one country, and another form in another country. — *Lect.* iv. p. 50. With these views, he proposes in his Lectures on Ecclesiastical History, "to speak out boldly what appears to him most probably to have been the case, without considering what sect or party it may either offend or gratify." — *Ib.*

The testimony of such a man certainly deserves great respect. The references in the following pages will show how his testimony corroborates the views of Congregationalists.

Again, it will be conceded, that it is an important part of every christian minister's duty to make disciples of those to whom he preaches (Matt. 28: 19), to gather these disciples into christian churches, and to administer to them the ordinances of baptism and the Lord's supper. Religion cannot long exist in the world, much less flourish, if these things are neglected. But, how can the ambassador of Christ discharge these important duties, if the Scriptures furnish no infallible directions for the organization of churches? And, if he is left in ignorance of the Divine will respecting these matters, how can it be true, as the apostle asserts, that "All Scripture is given by inspiration of God . . . . that the man of God may be perfect [ἄρτιος, prepared for every emergency] *thoroughly furnished unto all good works*"—or, every good purpose that his ministry is intended to answer? 2 Tim. 3: 16, 17. Indeed, if "the house of God, which is the church of the living God, the pillar and ground of the truth" (1 Tim. 3: 15), should fail to be suitably organized and governed, would not one great end of the ministry of reconciliation itself fail?

Another view of this subject may be taken: It will be admitted that the apostles did organize, in different parts of the Roman Empire, what they called churches, and, that these were all formed upon the same general principles. Now, whatever these principles were, they may be fairly considered as descriptive of the term "church," as used by Christ and the apostles. If, then, we would understand what Christ and his apostles meant by *a church*, we must examine the peculiarities of those bodies which they called churches. And where shall we look for these, but in the New Testament of our Lord and Saviour Jesus Christ?

And furthermore, since the duty of men to become church members is now as imperative as when the apostles preached; and since God has given no other revelation of his will respecting the order of his churches than that which the New Testament furnishes;—it follows, that men should now become members of the same kind of churches—that is, churches built upon the same general principles—as those which the New Testament recognizes as christian churches. If, then, we can learn from the Scriptures what was the general polity of the *apostolic* churches, we can ascertain what should be the polity of *all churches*, in all ages of the world.

OBJECTIONS CONSIDERED.

Will it be said, in order to avoid the force of the above suggestions, that the circumstances of the apostolic churches were so unlike our own as to require an entirely different organization?

But in what respects were their circumstances peculiar?

"They were in their infancy."

So is every church when first formed.

"But, Christianity itself was then in its infancy."

So it is in every heathen land when the first missionary church is organized. Shall we, therefore, institute churches at our missionary stations, first, on the primitive plan; and afterwards, pull them down and put up those which some men consider an improvement on the Divine model?

If the churches and Christianity itself were in their infancy when the apostolic models were erected, *then*, surely, if ever, the churches should have been "under governors and tutors;" and should have enjoyed the least freedom of choice and liberty of action. But instead of this, those who object to the apostolic churches as models for us, are for restricting the liberties of the churches, and giving them less freedom, rather than more, and their governors more authority rather than less, as the churches and Christianity itself advance towards maturity. A strange procedure this. It is as though it should be said: "When you are a child, you may and ought to have your own way; but as you approach manhood, your liberty of choice and your freedom of action must be restricted."

But we are told: 'In the days of the apostles, Christians were hated and persecuted, and the outward form of the churches was adapted to this state of things; now, however, something more attractive, and better fitted to arrest the attention of men—something more congenial with the improved state of society, and the more prosperous condition of the churches, is required, to meet the taste and supply the wants of christian communities.'

In reply, we admit that the apostolic churches were adapted in their organization to the exigencies of their condition; but we regard it as a great mistake to suppose that their condition was so essentially unlike our own as to require of us any material modification of their church polity. It appears to us, that the difficulties which environed them were substantially those which surround us. The World, the Flesh, and the Devil were then leagued against Christ and his churches: the unholy league remains unbroken. The world yet hates all those who are not of the world; the carnal mind is still enmity against God; the flesh still lusts against the Spirit; our adversary, the Devil, still walketh about as a roaring lion seeking whom he may devour; "the Dragon" yet persecutes "the woman." It is indeed true, that the outward manifestation of this enmity against Christ and his churches is not now, and everywhere, the same that it was eighteen hundred years ago; but the source of this enmity and its spirit are still precisely the same; and the words of the Apostle are as true now as when first uttered: "All that will live godly in Christ Jesus shall suffer persecution."

The apostolic churches were, indeed, very simple and unostentatious in their constitution, discipline, and worship; and in this they were perfectly accordant with the spirit of Christianity. And furthermore, all history tells us that a departure from this simple order and worship has been attended with a parallel departure from the simplicity and godly sincerity of the apostolic faith and practice.

Men of fastidious taste may cry out against 'the literal, naked, bald character of the public religious services' of those churches which attempt to follow apostolic example. But they would do well to consider what have been the results of all attempted improvements on this example. The history of the

Church during the third and fourth centuries; the history of the Papacy; the history of the Church of England; are all instructive on this point — the danger of accommodating christian institutions to the taste of worldly men.

The truth is, that if we give up the principle, that the apostolic churches are the models after which all churches should be formed and regulated, we are at sea, with nothing better than an ignis-fatuus for our guide.

But let us not be misunderstood. We do not advocate an exact and entire conformity to all the peculiarities of the apostolic churches; for we know this to be impossible. We plead only for conformity in essentials, and so far as our circumstances are similar. And it is certainly possible to imitate the apostolic models thus far, without following them in all the minutiæ of their arrangements. Thus we interpret the instructions of Christ and his apostles, and the authorized example of primitive Christians in respect to other matters; why should we not in the case under consideration?

This, then, is the sum of our belief: We suppose that whatever was essential to a church of Christ in the days of the apostles, is equally essential in these latter days; that Christ designed that the principles of church order and discipline should remain essentially the same in all ages of the world; that his disciples have no liberty to adopt other principles; and, that these principles may be learned from the Scriptures; though not always from express injunctions and instructions, since the authorized example of the apostolic churches is equally authoritative with express commands, and a fair and legitimate inference from admitted premises, is of nearly equal weight.

In adopting and acting upon these views, Congregationalists regard themselves as thorough Protestants. The Bible is our infallible guide, in matters of church order and discipline, as well as in those of faith and religious practice. We cannot believe it to be necessary to resort to the writings of any men, as an authoritative and necessary "supplement to Scripture in these points." * Adopting this principle

---

* A dignitary in the Church of England (Dean of Worcester, in a sermon "Concerning Ecclesiastical Authority," published about the year 1738), has asserted, that "He must never have looked into Scripture who is capable of thinking it a perfect rule of worship, I mean external worship and discipline: but he that will take in the writings of the primitive church, as *a supplement to Scripture in these points*, cannot be at a loss to know what are the powers of church governors, or what the obedience due unto them." — See *Samuel Mather's Apology for the New England Churches*, p. 2, 3.

And yet this "supplement" to points of such vast importance to the Church, is found in tongues unknown to the great mass of its members — in the Greek and Latin languages; and in volumes of frightful magnitude, and inaccessible to the community generally. And more than all, many of the Fathers are so corrupt in their text, and so contradictory in their statements, that the most opposite testimonies have been drawn from them. The reader may find some of the errors of the Fathers pointed out in De Laune's Plea for the Non-conformists, p. 19–21. Mr. Taylor, in his Ancient Christianity, shows very clearly the extreme danger of taking the Fathers for our guides. Jortin, in his Remarks on Ecclesiastical History, says: "The Fathers are often poor and insufficient guides in things of judgment and criticism, and in the interpretation of the Scriptures, and sometimes in point of morality also, and of doctrine; as Daille, Whitby, and others have fully shown. The men themselves deserve much rewe are on firm and safe ground. All else is uncertain. "The very Papists do see and acknowledge this that I say, namely, both that these grounds of the Scripture's perfection in all ecclesiastical matters, whereon we exactly do stand, are the true and right principles of the Protestants' Religion; and also, that Diocesan Lord-Bishops do, and must needs turn away from these principles, and deny them when they deal with us; and must join plainly with the Catholics in their answers, if they will maintain themselves." *

Having settled in our minds this first and great principle — that the Scriptures should be our only infallible guide — we next inquire: What, according to them, is essential to the character of a christian church? I speak now of what is usually termed a visible, or organized church. The answer to this question will be the statement of the second principle of the Congregational system, namely: —

II. *A visible, christian church, is a voluntary association of professed Christians, united together by a*

---

spect, and their writings are highly useful on several accounts. It is better to defer too little, than too much to their decisions and the authority of Antiquity, that handmaid to the Scriptures, as she is called. She is like Briareus, and has a hundred hands, and these hands often clash and beat one another." — Vol. II. p. 57.

* *Henry Jacob's* "*Reasons*, etc. Proving a necessity of Reforming our Chhs. in England." A. D. 1604.

Jacob, though for a time opposed to those who advocated our principles in England, came at length to be a devoted defender of them. He was pastor of the first Congregational church in London which was formed on Mr. Robinson's plan, in 1616.

*covenant for the worship of God and the celebration of religious ordinances.**

---

* *Mr. Robinson and Church*, Prince, Chro. P. II. sect. 1, or *Hist. Congregationalism*, p. 362; *Hooker's Survey*, P. I. p. 14–16, 46, 47; *Mather's Ratio Dis.*, Intr. p. 8, 9; *Camb. Platf.* ch. 2, § 6; *S. Mather's Apology*, p. 1, 2. John Locke thus defines a church: "A church I take to be a voluntary society of men, joining themselves together of their own accord, in order to the public worshipping of God in such a manner as they judge acceptable to him and effectual to the salvation of their souls." — *Letter I. on Toleration.*

The whole body of believers in the world, constitute *The Church* general or universal; but such of them as may be at any time and in any place organized into a distinct body in order to profess their faith in Christ more openly and distinctly, and to worship God and celebrate christian ordinances more effectually and profitably — are called the *visible* church.

In 1589 a tract was published in England entitled, "A True Description out of the Word of God, of the Visible Church." Though anonymous, its authorship was ascribed at the time to "Robinson's Pastor;" that is, to either Mr. Clyfton, or Mr. Smyth, who were both pastors of Congregational churches in the north of England, of which Robinson, and what was subsequently "the Leyden Church," and finally the "Church of Plymouth, Massachusetts Bay," were members. This rare and valuable tract thus discriminates between the Church *universal* and the Church *visible*: —

"As there is but one God and Father of all, one Lord over all, and one Spirit; so is there but one Truth, one Faith, one Salvation, one Church — called in one Hope, joined in one Profession, guided by one Rule, even the Word of the Most High. This Church, as it is universally understood, containeth in it all the Elect of God that have been, are, or shall be: but being considered more particularly, as it is seen in this present world, it consisteth of a Company and Fellowship of faithful and holy people, gathered in the name of Christ Jesus, their only King, Priest, and

1. When we use the expression *voluntary association*, we do not mean that Christians are under no obligations thus to associate together; for we believe that every disciple of Christ is bound by the most solemn obligations, to separate himself from the world and to unite with a visible church of Christ; but we mean, that in doing this, it is essential that every person should act freely, under the influence of motives; and that no circumstances of birth, no civil law, no ecclesiastical regulations, should be thought sufficient to constitute a church, or entitle a person to church membership.

We think it manifest, that the apostolic churches were, in this sense, *voluntary associations*. A whole province was not organized into a church; neither were entire cities; and even all the members of the same family were not of course church members. But the churches were composed of such persons as on embracing Christianity separated themselves from the Jewish or Heathen communities in which they lived, and for Christian purposes, and of their own free-will, associated and united together. These things seem to us to lie upon the very face of the New Testament account of christian churches.

2. But, voluntary association for religious purposes is not all that is requisite to constitute a church of Christ. The persons thus associated must be *pro-*

Prophet; worshipping Him aright, being peaceably and quietly governed by his officers and Laws; keeping the unity of Faith in the bond of Peace, and love unfeigned." — See *Hanbury*, Vol. I. p. 28; *History of Congregationalism*, Appendix.

fessing Christians: that is, persons who avow openly their repentance for sin, their faith in Jesus Christ, and their cordial submission to the laws of Christ's kingdom.

The entire system of church government which we advocate is based on the presumption, that those who adopt it will be governed by religious principle. The system is as unsuited to irreligious men, as a republican form of civil government is to ignorant men. All power being vested in the hands of the church, for the glory of God and the good of man, it is indispensable that the members of the church should understand and appreciate the principles and design of their organization. But no unregenerate mind can fully understand and appreciate these spiritual, religious principles. 1 Cor. 2: 14–16. You can never make such an one feel the importance of that purity of heart, thought, word, and action which God's law requires, and by which the members of his churches are expected to be governed. Ignorant and regardless of the principles of God's moral law, he is utterly disqualified to administer a government based on these holy principles, and having for its great end the recognition and establishment of these principles throughout the world. Hence appears the reasonableness and necessity of this requisition for church membership — a profession of repentance for sin, of faith in Christ, and of submission of soul to God.

This peculiarity of our church polity, so far from being an objectionable feature, as some regard it, is one of its highest recommendations. It proves it to be in harmony with the whole spirit of the gospel; and thus furnishes very strong presumptive evidence of its truth.

3. As it respects the matter of *covenanting*, it may be remarked, that wherever there is a union of individuals for particular purposes, there must be of necessity a covenant among them, either expressed or implied. The very act of associating for specific purposes implies a covenant or agreement on the part of those who associate, to coöperate in effecting the specified purposes of their association. And if, to obviate all misapprehension, the character and design of the association be expressed in words, and each member of it be required to assent to these, the words are only a translation of the original act.

The manifold advantages of an expressed covenant are such as to have induced Christians, associating for church purpcses, to adopt this form of covenanting together, from a very early period, if not from the times of the apostles themselves.* And in this practice they were countenanced by the church of God under previous dispensations. The Old Testament abounds with notices of the covenants which the ancient people of God made and renewed from time to time, to walk together before God in obedience to his requisitions. In Gen. xvii. we have an account of the covenant made with Abraham and his seed. The book of Exodus, from the nineteenth chapter to

---

* Lord Chancellor King gives us no less than ten creeds and parts of creeds which are found in the writings of the Fathers of the first 300 years, A. D.—"*Primitive Church*," Part II. ch. 3. The entire chapter illustrates the subject discussed in the text.

the end of the book, contains the written Covenant and Articles of Faith, Order, and Discipline to which the church in the wilderness was required to assent and walk by, under the pain of God's displeasure. Another covenant is mentioned and described Deut. xxix. and xxx. See also 2 Kings 23: 1–3. 2 Chron. xv. and 29: 10. Here and elsewhere we have accounts of covenants made and written. In Nehemiah ix. we have a long covenant which was made, written, signed, and sealed by the children of Israel after their return from captivity; which illustrates, doubtless, Isaiah's words (44: 5), who, in predicting the restoration of the Jews from Babylon, and their religious condition, and at the same time probably glancing at the state of things under the the Messiah's reign, says: "One shall say, I am the Lord's; and another shall call himself by the name of the God of Jacob; and another shall *subscribe* with his hand unto the Lord, and surname himself by the name of Israel."

4. In regard to the *purposes* for which these associations should be formed: it is obvious, that they should be exclusively religious. They are churches of God—*christian* churches; and the worship and glory of God, the celebration of christian ordinances and the extension of christian influences are the ends contemplated in their organization. All this appears from the duties enjoined, and the directions given in the several epistles addressed to the apostolic churches and to their teachers. As a sample, read 1 Cor. xiv. and the epistles to Timothy and Titus. It is very apparent from the New Testament, that all who were connected with the apostolic churches voluntarily

and publicly professed their faith in Christ and their cordial submission to the principles of the gospel; and virtually covenanted, or agreed with each other, to walk together in accordance with this faith and these principles.

In the second chapter of Acts we have the following account of the first admission of members to the christian church, after the Saviour's ascension: "And when the day of Pentecost was fully come, they (i. e. the 120 disciples, who constituted the first christian church at Jerusalem) were all with one accord in one place. And suddenly there came a sound from heaven as of a rushing, mighty wind, and it filled all the house where they were sitting. And there appeared unto them cloven tongues like as of fire, and it sat upon each of them. And they were all filled with the Holy Ghost, and began to speak with other tongues, as the Spirit gave them utterance." This being noised abroad, a multitude of persons came together. "And they were all amazed, and were in doubt, saying one to another, What meaneth this? Others mocking, said, These men are full of new wine. But Peter, standing up with the eleven" apostles, addressed the assembled multitude in the most instructive and affecting manner. He concluded his address, by charging those before him with having crucified the Lord Jesus Christ. "Now when they heard this, they were pricked in their heart, and said unto Peter and to the rest of the apostles, Men and brethren, what shall we do? Then Peter said unto them, Repent and be baptized every one of you in the name of Jesus Christ, for the remission of sins, and ye shall receive the gift of the

Holy Ghost. For the promise is unto you, and to your children, and to all that are afar off, even as many as the Lord our God shall call. And with many other words did he testify and exhort, saying, Save yourselves from this untoward generation. Then they that gladly received his word, were baptized: and the same day there were added unto them, about three thousand souls. And they continued steadfastly in the apostle's doctrine and fellowship, and in breaking of bread, and in prayers. And fear came upon every soul; and many wonders and signs were done by the apostles, and all that believed were together, and had all things common; and sold their possessions and goods, and parted them to all men, as every man had need. And they continuing daily with one accord in the temple, and breaking bread from house to house, did eat their meat with gladness and singleness of heart, praising God, and having favor with all the people. And the Lord added to the church daily such as should be saved."

From this account it is evident, that the church at Jerusalem was a voluntary association. Motives were presented, arguments were employed, truth was urged; then it was left to every hearer to decide on the course he would take. Those who were persuaded — whose hearts were touched — who gladly received the word — came forward and offered themselves for baptism; after receiving which, they were "added to the church."

It also appears from this account, that the apostles received none into the church at that time, but those who publicly professed their repentance for sin, and their faith in Christ; none but those who "believed"

—"who gladly received the word." That they *professed* this belief, and this reception of gospel principles, is clearly implied in the declaration, that "they were baptized;" for christian baptism was a solemn renunciation of previous opinions, so far as these were inconsistent with the gospel, and an open profession of faith in Christ. And furthermore, we are told, that these penitent, believing, and baptized persons "were added unto them"—i. e. to the disciples who composed the church—and were thus separated from the unbelieving world. The subsequent conduct of these converts confirms this interpretation; for, in the forty-second verse and onward we read: "And they continued steadfastly in the apostle's doctrine and fellowship, and in breaking of bread, and in prayers. And fear came upon every soul: and many wonders and signs were done by the apostles. And all that believed were together, and had all things common; and sold their possessions and goods, and parted them to all men as every man had need. And they, continuing daily with one accord in the temple, and breaking bread from house to house, did eat their meat with gladness and singleness of heart, praising God, and having favor with all the people. And the Lord added to the church daily such as should be saved."

If all this was not a renunciation of their Jewish prejudices and a public profession of faith in Christ, actions have no significancy. And that there was a virtual covenanting, or agreeing to walk together on certain common principles of belief and practice, appears from the declaration that "they continued steadfastly in the apostles' doctrine and fellowship, and in breaking of bread, and in prayers."

Here we have, as I conceive, the outline of their covenant: they entered into *fellowship* with the apostles and with one another, professing to believe the *doctrines taught by the apostles;* (which were the "form of doctrine," or "sound words," delivered to all the churches. See Rom. 6: 17. 2 Tim. 1: 13,) and engaging to commune together in the *breaking of bread* sacramentally, and in social *prayer*. And notwithstanding all their temptations to violate this covenant, "they continued *steadfastly*" in the same.*

---

* I am aware that commentators do not agree in the exposition of this passage; some supposing that the "breaking of bread" spoken of in the text was *social*, and not *sacramental*. I prefer the interpretation in the text: (1) Because of the use of the word *fellowship* (Κοινωνίᾳ, communion,) which is generally used in application to acts strictly religious: as in 1 Cor. 10: 16. 2 Cor. 6: 14. Phil. 1: 5. 1 John 1: 3, 6, 7, etc. (2) Because the act of *breaking bread* stands in immediate connection with two others — the one before and the other after it — which are confessedly *religious* acts: namely, the belief of the apostles' doctrine, and the practice of prayers. The passage in the text, may perhaps be illustrated by 2 Cor. 8: 5.

Neander supposes that every daily meal was followed by the eucharistic use of bread and wine: "At the close of the meal, the president distributed bread and wine to the persons present, as a memorial of Christ's similar distribution to the disciples. Thus every meal was consecrated to the Lord, and at the same time was a meal of brotherly love." — *Hist. of the Planting and Training of the Christ. Chh.* Vol. I. p. 27, 3d Ed. Edinb. Bloomfield suggests that the meaning of Luke is, that their ordinary meals were taken "in charitable communion and religious thankfulness, and followed by prayer." — *Note on Acts* 2: 42. Mosheim would make

And here we have, also, the sacred *purposes* for which these good people associated and covenanted together: namely, the maintenance of the apostles' doctrines, and the practice of christian rites and duties.— See Acts 20: 7. 1 Cor. 11: 17–34.

Here then, we find in this single chapter, a confirmation of all the specifications in our second great principle of church organization. For, though this is but a brief account of one of the many churches organized by the apostles, yet we may believe that after this model all their churches were constituted. We are not, however, to be confined to this chapter.

By referring to other parts of the New Testament, we find the view we have taken of the above account confirmed. Thus, the position that piety and the profession thereof are both requisite to church membership, receives further confirmation from the language of the apostle, Rom. 10: 8–10; "This is the word of faith" [or the faithful word—the gospel] "which we preach; that *if thou shalt confess with thy mouth* the Lord Jesus Christ, and *shalt believe in thy heart* that God has raised him from the dead, thou shalt be saved. For with *the heart man believeth* unto righteousness; and with *the mouth confession is made* unto salvation." The words of the Saviour himself, Matt. 10: 32, inculcate the same doctrine: "Whosoever shall *confess me before men*, him will I confess also before my Father which is in heaven."

The manner in which the apostles speak of, and

Κοινωνίᾳ, *fellowship*, *communion*, refer to the particular act of presenting gifts and offerings for the relief of the poor.— *Commentaries*, Vol. I. p. 194, note.

to the churches in their epistles, clearly proves that these churches were composed of persons who had made a credible profession of faith in Christ. Paul, in his epistle to the church at Rome, addressed them as "*beloved of God, called to be saints;*" and says: "I thank my God that your faith is spoken of throughout the world." — Rom. 1: 7, 8. But how could this be, if they had not made a public profession of their faith? To the Corinthians, Paul wrote: "Unto the church of God which is at Corinth, to them that are sanctified in [or through faith in] Christ Jesus, called to be saints." . . . 1 Cor. 1: 2. See also Gal. 4: 28. Eph. 1: 1. Phil. 1: 1, 5, 7. 1 Thess. 1: 1–10. "Unto the Church of the Thessalonians, which is in God the Father and in the Lord Jesus Christ," Paul wrote: "Remembering without ceasing your work of faith, and labor of love, and patience of hope in our Lord Jesus Christ, in the sight of God and our Father; knowing, brethren beloved, *your election of God.*" He then declares to them: "Ye became *followers of us and of the Lord,* having received the word in much affliction, with joy of the Holy Ghost; so that ye were *ensamples to all that believe* in Macedonia and Achaia. For, from you *sounded out the word of the Lord* not only in Macedonia and Achaia, but also, in every place *your faith to God-ward is spread abroad.*" — 1 Thess. 1: 1–10. All this could not have been said of them, had they not publicly professed their faith in Jesus Christ.

In the 2 Cor. 6: 14–18, is this remarkable passage: "Be ye not unequally yoked together with unbelievers; for what fellowship hath righteousness with unrighteousness? and what communion hath light with darkness? and what concord hath Christ with Belial? or what part hath he that believeth with an infidel [ἀπίστου, an *unbeliever*].* And what agreement hath the temple of God [or the church of God,—Eph. 2: 19–22] with idols? For, ye are the temple of the living God; as God hath said: 'I will dwell in them and walk in them [see Rev. 2: 1]; and I will be their God and they shall be my people. Wherefore, COME OUT FROM AMONG THEM, AND BE YE SEPARATE, saith the Lord, and touch not the unclean thing; and I will receive you, and be a God unto you, and ye shall be my sons and daughters, saith the Lord Almighty." This passage furnishes direct and positive proof, that a christian church should consist of believers in Christ, who have openly professed their faith in him and separated themselves from the unbelieving world. Such an interpretation of the passage harmonizes with the design of the apostle as expressed in the context, and with his instructions elsewhere, and is required by the natural and obvious meaning of the words of the text.† Philip acted on this principle, when he required of the Eunuch an open and solemn profession of faith in Christ, before he would baptize him and thus recognize him as a member of the Church of Christ.—Acts 8: 26–40. And so, doubtless, did all the apostles and disciples of Christ, who went forth preach-

* So the word is translated in the 14th verse, and elsewhere, and so it should be here.

† See *Dwight's Theology*, Sermon 149. Also, Preface to Owen on "*The Nature of a Gospel Church.*"

ing the gospel and gathering christian churches. It is perfectly evident from the passages which have now been quoted, and from the general tenor of the epistles, that the apostolic churches were composed of those only who were regarded as "saints," as penitent believers in Jesus Christ; and who associated together under the bonds of a covenant, expressed or implied, to worship and glorify God and to celebrate the ordinances of the christian religion. Read the tenth chapter of the epistle to the Hebrews, particularly from the sixteenth to the twenty-fifth verse.

Now, if all the members of the apostolic churches were required to make an open profession of their faith in Christ as a prerequisite to church-fellowship, and to enter into covenant with each other to walk together in the faith and ordinances of the Gospel; and no alteration has been made in the nature of a christian church, or in the terms of communion,—it follows, that *no person should now be admitted to a christian church unless he gives evidence of conversion of soul to God, makes a public profession of his faith in Jesus Christ, and of his own free-will enters into covenant with the people of God, to walk with them in accordance with the faith and ordinances of the gospel.*

III. Another principle of Congregationalism is, that *a church should ordinarily consist of only so many members as can conveniently assemble together for public worship, the celebration of religious ordinances, and the transaction of church business.**

---

* See *Hooker's Survey*, P. I. ch. 4, p. 45, 49; Principles of Mr. Robinson and Church, in *Prince's Chron.* P. II. sec. 1, or *Hist. Cong.*, p. 362; *Mather's Ratio*, Intr. p. 8, and art. 1; *Camb.*

The Greek work ἐκκλησία (ecclesia) commonly rendered *church*, literally signifies "a congregation, an assembly," "an assembly *called out* or *separated* from others;" and it is used in the New Testament, for the most part, to designate either the whole body of Christians, or a single congregation of professed believers, united together for religious purposes.* In this latter sense it seems to be used by the sacred writers in more than sixty different instances. In Acts 2: 47, we read: "The Lord added to *the church* daily such as should be saved." Now this church is expressly described as a single congregation, a voluntary association of persons for religious purposes, who could meet together to worship God and trans-

---

Platf. ch. 3, § 4; Bartlett's "*Model of the Primitive Congregational Way*," in Hanbury, Vol. III. ch. 72; *Congregational Manual*, prepared by Drs. Woods, Humphrey, Snell, Shepard, Cooley, Storrs, and Cooke, ch. 2, § 3.

* See *Campbell's Lectures on Ecclesiastical History*, Lect. vi. p. 100, 105, 106; *King's Prim. Chh.*, ch. 1, *particularly* § 2; *Neander*, Vol. I. p. 169. See on, Part III. of this work.

Henry Jacob, 'whose writings,' says Anthony Wood, 'bespeak him learned,' remarks upon the word ἐκκλησία as follows: "I appeal to all authentic Greek authors — Thucydides, Demosthenes, Plato, Aristotle, Socrates, etc. — out of whom plentiful allegations may be brought, all of them showing that this word Ecclesia (ἐκκλησία) did ever more signify *only one assembly*, and never *a dispersed multitude, holding many ordinary set meetings, in far remote places*, as Diocesan and larger churches do. Now according to these, and other Greeks, living in the apostle's days, do the apostles speak. And this, I have heretofore often propounded and affirmed, as a principal ground and cause of our dissent from the Church state in England. And the ground is certain: It cannot be with reason spoken against." — *Attestation*, p. 209, 210, 16mo, printed 1613.

act church business.—Acts 2: 44, 46. 4: 23–31. 5: 11–14 compared with 3: 2, 11. 6: 1–6. Such was the church at Jerusalem, the first christian church, and the *model* after which all the apostolic churches seem to have been formed.* This was a complete church; and was, therefore, called "the church at Jerusalem." Other churches are spoken of as equally complete; and are designated by the names of the several places in which they were formed; as, "the church at Antioch," "the church at Corinth," "the church at Ephesus," etc. If each of these companies of Christians had not been regarded as an entire and complete church, they certainly would not have been thus designated. Instead of such phraseology, we should have read of *that portion* of the church of Christ which resided at Ephesus, Corinth, or Antioch; and not of *the church* of Ephesus, etc. There was a church at Corinth, and another at Cenchrea, the port of Corinth, which, being but nine miles distant, was usually considered as the suburbs of the city itself. From the language of the apostle, it is evident that the associated believers at Cenchrea were as truly and completely *a church* as their more numerous brethren in the parent city: "I commend unto you Phebe our sister, which is a servant of the church which is at Cenchrea."—Rom. 16: 1. The obvious reason why the Christians in these two places were not united together in one church, was, that in the organization of churches the apostle proceeded on the principle that a church should consist of only

* See Gieseler's "*Text-Book of Ecclesiastical History*," translated by Mr. Cunningham, Vol. I. p. 56.

so many persons as could conveniently assemble together for public worship, the celebration of religious ordinances, and the transaction of church business; and, as these brethren were nine miles apart, though resident in the same city, and sufficiently numerous in each place to constitute a distinct church, he organized them separately. In the Epistle to the Colossians we have *three*, if not *four* distinct churches mentioned, all within a very short distance of each other, namely: that of Laodicea, that in the house of Nymphas, in Colosse, and in Hierapolis. The first and the last were about six miles apart, and Colosse was between them:—"Them that are in Laodicea and them in Hierapolis. . . . . Salute the brethren which are in Laodicea, and Nymphas, and the church which is in his house. And when this epistle is read among you, cause that it be read also in the church of the Laodiceans; and that ye also read the epistle from Laodicea." — Col. 4: 13–16.

Another consideration which goes to establish the position that the churches founded by the apostles were single congregations, is, that so many distinct churches are mentioned in the New Testament. Not less than thirty-five different churches are expressly named, or so referred to as to leave little doubt of their existence.* And yet these evidently constituted

* The following are the particular churches mentioned or referred to in the New Testament: Jerusalem — Acts i–viii; Samaria, 8: 5; Damascus, 9: 10, 19; Lydda, Saron, and Joppa, 9: 32, 38; Cesarea, x., 18: 22; Antioch, xi. Antioch in Pisidia, xiii. Iconium, 14: 1–4, 21–23; Lystra, 16: 2; Derbe, 16: 1, 2, 4–6; Philippi, 16: 12–40; Thessalonica, 17: 1–10; Berea, 17: 10–14;

but a small part of all the "churches of the saints" which were organized by the apostolic laborers; for the inspired writers often refer to "the churches" of certain districts of country, as if they were very numerous: thus we read of "the churches throughout all Judea, and Galilee, and Samaria"— Acts 9: 31; of the apostles going "through Syria and Cilicia, confirming the churches"—Acts 15: 40, 41; "of the churches [of Phrygia] being established in the faith and increased in number daily"— Acts 16: 1–6; in another place we read that Paul went "over all the country of Galatia and Phrygia *in order*, strengthening all the disciples."— Acts 18: 23. 1 Cor. 16: 1. Gal. 1: 2. In Pisidia and Pamphylia the apostles "ordained them elders in every church."— Acts 14: 23, 24. We read also of "the churches of Asia"— 1 Cor. 16: 19; of "the churches of Macedonia"— 2 Cor. 8: 1; and Paul's direction to Titus to "ordain elders in every city" of Crete— Tit. 1: 5. Now, these expressions clearly imply, that the number of individual churches in the days of the apostles was very great; so great as to constrain us to think that a church then consisted only of a single congregation of believers, and this not so numerous as to forbid a "*whole church*" from assembling together for public worship, the celebration of religious ordinances, and

---

Corinth, xviii.; Ephesus, xix.; Troas, 20: 5–11; Tyre, 21: 4; Ptolemais, 21: 7; Puteoli, 28: 13, 14; Rome, 28: 14, 16; Colosse, Hierapolis, Laodicea, Col. 1: 2. 4: 13–16; Cenchrea, Rom. 16: 1; Babylon, 1 Pet. 5: 13; Smyrna, Pergamos, Thyatira, Sardis, Philadelphia, Rev. 1: 11; the church in the house of Priscilla and Aquila, Rom. 16: 5; 1 Cor. 16: 19; Nymphas, Col. 4: 15; and Philemon, Phil. 2.

the transaction of business, sometimes even in a private house.—See Acts 14: 27. 1 Cor. 5: 4. 2 Thess. 2: 1. Rom. 16: 5. 1 Cor. 16: 19. Col. 4: 15. Philemon 2.

If, then, such was the character of the apostolic churches, we infer that such should be the character of all christian churches, in all countries, and all periods of time.

OBJECTIONS CONSIDERED.

It is objected to these views, that the *size* of some of the apostolic churches forbids us to believe that they were congregationally organized.* Milner says: "It is absurd to suppose that the great church at Ephesus, in the decline of St. John's life, should be only a single congregation; and, most probably, the same is true of all the rest." He then goes on to estimate the Christians of Ephesus at "many thousands," and the church at Jerusalem at the same. Hence he draws the inference, that their members could not all have met together for church purposes; and therefore, could not have been congregationally organized. And Slater insists, that it is highly improbable that the church at Antioch could have been a single congregation.

It is a sufficient reply to these objectors, to say, that two, out of the three churches which they have selected as examples for their purpose, are expressly declared to have been congregational in their char-

---

* See *Milner's Chh. Hist.*, Cent. III. ch. 20, and Slater's "*Original Draught*," Am. ed. p. 70–72.

acter, i. e. capable of assembling together in *one place* for religious purposes. It is true that three thousand were added to the church at Jerusalem, as the result of the preaching of Peter and the other apostles on the day of Pentecost, and two thousand or more afterwards.— Acts 4: 4. But it must be remembered that many of these were Parthians, and Medes, and Elamites, and dwellers in Mesopotamia, and in Judea, and Cappadocia, Pontus, Asia, etc. (Acts 2: 9–11), who had assembled at Jerusalem to keep the feast of Pentecost, and who soon left the city for their distant homes. Subsequently, additions were made to this church, from time to time, "of such as should be saved;" but how many of them were stated residents in the city, we are not informed. The following references will show, that however numerous this church may have been, its members could, nevertheless, assemble together for religious purposes, and often did.— Acts 2: 46. 5: 12, 42. 6: 2. 15: 4, 12. Dr. Bloomfield, in a note on Acts 5: 12–14, says, among other things: . . . "The words ἅπαντες and ἐν τῃ στοα Σολομῶνος ['all' and 'in Solomon's porch'] are added, because now that believers were become so very numerous, they could no longer hold any general assemblies for divine worship in the υπεροῶν, [upper chamber] which they had before occupied, but were obliged to resort to the portico of the Temple, here mentioned. Of course, by ἅπαντες [all] are meant the Christians at large; and not, as some have thought, the apostles."

Milner (ut sup.) and Slater (p. 32) both urge the expression in Acts 21: 20, addressed to Paul by the elders of the church at Jerusalem, to prove that there must have been more than one congregation of believers in that city: "Thou seest, brother, how *many thousands* of Jews there are which believe."

These learned men, in their eagerness to make up a diocesan church at Jerusalem, seem to have overlooked the fact, that, at the time these words were spoken, the city was full of Jews from all parts of the empire, come up to keep the feast of Pentecost. See Acts 21: 27 compared with 20: 16. Of Ephesus, we only know that Paul labored there "in season and out of season," "by the space of three years;" and that "mightily grew the word of God and prevailed." But Paul, doubtless, would have considered the encouragement to remain in this city ample, had he seen a few *hundreds* turning to the Lord, instead of "many thousands," as Milner supposes; and Luke would have been justified in declaring that "mightily grew the word of God," had some hundreds of souls been converted in that profligate city. It should be borne in mind, also, that Ephesus was a great mart for the country round about it, and a famous resort for the idolaters of Asia Minor, because here was that wonder of the world, the temple of Diana, the goddess of the Ephesians. For this reason, if for no other, the apostle might have thought it proper to devote special attention to Ephesus; since by being there, he could, in effect, preach the gospel throughout all Asia, as Luke tells us he did. See Acts 19: 10. And if there were "many thousands" converted in this city, multitudes of them, doubtless, were but temporary residents there.

Slater labors hard to rebut the idea that the church

at Antioch was a congregational church. For this purpose, he refers repeatedly to the 11th chapter of Acts. He quotes, however, only a few words from the sacred text under each specification: had he given the entire passage, he would have overturned his whole argument, so far as the testimony of Scripture goes. In reference to the religious excitement among the Antiochians, he says: "Tidings of this came to the church of Jerusalem, where the whole college of apostles were in readiness to consult for them. They send Barnabas, a good man, etc. . . . to improve this happy opportunity." . . .

Was it by design, or accident, that we are thus left to understand that *the apostles* sent Barnabas to Antioch? However this may be, certain it is, that the sacred text gives no countenance to such a representation. It reads thus: "Then tidings of these things came unto the ears of THE CHURCH which was in Jerusalem: and THEY sent forth Barnabas, that he should go as far as Antioch."— Acts 11: 22. Not one syllable is said of "the whole college of apostles;" but the whole matter is spoken of as one in which "THE CHURCH which was in Jerusalem" was concerned. It was the church that received the glad news, and it was the church that sent forth Barnabas.

Notice, again, the representation in the next paragraph of the "Draught:" "But to forward this work, . . . Barnabas travels to Tarsus, and joins Saul, . . . and returning with him to Antioch, they continue a whole year together in that populous city, teaching much people." Now, compare this passage with the text, of which it is a paraphrase: "And it came to pass, that a whole year they [Barnabas and

Saul] assembled themselves with the church,* and taught much people," ὄχλον ἱκανὸν, a great multitude. Acts 11: 26. It is evident, from this passage, that large as was the multitude, the church at Antioch at this time was not so large but that it could assemble together with their teachers for public worship.

Another observation of Slater's respecting the "harvest of christian converts those apostolical laborers made, assisted by all that fled thither from Jerusalem, besides by the men of Cyprus and Cyrene," etc. deserves remark. This observation, designed evidently to carry the impression that there must have been a sort of diocesan church at Antioch, even in the apostles' days, receives a satisfactory answer from two or three texts of Scripture. Not to urge Acts 13: 1–4, where we are plainly taught that the whole church of Antioch were assembled, and were concerned in the work of setting apart Barnabas and Saul as missionaries to the Gentiles — we may refer to Acts 14: 25–27; "And when they [Barnabas and Saul] had preached the word in Perga, they went down into Attalia; and thence sailed to Antioch, from whence they had been recommended to the grace of God for the work which they fulfilled;" that is, the work of preaching the gospel to the Gentiles, to which they had been set apart, as I suppose, by the church of Antioch. "And when they were

---

* Συναχθῆναι ἐν τῇ ἐκκλησίᾳ. Bloomfield would render it, "were associated in the congregation [as colleagues]." Kuinoel however, sanctions our translation: "*conveniebant cum coetu,*" says he — they assembled with the church. It is not, however, material to our purpose which interpretation we adopt.

come, and had *gathered the church together*, they rehearsed all that God had done with them." . . . Now, here we have "*the church* that was at Antioch," "*gathered together.*" It was not the *elders* of the church that were gathered together, but—*the church* itself. We are thus taught, that all the "harvest of christian converts" which had then been reaped, could as yet be gathered into one place.

And even at a somewhat later period, after the division of the church about the question of circumcision, to which Slater refers as a further evidence that the converts at Antioch were too numerous to be included in a single congregational church — even after this, we learn that the whole multitude could be *gathered together.* In the 15th chapter we read, that it pleased "the apostles and elders, *with the whole church*" at Jerusalem, "to send chosen men of their own company to Antioch," to carry the opinion of the Jerusalem church upon the agitated question: "So when they were dismissed [by the church at Jerusalem] they came to Antioch; and when they had *gathered the multitude together* they delivered the epistle," etc. See Acts 15: 22–30. By "the multitude," no one can doubt but that the whole body of believers is intended; for the same expression is used in the 12th verse of this chapter to denote the whole body of Christians at Jerusalem. Compare 4th, 6th, 12th, 22d and 23d verses.

Now, I would "refer to the sober judgment of all" impartial men to say, whether the Scriptures must not be wrested from their natural and obvious meaning, in order to make the church at Antioch any thing more than a *congregational* church? — that is, a body of believers who could assemble together in one place for religious purposes? As to what is true of this church after the apostles' times — whether Antioch contained *one* or *fifty* congregations of Christians — I am not concerned just now to know; but if any man will open the Acts of the Apostles and read from the 11th to the 16th chapter, and find any thing that savors of Diocesan Episcopacy, or any thing that contradicts the idea that the church at Antioch and the others there spoken of were *congregational* in their character, he must understand language very differently from what I am able to do.

The church in Corinth, which we may reasonably suppose was not the least among the apostolic churches, was yet, evidently but a single congregation; for the apostle speaks of their coming "*together into one place*" to eat the Lord's supper, — 1 Cor. 11: 20, 33; and of "*the whole church*" coming "together into one place" for public worship, — 14: 23, 26.

Thus it appears, from the express words of the New Testament, that the church at Jerusalem, though large, yet consisted of but a single congregation; and that "the whole multitude of the disciples" composing it could, and did meet together for public worship and the transaction of church business. The same is true of the church at Antioch, and of the church at Corinth; and if so, we may reasonably believe, of all the churches mentioned in the New Testament.

So clear is the testimony of Scripture upon this point, that many Episcopal and Presbyterian writers have been constrained to admit, that the apostolic churches were congregational in their organization and practice, and so continued until their inspired teachers were removed. But these writers object to the inference, that *all churches* should be modelled after these primitive patterns; because they regard these as adapted to the apostolic age alone.*

But why, we ask, did the apostles organize churches throughout the Roman Empire upon a plan which they must have known (according to the supposition under consideration) would be adapted to their circumstances for a very few years only? Could Paul have regarded himself as "a wise master-builder" when laying the foundation, and framing together a "house" which would require an entire remodelling as soon as the grave should close upon himself and his inspired companions? — an event of which he lived in daily expectation. Can it be, that the apostolic organizations were no better than so many temporary sheds, constructed merely for the emergency of the times, and designed to be taken down, and replaced by the fair temple of Episcopacy or Presbyterianism so soon as the church should become sufficiently numerous and rich for this purpose, and her inspired guides should be removed? We cannot regard such a supposition as reasonable.

IV. It is a principle of Congregationalism, that *every church is competent to choose its own officers, discipline its own members, and transact all other appropriate business, independently of any other church,*

---

* See *Waddington's History of the Church,* (Harper's edition,) ch. 2, § 2. Maclane's note to Mosheim, Vol. I. P. II. ch. 2, n. 6. See also Part III. of this work. — "Modern Writers."

or ecclesiastical body or person; or, in other words — *that all church power is vested in the hands of those who constitute the church.**

This principle flows naturally and unavoidably from the preceding. If a church be an authorized, voluntary association, organized for specific and lawful purposes; then this association must have the right to choose such officers, make such regulations, and adopt such measures as are essential to the ends for which it is formed; all being done in accordance with the general directions of God's Word, or at least, in a manner consistent with the spirit of that Word.

(1) As to *the election of church officers.* We find this right fully recognized in the practice of the apostolic churches. For example: in Acts 1: 15–26 there is an account of the proceedings of the church at Jerusalem immediately after Christ's ascension, in choosing an apostle in the place of Judas. It is as follows: "And in those days Peter stood up in the midst of the disciples, and said, (the number of the names together were about a hundred and twenty,) men and brethren, this Scripture must needs have been fulfilled, which the Holy Ghost by the mouth of David spake before concerning Judas, which was guide to them that took Jesus. For he was numbered with us, and had obtained part of this ministry

---

* Robinson and Church — *Prince Chron.* Part II. sect. 1, and *Hist. Cong.*, p. 327, 330, 338, 339, 362; *Thomas Hooker*, P. I. ch. 11–13, partic. at p. 187, 188, 219, 220, 221, § 5; *Cotton's Way of the Cong. Chhs.*, ch. 1, sect. 1, and *Way of Cong. Chhs. Cleared*, P. II. ch. 1, partic. at p. 3, 5, 10, 19; *Keys of the Kingdom of Heaven*, p. 67–70, 76–91, 100; *Ratio Disc.*, p. 9; *Camb. Platf.* ch. 5, 8, 10, § 2, 5; *S. Mather's Apology*, ch. 1.

. . . Wherefore of these men which have companied with us, all the time that the Lord Jesus went in and out among us, beginning from the baptism of John, unto that same day that he was taken up from us, must one be ordained to be a witness with us of his resurrection. And they appointed two, Joseph called Barsabas, who was surnamed Justus, and Matthias. And they prayed, and said, Thou, Lord, which knowest the hearts of all men, shew whether of these two thou hast chosen, that he may take part of this ministry and apostleship, from which Judas by transgression fell, that he might go to his own place. And they gave forth their lots, and the lot fell upon Matthias; and he was numbered with the eleven apostles."

By "*lots*" (κλήρους) here, we may understand *votes* — they gave their votes. "And the lot fell upon Matthias; and he was numbered with the eleven" apostles: — συγκατεψηφίσθη, *chosen by a common suffrage*, says Wahl. That is, Matthias became one of the apostles by the common suffrage of the brethren of the church at Jerusalem.*

---

* Mosheim, in his "Commentaries on the Affairs of the Christians before the time of Constantine the Great," has a long note, in which he maintains the above view of the matter. He considers *κλῆρος, a lot*, as synonymous, in this connection, with *ψῆφος, a suffrage* or *vote;* and he supposes that Luke meant by the expression — "they gave forth their lots," simply this: — "and *those who were present gave their votes.*" He also supposes that the subsequent method of the most ancient christian churches, in *electing* their teachers and pastors, was founded on the manner of proceeding to which the apostles had recourse on this occasion. — Vol. I. p. 136–138.

Now, if the brethren of the church at Jerusalem, in the presence, and by the direction of the apostles themselves, were authorized to make such an election, are not those churches which are formed after the model of this primitive church, empowered to choose their own officers?

In Acts 6: 1–6, we have another instance in which this same model-church exercised the right of choosing ecclesiastical officers: "And in those days, when the number of the disciples was multiplied, there arose a murmuring of the Grecians against the Hebrews, because their widows were neglected in the daily ministration. Then the twelve called the multitude of the disciples unto them, and said, It is not reason that we should leave the word of God, and serve tables. Wherefore, brethren, look ye out among you seven men of honest report, full of the Holy Ghost and wisdom, whom we may appoint over this business. But we will give ourselves continually to prayer, and to the ministry of the word. And the saying pleased the whole multitude: *and they chose* Stephen, a man full of faith and of the Holy Ghost, and Philip, and Prochorus, and Nicanor, and Timon, and Parmenas, and Nicholas a proselyte of Antioch, whom they set before the apostles: and when they had prayed, they laid their hands on them."

But, why did not the apostles select these men? or the apostles and elders select them? Why was the matter submitted to "the whole multitude of the disciples?" For the very obvious reason, that it was, in the judgment of the apostles, the prerogative of the church to choose its own officers.

In Acts 14: 23, 24, we have an account of the

election and consecration of elders in the churches of Pisidia and Pamphilia, under the direction of Paul and Barnabas: "And when they had ordained them elders in every church [or as Doddridge renders it—*constituted* presbyters for them, etc.] and had prayed with fasting, they commended them to the Lord on whom they believed," etc. The Greek word here translated "ordained," is χειροτονήσαντες (cheirotonesantes), from χείρ (cheir) the hand, and τείνω (teino) to stretch out. Wahl renders the word, "to vote by holding up the hand." Schrevelius gives, as the meaning of the word, "to raise up and extend the hands—to elect by hand-vote—to vote by holding up the hand." Bloomfield, as we might expect, resists this interpretation; but admits that "several of the ablest commentators" adopt it. Doddridge has a long and able note upon this passage. He maintains that the Greek word employed in the text clearly denotes that the elders were elected by a vote of the several churches over which they were respectively placed. In this opinion agree Erasmus, Calvin, and Beza. Beza says: "The force of this word (χειροτονήσαντες) is to be noted, that we may know Paul and Barnabas did nothing by their private will, neither exercised any tyranny in the church."—Calvin says: "Luke relates that elders were ordained in the churches by Paul and Barnabas, but at the same time he distinctly marks the manner in which this was done, namely, *by the suffrages or votes of the people;* for this is the meaning of the term he there employs; χειροτονήσαντες πρεσβυτήρους κατ' ἐκκλησίαν. Acts 14: 23. Those two apostles, therefore, ordained; but *the whole multitude*, according to the custom observed in elections among the Greeks, declared by the elevation of their hands who was the object of their choice." *

Dr. Owen maintains the correctness of this interpretation, with great learning and ability.† "Χειροτονεῖν," says he, "is the same with τας χεῖρας αἱρειν [to raise the hands], nor is it ever used in any other signification." "He," continues Dr. Owen, "is a great stranger unto these things, who knoweth not that among the Greeks, especially the Athenians, from whom the use of this word is borrowed or taken, χειροτονια [the act of voting] was an act ὅλης της ἐκκλησῖας, 'of the whole assembly' of the people in the choice of their officers and magistrates." He quotes from Demosthenes and Thucydides in proof of this. It is clear that this word is employed 2 Cor. 8: 19, to designate such an act of the church—a popular vote. In speaking of Titus, the apostle says "he was *chosen* (or being chosen) of the churches (χειροτονηθεὶς υπό των ἐκκλησιῶν) to travel with us with this grace;" that is, with the collection made for the relief of the persecuted Christians in Judea. No one can doubt that Titus was chosen by a popular vote; and as the same word is used in both places, the inference is, that it designates the same act in both instances. The old English Bible translates the passage: "When they had ordained them elders by election." Harrington, in his Prerogative of Popular Government, renders the passage "Ordained them elders by the votes of the People." The Evangelist evidently

* *Institutes*, Book IV. ch. 3, § 15.

† *Owen's Works*, English edition, Vol. XX. p. 415–418.

meant to teach, that the ordinations in the several churches were in accordance with the wishes of the brethren of each church, *as expressed by their votes.*

Another instance of popular election is recorded in Acts 15: 22–29; where we read: "Then pleased it the apostles and elders, *with the whole church* [at Jerusalem] to send *chosen men* of their own company to Antioch with Paul and Barnabas; namely, Judas, surnamed Barsabas, and Silas, chief men among the brethren;" ἐκλεξαμένους ἄνδρας ἐξ αὐτῶν πέμψαι — "having chosen men from among themselves, to send [them]." — See also 25th verse. This was not an election of church officers exactly, but rather of church representatives. The proceedings of the church, nevertheless, furnish an important hint respecting the christian method of doing church business. The delegates were not appointed by the apostles, nor by the apostles and elders; but by "the apostles and elders, *with the whole church.*" Neander says: "Respecting the election of officers in the church, it is evident that the first deacons, and the delegates who were authorized by the church to accompany the apostles, were chosen from the general body. — 2 Cor. 8: 19. From these examples, we may conclude that a similar mode of proceeding was adopted at the appointment of presbyters." *

But, if it was the right and privilege of the churches formed by the apostles themselves, and while under their special supervision and instruction, to choose their own officers and representatives, can

---

* *History of the Apostolical Churches*, Vol. I. p. 181, 3d ed. So says Mosheim. — *Commentaries*, Vol. I. p. 219 and note.

this right and privilege be lawfully denied to any church founded on the same general principles, and composed of the same materials as were the apostolic churches?

(2) In proof that Christ has given to his churches the right to *discipline offending members*, may be adduced, first of all, that important passage in Matt. 18: 15–18, "If thy brother shall trespass against thee, [ἁμαρτήσῃ, *amartese*, commit a serious offence, *sin* against thee. The same word is used Matt. 27: 4. Luke 15: 18, 21. Rom. 2: 12. 3: 23. 1 John 1: 10, and is translated *sinned*,] go and tell him his fault between thee and him alone: if he shall hear thee, thou hast gained thy brother. But if he will not hear thee, then take with thee one or two more; that in the mouth of two or three witnesses, every word may be established. And if he neglect to hear them, tell it unto *the church*: but if he neglect to hear the church, let him be unto thee as a heathen man and a publican. Verily I say unto you, whatsoever ye shall bind on earth, shall be bound in heaven: and whatsoever ye shall loose on earth, shall be loosed in heaven:"—* that is, your doings as a church on earth shall be ratified by me in heaven.

To avoid the natural inference, that the power of excommunication is here put into the hands of the church, it has been said: that it is only the *aggrieved person* who is to count the obstinate trespasser "as an heathen man and publican;"—"let

* See an excellent sermon upon this text by Dr. Emmons, in which he terms the passage, "The Platform of Ecclesiastical Government, established by the Lord Jesus Christ."

him be unto *thee*," etc. To this it may be replied: that whatever the trespasser is to the offended brother, he is — after the course pointed out in the text has been pursued — to the whole church; for, when the matter is told to the church, and the church undertakes to reclaim the trespasser, then the trespass ceases to be *private*, and becomes the affair of the church; or, in other words, the church then takes the place of the offended brother. It would, therefore, be manifestly absurd to suppose that the church ought to retain in their fellowship one who had been guilty of such an offence as to render it the duty of a brother of the church to consider and treat him as a heathen and publican — i. e. as one destitute of religious principle, whose society should be shunned. The correctness of this interpretation of the passage is supported by the following texts. Rom. 16: 17. 1 Cor. 5: 9–13. 2 Thess. 3: 6, 14, 15. Tit. 3: 10. Any one who will examine these several passages will see, that they all relate to the duty of churches towards the disorderly, heretical, and ungodly among them. And they show, conclusively, that it is the duty of churches, after admonishing, and striving to reclaim trespassers against the laws of Christ's kingdom, without effect — to *purge them out* — to *put them away* from among them — to *withdraw themselves* from them — to *have no company with them, that they may be ashamed* — or to *reject them* from their number and fellowship, as no longer deserving the name of brethren, or the christian confidence of the churches. The passages here referred to may be regarded as a commentary on the common law of Christ's kingdom laid down in the 18th chapter of

Matthew; for it is reasonable to suppose that the directions of the Head of the Church are to be followed, substantially at least, by all churches, and in all ordinary cases before they put away from among them, or withdraw themselves from any man who has been called a brother. This view of the matter, while it furnishes a conclusive answer to the objection which has been stated above, and shows that the apostolic churches had the power of discipline in their own hands, also assists us in understanding this fundamental law of christian discipline in Matt. 18: 15–18.

In 1 Cor. 5: 1–8, we have Paul's instructions to the church at Corinth, to discipline, and even to excommunicate an offending member: "In the name of our Lord Jesus Christ, when *ye are gathered together*, and my Spirit, with the power of our Lord Jesus Christ" [being present to sanction your doings, I counsel and direct you] "*to deliver such an one unto Satan* for the destruction of the flesh, that the spirit may be saved in the day of the Lord Jesus:" [i. e. to cast him out of the church, which is the kingdom of Christ, into the world, which is the kingdom of Satan, there to experience the painful consequences of his fleshly lusts, until humbled and mortified by the fruits of his apostasy, he shall be brought back to Christ by sincere repentance.] . . . . "Know ye not that a little leaven leaveneth the whole lump? *Purge out, therefore, the old leaven*, that ye may be a new lump."

Having disposed of this particular case of flagrant sinfulness, the apostle is reminded of some instructions previously given the Corinthian church about the treatment of inconsistent church-members. These instructions they had somewhat misapprehended; he therefore explains more fully his meaning; showing that he spake not of irreligious and immoral men who were of the *world*, but of such as had crept unawares into the *church*. He tells the brethren, that they had power to pass judgment on such offenders, and requires them to put them away from among them: "I wrote unto you in an epistle, not to company with fornicators: yet not altogether with the fornicators of this world, or with the covetous, or extortioners, or with idolaters: for then must ye needs go out of the world. But now I have written unto you not to keep company, if any man that is called a brother be a fornicator, or covetous, or an idolater, or a railer, or a drunkard, or an extortioner: with such a one no not to eat. For what have I to do to judge them also that are without? do not ye judge them that are within? But them that are without God judgeth. Therefore put away from among yourselves that wicked person."

Is it not perfectly evident that the Corinthian church are here directed to perform acts of discipline of the highest and most solemn character? even to cut off, and to put away from among them, their own members.

See also, 2 Cor. 2: 6–11, where Paul gives intimations to the church respecting their duty to the incestuous person after his repentance for his sin: "Sufficient," says he, "to such a man is this punishment WHICH WAS INFLICTED OF MANY," [that is, doubtless, by a vote of the majority of the church,] "so that ye ought rather to forgive him and comfort him. . . . . Wherefore I beseech you that ye would confirm your love toward him." But how? Evidently by restoring him to their favor and communion. The apostle does not here speak as one having alone the key of the Corinthian church; but contrariwise, as one who recognized the power "of the many" (ὑπὸ τῶν πλειόνων, of the majority of the church) to act in the matter. He does not *command* the church to restore the penitent; but he "*beseeches*" them: much less does he restore the excommunicated person by the authority vested in himself as a minister of the gospel of Christ.*

In view of these facts, the inquiry arises: If the church at Corinth were authorized to perform these most solemn and most important of all ecclesiastical acts, were they not empowered to transact *all* appropriate church business? And if Paul himself, "the chiefest of the apostles," did not presume to act for the church, but contented himself with directing them how to act for themselves — not in his name, nor by his authority, but in the name of the Lord Jesus Christ, and by His authority — then, surely, no person has a right to control and dictate a church; but the power to act authoritatively must rest in the church alone, assembled together in the name, and by the authority of Jesus Christ.

If in these passages the keys of the church are not

---

* Calvin says: "It is to be marked, that Paul, though an apostle, yet did not excommunicate *alone*, after his own will, *but did participate the matter with the church*, that it might be done by common authority — *communi auctoritate*."

John Cotton takes substantially the same view of this case, in his "Keys of the Kingdom of Heaven," p. 87–90.

put into the hands of the church — if the power to discipline, and even to excommunicate (the most important of all church acts) is not committed to the associated brethren, called *the church* — there is no meaning in words.*

With what show of reason, then, can it be maintained, that the power of excommunication is here given to *the apostles;* and "*in a qualified sense*, may apply *to Christian teachers*, in all ages;" especially, when it is admitted by the same critic, that "tell it to the church," (εἰπὲ τῇ ἐκκλησίᾳ) must mean to the *particular congregation* to which you both, respectively, belong? †

What unprejudiced reader of the Saviour's directions will think of denying, that the power to bind and loose, — to receive and to excommunicate, — is here expressly given to the church, as such; that is, to the "*particular congregation*" of believers to which the trespasser and the complainant respectively belong; and, not to the apostles, as such, nor to christian teachers alone? The great Head of the Church knew that "offences must needs come." He knew, too, that a church could not long continue an organized and religious body, separate from the world, if destitute of power to "*purge out*" the leaven of impurity which would inevitably infuse itself into the mass. Knowing all this, can we believe that He has neglected to provide an effectual remedy? We

---

* Zuinglius says: "If we look thoroughly into the words of Christ which are in Matt. xviii. we may find him only to be excommunicated, whom *the common consent of that church in which the man dwelleth, hath shut out.*" — *Jacob's Attestation*, p. 30.

† See *Bloomfield's New Test.* in loc.

cannot. This remedy is pointed out in the passages which have been quoted. Here we have an infallible guide, unto which if we take heed we shall do well.

Admitting the Congregational principle — that every company of believers who have entered into covenant engagements for church purposes is a complete church, and authorized to transact all business, independently of the authoritative control or direction of any person or body of men whatever — admitting this, the directions of the Saviour are easily understood and obeyed. But, denying this principle, how can we proceed in cases of trespass? Who, and what is "the church," to which we are ultimately to carry our cause; and whose decision is to be final? If the apostles alone were intended, in the direction "tell it to the church," then there is no one now authorized to settle difficulties between church-members; yea, church discipline is out of the question; every member may walk as seemeth right in his own eyes, with none to say, "why do ye so?" Who can believe that Christ has left his churches in such a condition? But suppose it be said, that this disciplinary power is lodged with *the teachers* of the churches, as the successors of the apostles? Then I ask, What if a church be destitute of teachers, as some of our churches are for a succession of years? or what if the teachers themselves become corrupt? What then becomes of discipline? To avoid this difficulty, the power to discipline offenders may be committed to a "Church Session."* But is "a

* The Church Session consists of the Pastor or Pastors, and the Ruling Elders of a Presbyterian Congregation. — See *Con-*

church session" — i. e. the pastor and ruling elders of a particular congregation — "the church" of which Christ speaks in Matt. xviii. and to which Paul refers in his directions to the Corinthians? If it be, why then, we ask, did Paul (1 Cor. v.) direct the Corinthian church "gathered together," to pass an act of excommunication upon the incestuous person? Why were not his instructions addressed to the officers of the church alone? Is it not as clear that the apostles directed "*the church* which was in Corinth" — that is, "them that were sanctified in Christ Jesus, called to be saints" (1 Cor. 1: 2) — to perform this act of discipline, as it is, that his epistle was directed to the church as a body, and not to the officers merely? And if so, then have we not evidence from the Scriptures, that the power and right to exercise christian discipline were anciently vested in the congregated church? and that neither the elders of the church, nor any representatives of the body, could act independently of the brethren who constituted the church?

This is a principle of our system: that so far as the management of its own affairs is concerned,

---

fession of Faith of the Presbyterian Church, 18mo, p. 388, Phil. 1821. This body is constructively, *the church*, or *the congregation*. Dr. Campbell's remark upon such sort of churches, is worth repeating: "The notion . . . . of *a church representative*, how commonly soever it has been received, *is a mere usurper*" . . . . *Lectures on Ecc. Hist.* L. x. p. 166. Zuinglius says of a representative church — "ecclesia representiva." "Of this, I find nothing in the Holy Scriptures. Out of man's devices any may feign what they list. We rest in the Holy Scriptures." . . . *Jacob's Att.* p. 101.

every church is a little independent republic; invested by Christ with all needful authority to elect officers, to discipline offenders, to administer its own government, and to do all other things which are necessary to its individual welfare, and consistent with the general principles of the gospel.

The principles which have now been discussed, may be regarded as the corner-stones of the Congregational system. On these the whole edifice rests. Remove either of them, and the fair fabric of Congregationalism will be shattered. But the storms of centuries have beaten upon it in vain, and it is confidently believed, that nothing can move it, for it is "founded upon a rock."

PART II.

DOCTRINES OF CONGREGATIONALISM.

In the preceding pages we have considered what Congregationalists regard as the most essential characteristics of a christian church. In respect to these, we have ever been of one mind. But, in relation to what are here called (for the sake of a distinctive term, and for want of a better) the *Doctrines* of Congregationalism, it is somewhat otherwise. These have for the most part been gradually developed and adopted by the denomination, in connection with the practical application of fundamental principles. But the doctrines which will now be enumerated, are believed to be in accordance with our essential principles, and to have the very general, if not universal assent of consistent and intelligent Congregationalists of the present day.

Congregationalists maintain,

I. That there should be but two kinds of permanent church officers: ELDERS (sometimes called pastors, teachers, ministers, overseers, bishops,) and DEACONS.*

In the maintenance of this doctrine, modern Congregationalists differ materially from Episcopalians and Presbyterians, and even somewhat from the fathers of their own denomination.

As it is manifest to every reader of the New Testament that there were, in the apostolic churches, several orders of religious teachers and helpers, besides pastors and deacons; and, as we profess to copy after those churches, it is a reasonable question, "Why do you deviate from the inspired model?" We reply, Because we believe that all the official persons in the apostolic churches, except elders and deacons, were *extraordinary* assistants, designed to meet the peculiar exigencies of the churches in their early existence. This conclusion we think fully authorized by the Scriptures themselves. In the Epistles we are furnished with several distinct catalogues, more or less full, of those who were employed by the Holy Ghost in the days of the apostles, in converting men and in building up the churches. In 1 Cor. 12: 28 we have as complete and orderly an arrangement of these religious helpers as can anywhere be found. It is as follows: "God hath set some in the Church, first apostles, secondarily prophets, thirdly teachers; after that, miracles, then gifts of healing, helps, governments, diversities of tongues." We have here eight different sorts of spiritual men; and by com-

---

* See *Upham's Ratio Discip.* ch. 4; *Bacon's Chh. Manual,* p. 36–40, 1st ed.; *Pond's Church,* sec. 8; *Mitchell's Guide,* p. 38, 2d ed; *Congregational Dictionary,* Art. Officers.

paring this verse with the tenth verse we may, perhaps, add two more — those possessing the power of discerning spirits, and of interpreting tongues. But no one, it is presumed, will aver, that the apostle is here describing the ordinary and permanent officers of a christian church. He is evidently speaking of the supernatural gifts and graces of the Holy Spirit, and of the persons endowed with these several gifts and qualifications for usefulness. Compare 1–11 vs.* In Eph. 4: 11 we have another list of the gifts imparted by Christ to his Church: and "He gave some apostles [power and qualifications to become apostles]; and some prophets; and some evangelists; and some pastors and teachers; for the perfecting of the saints, for the work of the ministry, [διακονίας,] for the edifying of the body of Christ:" i. e. Christ, on leaving this world, authorized and instituted these several orders of religious teachers, namely, apostles, prophets, evangelists, pastors, and teachers; to the end, that their labors might perfect the saints in knowledge and holiness, and build up the Church in this apostate world.

This passage seems to imply, that the several religious teachers here named are essential to the accomplishment of the great work for which Christ came into the world; and that the churches will always need, and should always have these instrumentalities. This may be true, and yet it may not be true that the churches should always have *living*

---

* The reader will find an exceedingly interesting exhibition of these *charismata* (spiritual gifts) of the apostolic age, in *Neander's History of the Apostolical Churches*, Vol. I. ch. 5, bk. 3.

teachers answering to the four or five kinds above named. Indeed, from the very character of some of these teachers, it is a settled point that the churches cannot have them as permanent officers; I refer particularly to apostles and prophets. I know not that anybody pretends that there should be an order of prophets in our churches. Inspiration being indispensable to the prophetic office, prophets, of necessity, cease to exist so soon as the gift of inspiration is withdrawn. Still, the labors of prophets were essential to the establishment of Christianity, and their recorded predictions will be of great value to the Church in all periods of her existence.

APOSTOLIC SUCCESSION.

In respect to the apostolic office, some Episcopalians claim that this should be continued; and assert that in fact it is continued in their order of Bishops, so far as superiority in "ministerial power and rights" over the elders and the churches is concerned.

It will assist us in deciding this question, to inquire — What were the apostles? The Greek word translated *apostle* (ἀπόστολος, *apostolos*), means, "one who is sent with commands, or with a message." Thus it is used in John 13: 16, "The servant is not greater than his lord: neither is *he that is sent* (ἀπόστολος, *an apostle*), greater than he that sent him." And in 2 Cor. 8: 23, "Whether any do inquire of Titus, he is my partner and fellow-helper concerning you: or our brethren be inquired of, they are *the messengers* (ἀπόστολοι, *the apostles*) of the churches, and the glory of Christ." So Epaphroditus is called "*the messenger*, (ἀπόστολον, *the apostle*) of the church of Philippi." Phil. 2: 25. This title is, however, applied by way of eminence and distinction, to the twelve men whom Christ selected to be his personal attendants, and witnesses of all that he did, and said, and suffered; and eye-witnesses of his crucifixion, resurrection, and ascension; and his principal agents in establishing his kingdom in the world. This is expressed in Mark 3: 14, 15, "And he ordained twelve, *that they should be with him*, and that he might *send them forth* to preach, and to have power to heal sicknesses, and to cast out devils." So Matthew tells us: "These twelve Jesus *sent forth*," etc. 10: 5. See the whole chapter, which contains Christ's instructions to his apostles.

If from these instructions we turn to Christ's last interview with his chosen eleven — Judas having apostatized — we shall find the same character assigned to them. Having "opened their understanding, that they might understand the Scriptures," he said unto them: "Thus it is written, and thus it behooved Christ to suffer, and to rise from the dead the third day: and that repentance and remission of sins should be preached in his name among all nations, beginning at Jerusalem. *And ye are witnesses of these things.*" — Luke 24: 45–48. That the great design of their appointment was thus understood by the apostles, appears from the words of Peter when they were about to select one to fill the place of Judas, who had fallen by transgression from his high calling: . . . "Of these men which have companied with us *all the time that the Lord Jesus went in and out among us*, beginning from the baptism of John, unto that same day that he was taken up from us, must one be ordained to be *a witness, with us, of his resurrection.*" — Acts 1: 21, 22.

Now, from these passages it is evident, that the prominent and distinctive peculiarity of an apostle was this — HE WAS A WITNESS FOR CHRIST — a chosen messenger, sent forth to bear witness to what he had seen and heard of what Christ did and said during his public ministry, and particularly to his resurrection from the dead; for it was on this fact that the entire truth of the Christian System was made to rest. See 1 Cor. 15: 14, 17. In further confirmation of this view of the apostolic character and work, see Acts 2: 32. 3: 15. 4: 20, 33. 5: 30–32. 10: 39–41. 13: 31. 1 Pet. 5: 1. That Paul was not an exception, see Acts 22: 14, 15, and 26: 16, 22, 23. 1 Cor. 9: 1, 2. 15: 8.

So far then as the distinctive peculiarity of the apostolic office is concerned, it is manifest that the apostles can have no modern successors. We need their testimony to the important truths of Christianity; and in their inspired writings we have this testimony. But, as to such an order of living christian teachers as were the apostles, it is impossible, except by a miracle, that there should be any such now.

It may be asked: "Did not the apostles possess and exercise a superiority in 'ministerial power and rights' over other religious teachers, and over the early christian churches, which may be transmitted to modern successors?" In turn it may be asked: Did the apostles possess or exercise any superiority over other teachers, or over the churches, which was not founded on their peculiar relation to Christ as his chosen witnesses and specially commissioned and qualified agents? And, if they did not, could they transmit *this* superiority to any persons not holding this relation to Christ, and not possessing these supernatural qualifications?

That their authority over others was based exclusively on these extraordinary and incommunicable peculiarities, seems to us evident from the usual form of introduction in the epistles: "Paul, a servant of Jesus Christ, *called to be an apostle*," etc.—"Peter, *an apostle* of Jesus Christ." That it was on their character as the inspired apostles of Jesus Christ that they relied for authority over the churches, is further apparent from numerous express references to this fact: e. g. 2 Cor. 2: 10, where the apostle declares, that in granting forgiveness to the penitent offender, he acted "*in the person of Christ*,"—ἐν προσώπῳ Χριστοῦ—as the representative of Christ. The same idea is repeated in the 17th verse, "speak we *in Christ;*" i. e. "in the name of Christ, as his legates." In the 10: 8, Paul speaks of the "authority" which Christ had given him for the edification of the church; and in the 11: 5, he declares his belief that he "was not a whit behind the very chiefest of the apostles:" and this he gives as a reason why his authority should be regarded by the Corinthians. In the 12th chapter, throughout, he defends his claim to the confidence and obedience of the churches, by the evidence he had furnished of his apostolic and inspired character. He says: "In nothing am I behind the very chiefest apostles, though I be nothing. Truly *the signs of an apostle were wrought among you* in all patience, in signs, and wonders, and mighty deeds." See also 13: 2, 3, 10. Gal. 1: 11, 12. 2: 2, 6–10. 4: 14. Eph. 3: 1–7.

These texts seem fully to authorize the belief, that the apostles spoke and acted authoritatively, solely on the ground of their apostolic and inspired character. The reason why Paul had occasion to insist so much upon his apostolical character, was, that many persons, particularly the false teachers, questioned and denied his right to speak with authority in the churches; because, as they said, he was not an apostle, chosen of Christ, and empowered to act in his name. The fact that Paul deemed it sufficient to establish his apostolical character, in order to silence these opposers, proves conclusively, that the ground of the apostolical superiority over other teachers, and over the churches, was, that they, the apostles, were Christ's chosen witnesses and specially and divinely authorized and qualified agents. But for this, they would have possessed no more authority than other teachers. These peculiarities of character they could not, however, transmit to others: consequently, they could not, as apostles, have any successors.

It deserves remark, that Episcopalians, though in their controversies with Congregationalists and Presbyterians they assert that their bishops are successors of the apostles in their superiority over the churches and in "ministerial rights and power," yet, in arguing with the Papists, find it necessary to maintain the same views of the apostolic office which we do. For example, the learned Dr. Barrow, in his work on the "Pope's Supremacy," asserts, that "The apostolical office, as such, was *personal and temporary;* and therefore, according to its nature and design, *not successive or communicable to others,* in perpetual descendence from them. It was, as such, *in all respects extraordinary,* conferred in a special manner, designed for special purposes, discharged by special aids, endowed with special privileges, as was needful for the propagation of Christianity and founding of churches." He then goes on to specify — that it was necessary that an apostle should have "an immediate designation and commission from God" . . . "should be able to attest concerning our Lord's resurrection or ascension" . . . "be endowed with miraculous gifts and graces" . . . perhaps be able "to impart spiritual gifts" — that "his charge was universal and indefinite" — "that the whole world was his province;" . . . and that, by the "infallible assistance" afforded him, he could govern in "an absolute manner." He continues: "Now such an office, consisting of so many extraordinary privileges and miraculous powers, which were requisite for the foundation of the Church and the diffusion of Christianity, against the manifold difficulties and disadvantages which it then needs must encounter, *was not designed to continue by derivation;* for it containeth in it divers things which apparently were not communicated, and which no man, without gross imposture and hypocrisy, could challenge to himself.

"*Neither did the apostles pretend to communicate it;* they did indeed appoint standing pastors and teachers in each church; they did assume fellow-laborers or assistants in the work of preaching and governance; but they did not constitute apostles, equal to themselves in authority, privileges, or gifts; for, 'who knoweth not,' saith St. Austin, 'that principate of apostleship to be preferred before any episcopacy?' '*And the bishops*,' saith Bellarmine, '*have no part of the true apostolical authority*.'" * — He elsewhere tells us, that "the most ancient writers, living nearest to the fountains of tradition" . . . "do exclude the apostles from the episcopacy," i. e. they do not reckon them as bishops; or "were not assured in the opinion, that the apostles were bishops, or that they did not esteem them bishops in the same notion of others." †

EVANGELISTS.

Having given our reasons for supposing that the authoritative and controlling power of the apostles over the churches and their ministers cannot be transmitted to successors, we may pass to the consideration of another order of religious teachers — that of Evangelists.

Evangelists are ranked next to prophets. There is much difference of opinion respecting the character and the work of an ancient evangelist. The Greek word (εὐαγγελιστής, *euángelistes*) means literally, "one

---

* See under Supposition II. § 4, Vol. VII. p. 201–203. Also Supp. I. Arg. I. § 13–15, p. 168 seq.

† Supp. IV. throughout, particularly § 6. Dr. Campbell presents very nearly the same general view of the apostolic character, etc., as Dr. Barrow does. See *Lecture* v.

who announces joyful news," a preacher of the gospel; hence, some have questioned whether it designated a distinct order of religious teachers. That it did, seems to me evident from the use of the term in Eph. 4: 11; "He gave some apostles, and some prophets, and *some evangelists*, and some pastors and teachers." Evangelists are thus made as distinct from apostles and prophets as pastors and teachers are. We find the word used in two other places, Acts 21: 8, where Philip is called an "evangelist;" and 2 Tim. 4: 5, where Timothy is exhorted to do "the work of an evangelist."

The best commentators agree that evangelists, in the apostolic age, were religious teachers who had not the permanent care of any particular church, nor any fixed place of abode; but were sent by the apostles into different cities, that they might either preach the gospel to the heathen, or carry on the work of evangelization already begun by the apostles.*

It is quite apparent that these important agents in promoting Christianity, so far as they were endowed with miraculous gifts, can have no successors: their office, in other respects, was substantially the same

---

* See *Kuinoel*, Acts 21: 8; *Bloomfield* on Eph. 4: 11; *Doddr.* ib; Macknight, Henry, Scott, Burkitt. Neander takes the same view of the Evangelist: "Next to these [the apostles] were the *missionaries* or *evangelists*." — *Hist. Apostolical Churches*, Vol. I. p. 173. So does Dr. Campbell, *Lect.* v. p. 78. This account agrees with what Eusebius tells us, Bk. III. ch. 37 of Cruse's Transl. or thirty-third chapter of Hanmer's. Mosheim (Vol. I. p. 66, 67, Harper's ed.) supposes that many of the original seventy disciples, chosen and sent forth by Christ, were evangelists.

as that of a missionary of modern days; whose ministerial work is the same as that of an ordained elder.

Entertaining such views as have now been submitted, Congregationalists can recognize but one order of religious teachers, namely, that of *Elders*, sometimes called pastors, teachers, bishops.

Thus far, Presbyterians and Congregationalists perfectly agree: and upon this point there has ever been an entire agreement among all who have advocated our denominational peculiarities. Upon some other points, modern Congregationalists differ from their Presbyterian brethren, and also from the fathers of their own denomination. To these points we will next attend.

TEACHERS, RULING ELDERS, AND DEACONESSES.

Our religious ancestors recognized a distinction, in office, not in grade, between Pastors and Teachers: they also admitted the office of Ruling Elder; though they gave the elders no such judicial power as Presbyterians do.* They had among them, too, the

---

* Governor Hutchinson, in his "History of Massachusetts Bay," gives the following account of the Ruling Elder. "Most of the churches, *not all*, had one or more ruling elders. In matters of offence the ruling elder after the hearing, asked the church if they were satisfied; if they were, he left it to the pastor or teacher to denounce the sentence of excommunication, suspension, or admonition, according as the church had determined.

"Matters of offence, regularly, were first brought to the ruling elder in private, and might not otherwise be told to the church. It was the practice for the ruling elders to give public notice of such persons as desired to enter into church fellowship with them; and of the time proposed for admitting them, if no sufficient objec-

office of Deaconess or Reliever, in conformity with the practice of the apostolic churches. These several offices were recognized in the Confession of the North of England Congregational church, as early as 1589. And (with perhaps the exception of Deaconess) by the London Congregational church, formed 1593.*

Thomas Hooker believed that the New Testament authorized these five church officers:—Pastors,

---

tion was offered; and when the time came, to require all persons who knew any just grounds, to signify them.

"When a minister preached to any other than his own church, the ruling elder of the church, after the psalm was sung, said publicly: 'If this present brother have any word of exhortation for the people at this time, in the name of God, let him say on.'

"The ruling elder also read the Psalm.

"When a member of one church desired to receive the sacrament at another, he came to the ruling elder, who proposed his name to the church, for their consent.

"At the communion they sat with the minister.

"They were considered, without doors, as men for advice and counsel in religious matters; they visited the sick; and had a general inspection and oversight of the conduct of their brethren.

"Every thing which I have mentioned, as the peculiar province of the ruling elder; so far as it was in itself necessary or proper, may with propriety enough be performed by the minister.

"It is not strange, therefore, that this office, in a course of years, sunk into an almost entire desuetude in the churches. Indeed, the multiplying unnecessary, and mere nominal offices or officers, whose duties and privileges are not, with certainty, agreed upon and determined, seems rather to have had a natural tendency to discord and contention, than harmony and peace."—Vol. I. p. 426, 427.

* *History of Congregationalism*, App. No. 1. Also, p. 277.

Teachers, Ruling Elders, Deacons, and Deaconesses.* The Cambridge Platform, framed the same year that Hooker wrote, mentions the same church officers; † though it speaks of the Deaconess as a church officer less essential to the interests of the churches than are the other officers. Its language is: "The Lord hath appointed ancient widows, *when they may be had*, to minister in the church, in giving attendance to the sick, and to give succor unto them and others in like necessities:" 1 Tim. 5: 9, 10.—Chap. 7, § 7. When the 'Ratio Disciplinæ, Frat. Nov-Anglorum' was published, in 1726, the office of Deaconess seems to have been entirely dropped; and that of Ruling Elder extensively questioned, and "almost extinguished." See Art. 7. Both were at length given up by our churches; as was that of Teacher, in distinction from Pastor: and now, but two kinds of church officers, Pastors and Deacons, are recognized by Congregationalists as *jure divino*—required by the Scriptures. Even from the time that the Cambridge Platform was laid, (1648,) there were some persons in our churches, according to Mather, who could not "see any such officer as we call a Ruling Elder, directed and appointed in the word of God." And as early as 1702, Cotton Mather wrote: "Our churches are now nearly destitute of such helps in government." ‡

Before we examine the evidence tending to show

---

* *Survey of Chh. Discip.* P. II. ch. 1. Printed in 1648.

† Chapters 6 and 7.

‡ *Magnalia*, Bk. 5, ch. 17, § 4.

that pastors and deacons are the only divinely constituted, permanent church officers, it may be well to consider, why our churches have given up the other officers: —

(1) As it respects the office of *Teacher.*

This office, in distinction from that of pastor, was built on what the apostle says, Eph. 4: 8, 11. "When he [Christ] ascended up on high, he led captivity captive, and gave gifts unto men: And he gave some, apostles; and some, prophets; and some, evangelists; and some, pastors and *teachers*," etc. This text was supposed to indicate that our churches should have *both* pastors and teachers. The very arrangement of the text, however, suggests, that a different interpretation ought to be given to the last clause. This does not read, as the preceding do, — some pastors; and *some* teachers; but "some pastors *and* teachers;" which arrangement certainly allows, if it does not require, that the same officer should be *both* pastor and teacher: especially, as *feeding* the church of God — i. e. instructing it — is declared to be an important part of the pastor's work. See Acts 20: 28. 1 Pet. 5: 1–4. Compare these passages with 1 Cor. 12: 28, where the apostle, in describing the provision made by God for the edification of his Church, enumerates — first, apostles, secondarily, prophets, thirdly, *teachers*, after that, miracles, etc. Now, unless he includes the pastor in the term teacher, he has entirely omitted this most important church officer. He, doubtless, used the term as synonymous with pastor. Indeed, the two offices seem naturally to run into each other: and this very difficulty of keeping them separate, may have helped to convince our fathers that they had misinterpreted the passage on which the distinction had been founded.

(2) We come next to speak of *Ruling Elders.*

The principal foundation on which this order of church officers is built, is 1 Tim. 5: 17—"Let the elders that *rule well* be counted worthy of double honor [διπλῆς τιμῆς may denote both competent reward and suitable respect]—especially they who labor in the word and doctrine."

This passage was supposed by our fathers, and is still believed by our Presbyterian brethren, to teach that there should be one order of elders who should be simply *rulers* in the churches; and another, answering to our pastors and teachers, who should labor in word and doctrine also. To this inference, it is objected: First, that the verse may be otherwise construed; and that, without violence to the original, thus: *especially as they labor in word and doctrine*—μάλιστα οἱ κοπιῶντες ἐν λογο καὶ διδασκαλία. The word rendered *labor* (κοπιῶντες) means literally, *wearing out*, *fainting through weariness;* and the expression, *especially those wearing themselves out*, etc., intimates that the apostle, instead of designating two kinds of elders, and saying that the *latter* had special claims on the bounty and respect of the churches, intended rather to be understood, that, though all their divinely constituted leaders and guides were deserving of a *liberal* support (for this is evidently the meaning of *double*) and the respect of the churches—yet, more especially did those spiritual guides and rulers (a general name for those who had the care of the churches) deserve this compensation and respect, who were *eminently faithful and laborious* in their pastoral and ministerial duties;—those who were *wearing out* their very lives for their people.*

Secondly. In support of the general position alluded to above, it may be further remarked: that, while there is scarcely another text which, independently of this, would even *suggest* that there should be an established eldership for ruling the churches merely, there are several passages which connect ruling and teaching together, as the appropriate work of those who have the care of the churches: e. g. 1 Thess. 5: 12, 13—"We beseech you, brethren, to know them which *labor among you* and *are over you* in the Lord—[the same words are here employed as in 1 Tim. 5: 17—κοπιῶντας . . . καὶ προϊσταμένους]—and *admonish you;* and to esteem them very highly in love for their works' sake." . . . The natural and obvious construction of this passage will teach us, that one and the same order of persons is here spoken of, namely, such as *labor* in word and doctrine—*preside* in the assemblies of the church, and act as the mouth of the church in admonishing the unruly; and if so, then this text throws light on that in 1 Timothy, and is very nearly a parallel.

Another passage of the same general import may be found in Heb. 13: 7, 17, 24; "Remember them which have *the rule over you,* who have *spoken unto you the word of God*" . . . or more correctly—"Remember those who, having presided over you,

* See *Upham's Ratio,* § 38. *Limborch,* in Doddridge; and *Scott,* and *Henry, in loc.*

have spoken to you the word of God."* These rulers (ἡγουμένων) are allowed by almost all expositors, to be the same as those spoken of in Timothy.† And to these rulers, presidents, or guides is expressly assigned the work of teaching the word of God. See also, verses 17, 24. Now, these passages furnish no intimation that there were any rulers established in the churches except such as *watched for souls*—*spoke the word of God*—*labored in the word and doctrine;* or, in other words, such as were the pastors and overseers of the churches.

Another text, somewhat relied on by the advocates of Ruling Elders, is 1 Cor. 12: 28; "God hath set some in the church, first apostles, secondarily prophets, thirdly teachers; after that, miracles, then gifts of healing, *helps*, *governments*, diversities of tongues." But this passage is too weak to stand alone in the controversy. The apostle indeed speaks of *helps* (ἀντιλήψεις, those who aid, assist, etc.); but we may just as well suppose this expression refers to any other kind of aid or assistance as that of ruling. The word *governments* (κυβερνήσεις), means the office of governor, director, or superintendent; but, why should we suppose a *ruling elder* referred to here, rather than a bishop or pastor, as Wahl supposes?

There is, however, another, and as it seems to me an entirely satisfactory way to dispose of this question. It is this: The apostle in the twelfth and thirteenth chapters of 1 Cor. is treating, not of the ordinary, and established, and permanent officers of

---

* See *Doddridge, in loc.*

† *Doddridge, Macknight,* and *Bloomfield.*

the churches of Christ, but of the spiritual and miraculous gifts, which, for wise and obvious reasons, God bestowed on many of the early Christians. This is perfectly obvious from the first eleven verses of the twelfth chapter. So that, should it be admitted, that among these diversified gifts of the Spirit, the gift of government — or eminent qualifications for administering the government of the churches — was imparted to some of the elders who had been ordained over them, it would by no means follow that these gifted ones were SIMPLY *rulers* or *governors*, and not *teachers;* much less would it follow, that there should be such an order of ruling elders in *our* churches. This passage, and one nearly parallel, in Rom. 12: 6–9, instead of authorizing the establishment of a bench of mere ruling elders in each church, would rather go to countenance the practice early adopted by the primitive churches, and which was the first step towards Diocesan Episcopacy — of choosing one of their several elders to act as a leader, guide, and governor, or overseer, in each church; who finally received the title of ἐπίσκοπος, *the bishop*, or προεστῶς, *the president.* But, to our minds, the passage furnishes authority neither for ruling elders nor diocesan bishops; but simply informs us, that among other miraculous gifts imparted to the early Christians was that of unusual skill in governing. And this, surely, was not less important to the welfare of the churches than the gift of healing, or of discerning spirits, or of interpreting tongues.

Thirdly. There is one other view of this controversy about ruling elders which we deem very important, and conclusive in our favor, namely: that no description of their qualifications, etc., is anywhere given in the New Testament; nor any directions for choosing and ordaining them. We certainly might reasonably expect that Paul in his directions to Timothy or Titus, who were employed in setting in order churches, would give some hint about this important order of church officers, if indeed they were *jure divino* and intended to be permanent in the churches. We find directions about elders, or pastors, and also about deacons; but nothing about the peculiar qualifications of an intermediate order. We feel justified, therefore, in the inference, that such officers as ruling elders are not, by Divine authority, established in christian churches.

I have now said what seems to be necessary to explain why modern Congregationalists cannot recognize the office of Ruling Elder. I might add to the above, as collateral considerations against this order — the danger of conflict with pastors in the administration of church government — the difficulty of procuring, in most of our churches, besides the necessary number of deacons, a sufficient number of persons suitably qualified for ruling elders — and yet further, that the deacons can ordinarily furnish the pastors with all needed counsel and help in the administration of church government; all these considerations might be urged as arguments against this office as a *prudential* arrangement. But I have already dwelt quite long enough upon this question. The conclusion of the whole matter is this: modern Congregationalists have dropped the office of ruling elder in their churches, because they cannot find satisfactory evidence that there ever was such an order of men in the churches; or, if there was, that they were other than miraculously qualified for their temporary work in the apostolic churches.*

(3) The same view substantially may be taken of another class of church officers mentioned in the New Testament — the *Deaconesses.* These were an order of helpers which the peculiarities of Eastern manners and customs rendered necessary to the primitive churches. Every reader of ancient history must be aware, that in most Oriental countries familiar social intercourse between the sexes is not allowed. Even to this day, an Eastern lady would regard herself as degraded were she exposed to the gaze of the other sex. Hence the practice of veiling the face, and in some instances even the whole person. To meet this state of things among the people to whom the gospel was first preached, it became expedient to appoint aged women, usually widows, to administer to the necessities of the female disciples; to visit them in sickness; to distribute among them the charities of the church; and in various other ways to minister to their wants, both temporal and spiritual. To these females, reference is perhaps made in 1 Tim. 5: 9, 10; "Let not a widow be taken into *the number* (that is, of the *deaconesses*) under threescore years old," etc. Phebe, spoken of by the apostle, Rom. 16: 1, was one of

* In *Mosheim's Commentaries*, or Larger History of the First Three Centuries, is a long note, in which this question of Ruling Elders is discussed, and the views expressed above, generally maintained.—Vol. I. p. 215–218.

this number: "I commend unto you (or I introduce to your christian confidence) Phebe, our sister, which is a *servant* (διάκονον, a deacon) of the church at Cenchrea."

From Ecclesiastical History we learn that these deaconesses were set apart to their office by imposition of hands. "Yet we are not to imagine, that this consecration," says Bingham, "gave them any power to execute any part of the sacerdotal office. . . . Women were always forbidden to perform any such offices as those." . . . "Some heretics, indeed," as Tertullian observes, "allowed women to teach, and exercise, and administer baptism; but all this," he says, "was against the rule of the apostle." . . . . Epiphanius, a Christian father who died about A. D. 403, says: "There is, indeed, an order of deaconesses in the church, but their business is not to sacrifice, or perform any part of the sacerdotal office, . . . but to be a decent help to the female sex in the time of their baptism, sickness, affliction, or the like." *

If the primitive churches were authorized to ordain these "female public servants, or deaconesses"— which, however, the Scriptures nowhere intimate— it is very obvious that they were, like several other servants of the churches in those days, *extraordinary*, and not designed for permanent church officers. They were appointed simply to meet the exigencies of the churches in Eastern countries; and consequently, when these exigencies ceased, or among a

* "*Antiquities of the Christian Church*," Book II. ch. 22, § 7. See a full account of this matter in *Coleman's Christian Antiquities*, p. 115–118.

people of different habits, the office itself should be discontinued.

Setting aside the apostles, and those spiritual persons and extraordinary assistants whose claims have been now considered, we have remaining, as constituted and permanent officers in the church of Christ: —

1. Elders. These were ordained persons, who had the charge of particular churches; and, so far as we are informed, had no ecclesiastical authority in any other church than that "over which the Holy Ghost had made them overseers."

The account of the second visit of Paul and Barnabas to the churches of Asia Minor (Acts 14: 21–23) confirms this view. We read: "*And when they had ordained them elders in every church*, and had prayed with fasting, they commended them to the Lord in whom they had believed." Now, the unavoidable inference from this passage is, that these churches, which were founded by the labors of the apostles, were *each* of them furnished with one elder or more. The number was probably regulated by the size of the church and the circumstances of the elders. It is probable that most of the primitive elders were men who labored at some trade or secular business most of their time. Hence, in part, the necessity of ordaining several elders over a single church, if that church was large. See Acts 14: 23. 15: 6. 20: 17. 21: 18. Phil. 1: 1. 1 Thess. 5: 12. Tit. 1: 5.

Another reason for the plurality of elders in the primitive churches, may perhaps be found in the fact, that the larger churches, in times of persecution particularly, were compelled to meet in small companies, in private houses, in vaults, or caves, and other places of security, in order to worship God unmolested: each of these assemblies would need an elder to conduct its religious services; and thus several overseers would be necessary for a single church of any considerable size. Then, again, the elders were specially exposed to be cut off by persecution; and if there had been but one in a church, that church might any day have been left destitute of a teacher and overseer.

In proof that the *elders* of the primitive churches were the same order of men that are sometimes called *pastors*, *overseers*, and *bishops*, reference may be made to the epistle of Paul to Titus. In chapter first, verse 5th, Paul says to Titus: "For this cause left I thee in Crete, that thou shouldst set in order the things that are wanting" — that is, the things necessary to the complete organization and the spiritual improvement of the churches — "and *ordain elders in every city*, as I had appointed thee;" or, as I had previously instructed thee to do.

Paul, it seems, had visited Crete in company with Titus; and their united labors had gathered a number of christian churches on that island. But, as Paul was pressed for time, and the island was very populous — containing, according to Homer, one hundred cities — the apostle could not make all the necessary arrangements, and give all the needed instruction, for the complete organization of the numerous converts into distinct churches. He therefore left Titus in Crete, with instructions how to proceed in this important work. In the passage just quoted, these instructions are referred to and some of the more important items in them recapitulated. One of the most prominent of these was — to "*ordain elders* [πρεσβυτέρους — *presbuterous;* whence the English *presbyters*] in *every city*," — that is, in every city where there was a church: or, in other words, to supply every church with elders.* This is precisely what the Apostle and Barnabas did in the cities of Asia Minor, among which they had been preaching the gospel. See Acts xiv.

Having given this general direction, "to ordain elders in every city;" the Apostle next tells Titus what sort of men to select for elders: "If any be blameless, the husband of one wife [only], having faithful children, not accused of riot, or unruly." Then, in the following verse — as if purposely to show that an *elder and a bishop were precisely the same officer* — he continues: "For A BISHOP [ἐπίσκοπον

* In the spurious postscripts to the epistles of Paul to Titus and Timothy, these Evangelists are called *Bishops.* Timothy is said to have been "the first bishop of the church of the Ephesians;" and Titus to have been "the first bishop of the church of the Cretians." Now, in reference to these postscripts, "it is universally agreed, among the learned, that they are of no authority." They were probably annexed to the epistles as late as the fifth century. "Certain it is," says Dr. Campbell, "that in the three first centuries, neither Timothy nor Titus is styled *bishop* by any writer. It also deserves to be remarked, that in the island of Crete, of which Titus is said . . . to have been ordained the first bishop, there were no fewer, according to the earliest accounts and catalogues extant, than *eleven bishops.* Hence it is, that Titus has been called by some of the late fathers, an *archbishop;* though few of the warmest friends of Episcopacy pretend to give the archiepiscopal order so early a date." *Lec.* v. p. 79.

— *episcopon* — an inspector, an overseer] must be *blameless*, as the steward of God [of God's house, which is his church]; not self-willed, not soon angry," etc. Tit. 1: 5–7. Here we perceive that the words *elder* and *bishop* are used interchangeably, to designate the same church officer. Nothing can be more clear. In the same manner are the words used by the Evangelist, in giving an account of Paul's interview with the elders of the church at Ephesus, Acts 20: 17–28; "And from Miletus he sent to Ephesus, and called the *elders* of the church;"* — τούς πρεσβυτèρους τῆς ἐκκλησίας. In the 28th verse the same persons are called *overseers*, or bishops: "Take heed, therefore, unto all the flock over which the Holy Ghost hath made you *overseers* (bishops, ἐπισκόπους,) to feed the church of God, which he hath purchased with his own blood." The case is so plain that no one need doubt that the same order of men are called either *elders*, *bishops*, or *overseers*, interchangeably.

The same thing is apparent from the description of a good *bishop*, 1 Tim. 3: 1–7; which answers, exactly, to the requisite of a good *elder*, Tit. 1: 5–9.†

---

* The Syriac version, made probably early in the second century, and one of the most valuable of all the ancient translations, reads: — "*elders of the church of* EPHESUS, — Venire fecit presbyteros ecclesias *Ephesi*." A hint worth remembering, as an offset to the quotation from Irenaeus, designed to prove that these *elders*, or bishops, were from several *neighboring* churches, and not from Ephesus alone. — *Stillingfleet's Irenicum*, p. 292.

† The reader who wishes to examine this matter more fully, and especially, if he would know the sentiments of the fathers of the church, and the English Reformers upon this subject, is referred to *Dr. Dwight's Theology*, Ser. 150 and 151, to Prof. Pond's

The Greek word πρεσβύτερος, translated presbyter or elder, means literally, *an older*, or *an old man;* being the comparative of πρέσβυς, *old.* The term was originally applied to the heads of the tribes of Israel, and to the members of the Jewish Sanhedrim or high court of the nation. These were generally men advanced in life, and distinguished for sobriety, knowledge, and sound judgment. The term is applied to the teachers of the christian church, because these were at first selected from the more aged, experienced, and intelligent converts to Christianity. The first place in which the term *elder* is used in the New Testament to designate a christian teacher, is Acts 11: 30; "The disciples, every man according to his ability, determined to send relief unto the brethren which dwelt in Judea. Which also they did, and sent it to *the elders*, by the hands of Barnabas and Saul." We find the term in numerous other places, in such connections as to prove conclusively that the same order of persons is designated by the term *presbyters*, or *elders*, as is elsewhere called *bishops*, *overseers*, or *pastors*. The first epistle of Peter 5: 1–4 very clearly illustrates this. "*The elders* (πρεσβυτὲρους) which are among you, I exhort, who am also an elder" (or co-elder) . . . "*Feed the flock* of God which is among you";—ποιμάνατε, act the part of a pastor towards the flock. Here we have the *pastoral* character introduced; the *elders* are spoken of as *pastors;* allusion being made to

---

most satisfactory exhibition of the matter, in the 8th chapter of his book, "*The Church*," and *Dr. Campbell's Lectures on Ecc. Hist.* See also *History of Congregationalism*, p. 162, 195–198.

such passages as Jer. 3: 15; "I will give you *pastors* according to my heart, which shall *feed* you with knowledge and understanding." These *pastors*, or *elders*, are next described as *bishops*, "taking *the oversight* thereof, [ἐπισκοποῦντες, *acting the bishop, overseeing the church*], not by constraint, but willingly; not for filthy lucre, but of a ready mind; neither as being *lords* over God's heritage, but being *ensamples to the flock*. And when the chief Shepherd shall appear, ye shall receive a crown of glory that fadeth not away." Which is as if the apostle had said: The elders or pastors are to act the part of *bishops* in the church — they are to govern the church; not, however, with lordly authority, but rather by the weight of their holy example, and their strict conformity to the directions and spirit of the Chief Shepherd and Bishop of souls.

How the apostle could teach the identity of the office of presbyter or elder and bishop or overseer, with that of pastor and teacher, more clearly than he does in this passage, it would be difficult to conceive. Dr. Bloomfield in his note upon this chapter seems to admit this identity. His words are: "The apostle now gives particular injunctions to the *presbyters*, i. e. the bishops and pastors of the church." . . .

The titles *pastor* and *teacher* designate "the office-work" of elders or bishops; namely, to guide the flocks, to preside over them, and to feed them with knowledge and wisdom. Jesus Christ is the Chief Shepherd and Bishop of souls (1 Pet. 2: 25); and every elder in his church is an under bishop and shepherd, or pastor, of a portion of his flock.

Can any thing be made more plain, by Scripture

testimony, than the correctness of this doctrine of Congregationalism — that *elder*, *pastor*, *bishop*, *are different titles of the same church officer?*

Dr. Bloomfield himself, though a devoted churchman, is constrained to admit, that "the best commentators, ancient and modern, have, *with reason*, inferred that the terms [elder and bishop] as yet denoted the same thing." *

If, then, these terms "*as yet*," (that is, during the lifetime of the apostles) signified the "*same thing*," by what authority are they *now* made to signify *different things?*

Waddington, another Episcopal writer, admits that "it is *even certain*, that the terms *bishop*, and *elder*, or *presbyter*, were, in the first instance, and for a short period, sometimes used synonymously, and indiscriminately applied to the same order in the ministry." † Bishop Onderdonk, fully admits that the word *bishop* and *elder* have *uniformly*, and precisely, the same meaning in Scripture. He says: "The *name* Bishop, which now designates the highest grade of the ministry, is not appropriate to that office in Scripture. That name is given to the middle order, or Presbyters; and all that we read in the New Testament concerning 'Bishops' . . . is to be regarded as pertaining to that middle grade" — that is, to presbyters, or elders.‡

If this be an admitted fact, and the soundness of the first principle of Congregationalism be allowed —

---

* *Bloomfield's New Testament*, Acts 20: 17, note.

† *History of the Church*, ch. 2, § 2.

‡ *Episcopacy Tested by the Scripture*, p. 12.

that the Scriptures are our safe and only guide in respect to church polity — then it must follow, that no distinction should now be made between elders and bishops. This is Congregational doctrine.

2. DEACONS are the only other permanent church officers recognized by CONGREGATIONALISTS.

The original appointment of deacons is given in Acts 6: 1–6; "In those days, when the number of the disciples was multiplied, there arose a murmuring of the Grecians against the Hebrews, because their widows were neglected in the daily ministration;" that is, in the daily distribution of the charities of the church. "Then the twelve called *the multitude of the disciples* unto them," — that is, all the professing Christians of the city, or *the church* — "and said: It is not reason that we should leave the word of God and serve tables" — or, leave the preaching of the gospel to attend to secular business. "Wherefore, brethren, *look ye out among you* seven men of honest report, full of the Holy Ghost and wisdom, whom we may appoint over this business" — or set apart, ordain, (καταστήσομεν) to this work; — "but we will give ourselves continually unto prayer and the ministry of the word. And the saying pleased the *whole multitude* (παντός τοῦ πλήθους), and *they chose* Stephen, a man full of faith and of the Holy Ghost, and Philip, and Prochorus, and Nicanor, and Timon, and Parmenas, and Nicholas, a proselyte of Antioch. Whom they set before the apostles; and when they had prayed, they laid their hands on them"; — or, in other words, *ordained* them.

The specific object for which these men were selected and ordained, explains the nature of their office, and furnishes a conclusive argument for its perpetuity. The primitive churches were accustomed to take up weekly contributions for the relief of the widows and the fatherless, and the sick and necessitous among them. See 1 Cor. 16: 1–3. 2 Cor. viii. and ix. 1 Tim. 5: 16. This care of the poor was specially important in times of persecution, when Christians were liable to be stripped of their property, driven from their homes, shut up in prison, and even martyred for the truth. Thus were many families deprived of their supporters; wives were made widows, and children, orphans. It became, therefore, the imperative duty of the church, for whom these persons suffered, to minister to their necessities. While the Christians were few in number, the apostles and elders could easily take charge of these charities; but when "the number of the disciples was multiplied," the teachers of the churches could not do this work, without neglecting their appropriate and peculiar business of teaching and ruling. Under these circumstances, the apostles, acting by Divine authority, directed the church at Jerusalem to choose from among themselves a suitable number of persons, who might be set apart to this particular and important work; and thus a new order of church officers was established.*

---

* It is the opinion of some commentators, that this was not the *origin* of the deacon's office; but, rather, that after the example of the Synagogues, there had from the beginning been such servants in the christian churches as deacons. And, that these seven deacons were *added* to those already existing in the church at Jerusalem; and were selected from among the *foreign* Jews in order to obviate complaints of inattention to their widows.— See

That the office of a deacon was not confined to the church at Jerusalem, where it was first introduced, is apparent from the repeated mention of this church officer in other connections. Thus Paul addresses the "saints at Philippi, with the bishops and *deacons*." Phil. 1: 1. And in his letter of instructions to Timothy respecting the proper organization of christian churches, he expressly specifies the office of the *deacon:* "Likewise must the *deacons* be grave, not double-tongued, not given to much wine, not greedy of filthy lucre; holding the mystery of the faith in a pure conscience. And let these also first be proved; then let them use the office of a deacon, being found blameless." See 1 Tim. 3: 1–15.

It is true, that the necessity of "daily ministrations" among the poor of our churches may not be now so great as it was in apostolic times; but the poor, the churches will always have among them; for unto the poor the gospel has always been most successfully preached; and the poor in this world are still those whom God hath chosen to be rich in faith. So long as these things shall be true, so long will there be occasion for the apostolic deacon.

It is not, however, to be inferred that the whole

Mosheim, Vol. I. p. 69, 70. He supposes the "*young men*" mentioned Acts 5: 6, 10 and 1 Pet. 5: 5—were deacons. *Kuinoel* and *Bloomfield* agree with Mosheim, so far as the first opinion is concerned.

The question respecting the design of the deacon's office, and the manner of selecting and inducting into office is not affected by the opinion of these writers. Neander rejects this theory of Mosheim and others; and maintains that of the text.—See *Hist. of the Apostolical Churches*, Vol. I. p. 34–41.

office-work of the deacon was confined to the care of the poor. The reason assigned by the apostles for the selection of "the seven," was: "It is not reason [ἀρεστόν, right; fit, proper] that we should leave the word of God, [the preaching of the gospel] *and serve tables:*" — διακονεῖν τραπέζαις, to administer tables; i. e. by implication, to take care of pecuniary affairs.*

Hence our churches have judged it to be proper to commit to their deacons the care of their funds, if any they chance to have, and their pecuniary matters generally. They reason thus: If it was wrong for the apostles "to leave the word of God to serve tables," it must be equally so for any preachers of the gospel. And, if it is wrong for ministers of the gospel to neglect their appropriate work to attend to pecuniary affairs, it must be equally so for them to be cumbered about any secular business, even though connected with the welfare of the church. But every person at all conversant with church affairs is aware, that there are many things of a secular character which must be attended to, or the interests of the church will materially suffer. This being true of every church, in every age, it is evidently suitable and proper that there should be permanent church officers set over "this business." The importance of this office in the churches is acknowledged by the conduct of those denominations, even, who deny its scriptural authority. No church, it is believed, has found it convenient to dispense with the services of secular agents in church affairs. Some have their

* See *Wahl's Lexicon.* The same view is taken by Neander. — *Hist. of Apost. Chh.* Vol. I. p. 38, note.

church-wardens, others their stewards. Congregationalists prefer to follow apostolic example, and choose, as permanent officers, a sufficient number of deacons, who are set apart to the work of serving tables, and in other ways relieving their pastors and assisting their brethren.

OBJECTIONS CONSIDERED.

It has been objected to this view of the deacon's office, that Stephen and Philip, two of the primitive deacons, were found, soon after their ordination, *preaching the gospel;* and one of them, *administering* the *ordinance* of *baptism.* Hence it is inferred, that *a deacon* should be *a preaching* church officer.

In reply, it may be said, that it is obvious, on the slightest examination of the subject, that the apostles directed the church at Jerusalem to elect deacons for *secular purposes.* "Look ye out among you seven men of honest report, etc., whom we may appoint [καταστήσομεν, set apart, ordain] over *this business,"* — namely, the distribution of the charities of the church, and the necessary secular work connected therewith. But, if these deacons were chosen by the church to *preach the gospel;* then, in order to have administered the charities of the church, and to have done other secular work, *they* must have left "the word of God to serve tables," as really as the apostles had previously been required to do; otherwise, the evils which their appointment was designed especially to remove, must have remained unremedied: and if so, what was gained by this election of deacons?

This argument is so conclusive, that candid and

learned churchmen have felt and admitted its force. Thus *Bishop White*, in a letter to Bishop Hobart, says: "But can it be imagined that an order instituted for the purpose of 'serving tables' should, in the very infancy of its existence, have the office of the higher order of the ministry committed to them? I do not deny either the right or the prudence of allowing what has been subsequently allowed to this lowest order of the clergy. All I contend for, is, that at the first institution of the order there could have been no difference between them and laymen, in regard to the preaching of the word and the administering of the sacraments." * Bishop Croft, in his "Naked Truth," is equally explicit in declaring that the original institution of the Deaconship was to be overseers of the poor. He says: "Their office was 'to serve tables,' as the Scripture phrases it; which, in plain English, is nothing else but overseers of the poor, to distribute justly and discreetly the alms of the Faithful; which the Apostles would not trouble themselves withal, lest it should hinder them in the ministration of the Word and prayer. But, as most matters of this world in process of time deflect much from the original constitution, so it fell out in this business; for the Bishops who pretended to be successors to the apostles, by little and little took to themselves the dispensation of alms, first, by way of inspection over the deacons, but at length the total management; and the deacons, who were mere lay officers, by degrees crept into the church ministration and

* *Wilson's Memoir of Bishop White*, p. 365; quoted in Smyth's "Apostolical Succession," p. 150.

became a reputed spiritual order, and a necessary degree and step to the priesthood, of which I can find nothing in Scripture and the original institution, not a word relating to any thing but the ordering of alms for the poor. And the first I find of their officiating in spiritual matters, is in Justin Martyr, who lived in the second century." * *Father Paul*, in his "Treatise of Ecclesiastical Benefices," etc., explains the change referred to by Bishop Croft, whereby the Bishops gradually assumed to themselves the deacons' work, and applied themselves "to the sole government and care of their temporals, leaving the other part of their function of teaching the word of God, as a lesser care, to the monks and priests of the lowest order in the church." †

But it is asked: "Why need these men be full of the Holy Ghost and wisdom, if they were designed merely to superintend the temporalities of the church?" The answer is: Because eminent piety, as well as honesty and wisdom, was necessary to a faithful, fearless, and successful discharge of their official duties as stewards of the charities of the church and guardians of its secular interests. Furthermore, these deacons were to mingle extensively with the Jewish and Heathen population of the city, in their visits from house to house and in the transaction of their secular business; and by the people generally, would be regarded as representatives of the entire christian church. Hence the necessity that

---

* Quoted by Smyth, p. 150, from Scott's Coll. of Tracts, Vol. VII. p. 307, 308.

† See Chaps. I.— II. inclusive.

they should be men "full of the Holy Ghost and wisdom;" — men of eminent piety and devotion to God, tempered with much of that "wisdom which cometh down from above, and is profitable to direct." Besides this eminence in personal piety, it is by no means unlikely that "the seven," who were selected for deacons in the Jerusalem church, were distinguished among their brethren for the possession of some of those miraculous gifts of the Spirit which were early vouchsafed to the churches. — See 1 Cor. xii. These would be specially valuable to men who were to sustain that relation to the churches and the world which the primitive deacons are supposed to have held. This is certain, that whatever this "fulness of the Holy Ghost" was, it was not imparted by the laying on of hands of the apostles at the time of the ordination of the deacons, but was possessed by "the seven," probably in common with many of their christian brethren, previously to their ordination.* It was, undoubtedly, that full and constant

---

* It seems evident that the first deacons were *ordained.* For we read: "When they" — the apostles — "had prayed, they *laid their hands upon them,*" Acts 6: 6. Compare v. 3.

Upon this passage *Bloomfield* remarks: "Selden and Wolf deduce the origin of laying on of hands from the age of Moses, ... Num. 27: 18. Hence the custom obtained in the Jewish church, and was thence introduced into the Christian. As laying on of hands had always been used in praying for the good of any person present, in order to show δεικτικῶς, *for whom* the benefit was entreated; so it was, also, from the earliest ages, a rite of institution to office, which is conferred *by symbol.*"

The *Cambridge Platform,* which contains the articles of "Church Discipline agreed upon by the Elders and Messengers of the Churches, assembled in the Synod at Cambridge in New England,

enjoyment of the Divine presence which rendered them eminently holy and wise, and in other respects peculiarly fitted them for the service assigned them.

But it is said, that Philip and Stephen certainly exercised the prerogatives of eldership; that they preached the gospel and, one of them, administered the rite of baptism. As it respects Stephen, this is not asserted by the sacred historian. It is said, indeed, that "Stephen did great wonders and miracles among the people;" and, that he "*disputed*" with various opposers of the gospel (Acts 6: 8, 9); but all this he might have done while employed in the work of distributing to the necessities of the poor saints. As he went from house to house on these errands of mercy, he was quite as likely to fall in with the Libertines and Cyrenians, and them of Cilicia, and of Asia, with whom he disputed, as he would have been in publicly preaching the gospel. In

---

Anno 1648 —" expressly recognizes the propriety and duty of ordaining deacons. "Church officers," says the Platform (ch. 9, § 1), "are not only to be chosen by the church, but also to be *ordained by imposition of hands and prayer*." In the 6th and 7th chapters of the Platform, the officers of the church are designated; and among them is the deacon. Its language is as follows: "The office of deacon is instituted in the church by the Lord Jesus. . . . The office and work of a deacon is to receive the offerings of the church and gifts given to the church, and to keep the treasury of the church, and therewith to serve the tables which the church is to provide for."

The practice of ordaining these officers has, to some extent, gone into disuse among Congregational churches. It is an important question, however, whether we have not in this particular departed from "the right way;" — from the doctrine of our fathers and the example of the apostles? — *See on, Part* IV. § 2.

respect to Philip, the case is somewhat different. "Philip," we are told (Acts 8: 5), "went down to Samaria and preached Christ unto them." But this will not prove that even Philip was *ordained* "to this business." If the fact that he went down to Samaria and preached the gospel proves that he was an ordained preacher of the gospel, then by the same argument we can prove that the *whole church at Jerusalem* were ordained preachers of the gospel; for it is expressly said that *all the brethren* of the church at Jerusalem, when driven abroad by the persecution which followed Stephen's martyrdom, preached the word: "At that time," says Luke, (Acts 8: 1–4,) "there was a great persecution against *the church* which was at Jerusalem; and they were *all scattered abroad* throughout the regions of Judea and Samaria, *except the apostles*. . . . . Therefore they that were scattered abroad, went everywhere *preaching the word*."

It is said, however, that Philip administered the ordinance of baptism; which, even on Congregational principles, a deacon is not authorized to do. It is true, that Philip did baptize the converts of Samaria and the eunuch of Ethiopia; and it is equally true, that the Holy Ghost authorized him so to do, by *special directions* given to him. He was endowed with the power of working miracles in Samaria, (see Acts 8: 6, 7,) and was especially commissioned to disciple the eunuch, as we learn from Acts 8: 26–28. This being the state of the case, could Philip doubt that he was authorized to *baptize* the converts thus made? since Christ had enjoined upon all those whom he had commissioned to "*teach*," the duty of *baptizing* also: — "Go ye and *teach* (or disciple) all nations, *baptizing* them into the name of the Father, and of the Son, and of the Holy Ghost." — Matt. 28: 19. It is not unlikely that others of the scattered brethren of the church at Jerusalem performed the same ministerial acts. Wherever they went preaching the word, and the Holy Ghost accompanied their labors, it is highly probable that they administered baptism and gathered the converts into churches; and, under similar circumstances, any layman of our churches would be authorized to do the same things. This, however, would by no means sanction this course of procedure under ordinary circumstances.*

In addition to what has been already said upon this subject, it ought to be remarked, that the Scriptures warrant the supposition that Philip, subsequently to his ordination as a deacon, was set apart to the work of an *evangelist*. That this was not unfrequently done by the primitive churches, is perhaps intimated by the apostle, 1 Tim. 3: 13; "They that have used the office of a *deacon* well, purchase to themselves *a good degree;*" that is, a higher degree, or office, in the church.† That Philip had been thus

---

* *Mosheim* says: "at first, all who were engaged in propagating Christianity, administered this rite [baptism]; nor can it be called in question, that whoever persuaded any person to embrace Christianity, could baptize his own disciple." — *Murdock's Mosheim*, Vol. I. p. 105–6, 1st Ed. See also *Eusebius*, *Ecc. Hist.* Lib. II. ch. 1; *Waddington*, *Hist. Chh.* p. 43; *Campbell's Lec. on Ecc. Hist.* Lec. iv. p. 62–65; Lec. 8, p. 125–127; Lec. 9, p. 151–155, Phila. Ed. 1807; *Sailor's Magazine* for Dec. 1843, p. 108.

† See *Doddridge*, *and Bloomfield.*

promoted, appears from Acts 21: 8, . . . "We that were of Paul's company departed, and came unto Cesarea: and we entered into the house of *Philip the Evangelist*, which was one of the *seven*" — deacons.

From whatever point of view, then, we contemplate this subject, we can see no evidence that the primitive deacons were an order of the *clergy;* but rather, that they were substantially like Congregational deacons, chosen and set apart to "serve tables."

That elders and deacons are the *only* officers which Christ designed to have permanently connected with his churches, and that their authority should extend no further than to the particular churches which elect them, may be inferred from the nature of the case; from the considerations which have been offered upon the general topics already discussed; and from the manner in which these church officers are spoken of in Scripture. Take, for example, the address of Paul to the Philippians, 1: 1; "Paul and Timotheus, the servants of Jesus Christ, to all the saints in Christ Jesus which are at Philippi, with *the bishops and deacons.*" Now, had there been in the church at Philippi any other officers than bishops and deacons, would they not have been mentioned by the apostle ?* And if there were no other officers in that church, what reason have we to suppose there were in any of the apostolic churches?

---

* It is worthy of remark, that *Polycarp*, writing to this church more than fifty years after the apostle, mentions the same two officers, and *only* the same, namely, *presbyters* and *deacons.* — See extracts from the *Apostolic Fathers* in this work

And, if in none of the apostolic churches, why should there be in any of our modern churches?

In further confirmation of this doctrine, we may refer to Paul's first epistle to Timothy. This was written to give the young evangelist such instructions as would guide him in arranging the affairs of the church at Ephesus, and probably, also, of the neighboring churches. Among other important items, Paul instructs Timothy how to proceed in the choice and ordination of church officers. First, In respect to *bishops:* "This is a true saying, if a man desire the office of a bishop, he desireth a good work. A bishop, then, must be blameless, the husband of one wife, vigilant, sober, of good behavior, given to hospitality, apt to teach; Not given to wine, no striker, not greedy of filthy lucre; but patient; not a brawler, not covetous; One that ruleth well his own house, having his children in subjection with all gravity; (For if a man know not how to rule his own house, how shall he take care of the church of God?) Not a novice, lest being lifted up with pride he fall into the condemnation of the devil." 1 Tim. 3: 1–6. Secondly, In respect to *deacons.* "Likewise must the *deacons* be grave, not double-tongued, not given to much wine, not greedy of filthy lucre; holding the mystery of the faith in a pure conscience. And let these also first be proved; then let them use the office of a deacon, being found blameless. Even so must their wives be grave, not slanderers, sober, faithful in all things. Let the deacons be the husbands of one wife, ruling their children and their own houses well. For they that have used the office of a deacon well, purchase to themselves a good degree, and great boldness in the faith which is in Christ Jesus. These things write I unto thee, hoping to come unto thee shortly: *but if I tarry long, that thou mayest know how thou oughtest to behave thyself in the house of God, which is the church of the living God, the pillar and ground of the truth.*" 1 Tim. 3: 8–15.

It deserves notice, that not one word is here said about any qualifications to *teach.* The *bishop* must be "*apt to teach:*" but the *deacon* must be, simply, grave, sincere, temperate, moderate in his desires for wealth, and of intelligent and deep-toned piety. It being the special design of Paul in this epistle, to instruct Timothy how to *behave himself in the Church of the living God;* that is, how to order and arrange the affairs of the churches — what errors to oppose, what duties to inculcate, what officers to ordain, and what kind of men to select; — this being the special object of the apostle in writing to Timothy, it is inconceivable that he should have omitted to mention any of the officers which were to be chosen of men, and set apart to the service of the churches. Only two, however, are named by him, — BISHOPS and DEACONS. The unavoidable inference is, *that no others were required by the apostolic churches as permanent ecclesiastical officers.* And if not by the apostolic churches, why by any churches?

Further, we may add, that in no part of the New Testament have we any directions about the qualifications of other church officers, or any account of the manner of setting them apart to office. But, is it reasonable to believe that the Scriptures would be thus silent, if other officers were important to the churches? — if the great Head of the Church required their selection and consecration? and more especially, if men must be left to the "uncovenanted mercies of God," however sincerely devoted to him, if not organized into churches having divers other officers? and the sacraments of the church be "mock sacraments," when administered by any except those who recognize three orders in the ministry? It seems to us perfectly plain, that, since only two kinds of church officers are described in the New Testament, two only should be retained by the churches of Christ; and that all else is of human, not of Divine appointment.

It may be thought that the subject of church officers has received an undue proportion of attention; but the fact that the controversy upon church polity mainly turns upon this question, will suggest a sufficient apology for the course I have pursued.*

II. Another important doctrine, upon which there is a very general agreement among Congregation-

---

* The reader who wishes to examine this subject more fully will find many valuable remarks in Macknight's notes on the Epistles to Timothy and Titus; particularly, 1 Tim. 3: and 5: 17, 18; and in Prof. Pond's work, "The Church." Dr. Bloomfield, in his Notes on the New Testament, presents the Episcopal side of the question, as does *Bingham*, in his Antiquities of the Christian Church, Book II. chaps. 1, 2, 3. *Dr. Owen* discusses this subject with his usual ability in the 4th chapter of his learned work, on "The true Nature of a Gospel Church and its Government." Doddridge's remarks upon many of the texts which have been quoted, will be found candid and learned. The reader will find some of the points ably discussed in Bishop Onderdonk's Tract on Episcopacy Tested by Scripture, and Rev. Albert Barnes' Review of the same.

alists, is, *that ecclesiastical councils, both mutual and ex parte, are in cases of necessity, suitable and important helps in the administration of church government.*

Our councils are usually composed of the pastor and one of the brethren from each of several neighboring churches. They are called to organize churches, to ordain and dismiss pastors, to depose from the ministry, and to assist in the settlement of difficulties. They are brought together, as occasion requires, by what are termed "Letters Missive" sent to the churches. Not only may churches and their pastors call councils, but either, without the concurrence of the other; and also any number of church members, with, or without the concurrence of their brethren or their pastor. A *mutual* council is one in which the parties on whose behalf the council is called, are agreed. An *ex parte* council is called by one of the parties, the other refusing to unite in a mutual council.

The general doctrine of advisory councils was broached even by Robert Browne, though a most zealous advocate for independency.* Mr. Robinson and his church admitted the same doctrine. The Amsterdam and London Congregational church distinctly recognized the propriety of such councils.† Thomas Hooker allowed the same; ‡— also John Cotton; § so does the Cambridge Platform.||

* *Hanbury*, Vol. I. ch. 2.

† Ib. p. 359, 360. See over, p. 114, note.

‡ *Survey*, P. 4, ch. 2, p. 19, and Appendix, passim.

§ *Cotton's Keys of the Kingdom of Heaven*, p. 43–46, 101–108. Printed 1644, Reprinted 1843, by Tappan and Dennet.

|| *Chaps.* 15, 16.

That it has long been the belief of Congregationalists that *ex parte* councils may, in certain emergencies, be called, will appear on reference to the authorities below.* Congregationalists, however, agree in asserting, that councils have neither legislative nor executive authority over the churches. Their decisions are generally left with the churches in the form of counsel and advice, which the churches are free to accept or reject, as they may judge most agreeable to the Divine will. But, in deposing from the ministry unworthy incumbents, councils act authoritatively and conclusively.

The Congregational doctrine respecting councils, is, that they derive all their authority to act in any given case, from the churches which are represented in them; the churches themselves being constructively present in the persons of their delegates.† And,

---

* *Mather's Ratio*, Art. 9, § 1; *Upham's Ratio*, ch. 17.

† Our fathers were very particular to have lay delegates in their councils. See *Mather's Ratio*, p. 175; *Wise's Vindication*, p. 18; *S. Mather*, p. 117.

The *pastor* of a church is as truly a *delegate* of the church which sends him, as is the lay brother who accompanies his pastor. The Cambridge Platform holds the following language upon this point: "Because it is difficult, if not impossible, for many churches to come together in one place, in all their members universally; therefore, they may assemble by their delegates or messengers; as the Church at Antioch went not all to Jerusalem, but some select men for that purpose. Because none are, or should be, more fit to know the state of the churches nor to advise of ways for the good thereof, than elders; therefore, it is fit that in the choice of the messengers for such assemblies, they (the churches) have special respect unto such; yet, inasmuch as not only Paul and Barnabas, but certain others also, were sent to Jerusalem from Antioch; and when they were come to Jerusalem, not only the

as no Congregational church claims any authority over a sister church, it cannot of course communicate to its delegates any such authority. Councils are called to advise the churches, not to make laws for them; on the ground, that "in the multitude of counsellors there is safety." Their influence over the churches is exclusively moral; such as arises from the combined wisdom of intelligent, unprejudiced, and pious men. "They pretend unto no judicial power, nor any significancy, but what is merely instructive and suasory. . . . They have no secular arm to enforce any canons. They ask none; they want none."* The churches hold fast the power

---

apostles and elders, but other brethren also, did assemble and meet about the mattter; therefore synods [and, upon the same grounds, *all councils*] are to consist both of elders and other church members endued with gifts and sent by the churches, not excluding the presence of any brethren in the churches, Acts 16: 2, 22, 23."—*Platform*, ch. 16, § 6.

* *Mather's Ratio*, p. 172, 173; *S. Mather's Apology*, p. 18-25, 118.

The English Congregationalists agreed with the N. E. fathers in this respect. Take for illustration, the 38th article of the Confession of the London Cong. Chh., published in Amsterdam, 1596-1598, "XXXVIII. And, although the particular congregations [churches] be thus distinct and several bodies, every one as a compact and knit city in itself, yet are they all to walk by one and the same rule; and, by all means convenient, to have the counsel, and help one of another in all needful affairs of the church, as members of one body in the common faith, under Christ their only Head."—*Hanbury*, Vol. I. p. 97.

The Savoy Synod of 1658, while it "disallows the power of all *stated* synods, presbyteries, convocations, and assemblies of divines, over particular churches; admits, that in cases of difficulty, or difference relating to doctrine or order, churches may meet

which Christ has given them in Matt. 18: 18, to "open and shut, to bind and loose."

"The truth is," says Thomas Hooker, "a particular congregation [church] is the highest tribunal to which an aggrieved party may appeal in the third place;"—alluding to the steps in Matt. xviii.: . . . "If difficulties arise in the proceeding, the council of other churches should be sought to clear the truth; but the power of censure rests still in the congregation, where Christ placed it." * So Samuel Mather says: "When they [the Councils or Synods] have

---

together by their synods or councils, to consider and give advice, *but without exercising any jurisdiction.*"—*Neal's Puritans*, Vol. IV. p. 216, 217.

The celebrated John Cotton, in his work on the Keys of the Kingdom of Heaven, seems to give more power to Synods and Councils than any other standard writer with whom I have consulted. He says: "We dare not say that their power reacheth no further than giving counsel."—p. 59. Yet, on the 60th page he concedes, that the churches may judge of the decisions of synods and councils, whether "prejudicial to the truth and peace of the Gospel," . . . "and may refuse such sanctions as the Lord hath not sanctioned." And further on, in answer to the question —"Whether the Synod hath power of Ordination, and Excommunication," he says: "We should rather choose to *determine*, and to *publish* and *declare* our determination—That the ordination of such as we find fit for it, and the excommunication of such as we find do deserve it, would be an acceptable service both to the Lord, and to his Churches: but the administration of both these acts we should refer to the Presbyterie of the several churches whereto the person to be ordained is called, and whereof the person to be excommunicated is a member: and both acts to be performed in the presence, and *with the consent* of the several churches to whom the matter appertaineth."—p. 62, 63.

* *Survey*, Part iv. p. 19.

done all, the churches are still free to accept or refuse their advice." * In the Platform the same doctrine is recognized, though not quite so distinctly. Its language is: "The Synod's [or council's] directions and determinations, so far as consonant with the Word of God, are to be received with reverence and submission." . . . . .† This passage, though it may seem to give more power to councils, than Hooker or Mather allow; yet, as it evidently submits the question whether the determinations of the council are "consonant with the Word of God," to the churches — in effect takes the same ground. This appears more clearly by comparing section four, where we read: "It belongeth unto Synods and councils to debate and determine controversies of faith and cases of conscience, etc., . . . not to exercise church censures in way of discipline, nor any act of church authority or jurisdiction."

That acute reasoner and learned theologian, Dr. Emmons, maintains with great earnestness, the supremacy of individual churches in matters ecclesiastical: "No ecclesiastical decision," says he, "ought to be taken out of the hands of a particular church, where Christ has lodged it; for he has appointed no ecclesiastical tribunal superior to that of an individual church." ‡ . . .

This, then, I suppose to be the doctrine of ancient and modern Congregationalists: — In cases of diffi-

---

* *Apology*, p. 118, 133. The Synod of 1662 maintained the same doctrine. Quest. 2, Ans. 1; *Hubbard's N. E.* p. 589.

† *Chap.* 16, § 5.

‡ *Platform of Ecc. Gov., a Discourse*, etc. p. 19–23.

culty, a church, or the aggrieved members of a church, may call for the advice of a council of sister churches; and this advice the church is bound respectfully to consider and cheerfully to follow, unless manifestly contrary to what is right and scriptural; but of this, the church has an undoubted right to judge; and to act in accordance with its deliberate judgment.*

But, suppose a church, in the exercise of her sovereignty, should obstinately refuse to follow the reasonable and scriptural advice of a council? She would then become liable to discipline, as will be hereafter specified, and would forfeit the confidence and fellowship of sister churches.

The Consociational doctrine, adopted by most of the Congregational churches of Connecticut, may, perhaps, be regarded as an exception to the above statement. In that State there are what are called "Consociations of Ministers and Churches," composed of pastors and delegates from all the churches within convenient distances. These are standing councils, to which all unsettled difficulties in the churches within their several districts may be referred. The decisions of these bodies are final and authoritative.†

This plan of consociation was designed to break up the practice of calling *ex parte* councils. Wise and good men framed this consociational system; and it possesses, apparently, some important advantages over the usual method of calling councils as

---

* *See Mather's Ratio*, p. 173, 174; *Upham's Ratio*, ch. 15, § 152–154, ch. 18, § 178.

† *Saybrook Platform*, Art. II. III. V. XII. XIII.

occasions require. Still, I must regard it as a departure from strict Congregational principles, and of very questionable tendency. The principle that every church is authorized to act authoritatively and conclusively in relation to all matters of personal concern, is of great importance. Any thing tending to undermine this principle should be deprecated. For this very reason *all* councils to settle church difficulties should be avoided as much as possible; and most especially, *standing* councils; for such councils are a sort of standing invitation to the churches not to adjust their own difficulties.

It is a serious question, too, whether the churches have the right to commit the work of Christian discipline to delegated hands; whether they can perform this duty by proxy. Christ has said of the obstinate offender: "If he hear not *the church*, let him be to thee as an heathen man and a publican." Consistently with this direction, a church may take advice and counsel; but, for a church to surrender to a council the right to "*hear*, *judge*, DETERMINE, and FINALLY ISSUE" any case, (as the Saybrook articles of discipline expressly do) * seems utterly inconsistent with the "Magna Charta" of Christ's churches.†

The above remarks are, perhaps, after all, more appropriate to the letter of the Saybrook articles than to the practical application of them which extensively prevails in Connecticut. From the time of their origin, the churches have manifested consid-

---

* See *Article* VII.

† Samuel Mather is very explicit upon the danger of councils, for the purpose of settling church difficulties. See *Apology*, ch. 7.

erable solicitude lest they should interfere with their Congregational rights. Many have, therefore, given a very liberal interpretation to the most objectionable of these articles. Thus they choose to interpret the third article, which says, "that all cases of scandal that fall out within the circuit of any of the associations, shall be brought to a council of the elders, etc. [i. e. to a consociation] when there shall be need of a council for the determination of them,"—as allowing them to judge when it is necessary to call the Consociation, and as permitting them to call a mutual council if they choose, or even a select council, reserving the right to the censured party of appeal to the Consociation. So also, some of the Consociations choose to call their decisions *advice*, rather than authoritative determinations. And in other particulars, "the increasing independency of views cherished by the churches" has materially modified the objectionable letter of the Saybrook Platform.*

To any form of consociation or confederation among the churches, which removes from them individually the right of final decision in all cases affecting their personal interests, we conceive there are most serious objections.

INFLUENCE OF CONSOCIATIONS ON THE ANCIENT CHURCHES.

The general correctness of the views above expressed, is corroborated by the remarks of Mosheim

* See "*Congregational Order*," or the Ancient Platforms of the Cong. Chhs. with a Digest of Rules and Usages in Conn. Published by the Gen. Ass. of Conn. 1843.

upon the influence of councils on the primitive churches. Having stated that all the churches in the first centuries "had equal rights, and were, in all respects, on a footing of equality," he adds: "Nor does there appear in this century, any vestige of that Consociation of the churches of the same province, which gave rise to ecclesiastical councils and metropolitans. Rather, as is manifest, it was not till the second century, that the custom of holding ecclesiastical councils began in Greece, and thence extended into other provinces." *

Again, in speaking of the second century, he says: "During a great part of this century, all the churches continued to be, as at first, independent of each other; or, were connected by no consociations or confederations." "Each church was a kind of little independent republic, governed by its own laws, which were enacted, or at least sanctioned by the people. But, in process of time, it became customary for all the christian churches in the same province to unite, and form a sort of larger society or commonwealth; and, in the manner of confederate republics, to hold their conventions at stated times, and there deliberate for the common advantage of the whole confederation. This custom first arose among the Greeks, among whom a [political] confederation of cities, and the consequent convention of their several delegates, had been long known; but afterwards, the utility of the thing being seen, [we shall see directly how useful these conventions were,] the custom ex-

* Vol. I. p. 86, *Murdock's* 1st Ed.

11

tended through all countries where there were christian churches. These conventions of delegates from the several churches, assembled for deliberation, were called by the Greeks *synods*, [from *σύνοδος*, an assembly] and by the Latins, councils [from concilium, an assembly] and the laws agreed upon in them, were called canons, that is, rules, [from *κανών* canōn]. These councils, of which no vestige appears before the middle of this century, (i. e. the second) CHANGED NEARLY THE WHOLE FORM OF THE CHURCH. For, in the first place, the ancient rights and privileges of the people were by them very much abridged; and, on the other hand, the influence and authority of the bishops were not a little augmented. At first, the bishops did not deny that they were merely representatives of the churches, and acted in the name of the people, but, by little and little, they made higher pretensions, and maintained, that power was given them by Christ himself, to dictate rules of faith and conduct to the people. In the next place, the perfect equality and parity of all bishops, which existed in early times, the council gradually subverted. For, it was necessary that one of the confederated bishops of a province, should be intrusted with some authority and power in those conventions, over the others; and hence originated the prerogatives of Metropolitans. And lastly, when the custom of holding these councils had extended over the christian world, and the universal church had acquired the form of a vast republic, composed of many lesser ones, certain head men were to be placed over it in different parts of the world, as central points in their respective countries. Hence came the *Patriarchs;* and ultimately a *Prince of Patriarchs* — the ROMAN PONTIFF." *

Waddington, (*Ecc. Hist.* p. 44), admits the correctness of Mosheim's account. He says: "Though these synods were doubtless indispensable to the well-being of Christianity, they seem to have been the means of corrupting the original humility of its ministers." If this be true, and if it be also true that "like priest like people," and that like causes tend to like effects — then, I ask, If synods or councils to assist in the administration of church government are sometimes necessary, ought they not at least, to be *occasional* bodies, called as seldom as the necessities of the churches will permit; and so limited in their authority as not in the least to interfere with the sovereignty of individual churches? And, if the plan of consociation has occasioned such countless evils in the churches in past ages, ought not we to regard it with a jealous eye? And, is not the doctrine, that no ecclesiastical council shall have any authority to enforce its decisions on the churches — highly important, yea essential to the independence and the permanent welfare of the churches?

III. Another Congregational doctrine of considerable importance, is, that *an ex parte council cannot be regularly called, until a mutual one has been refused by one of the parties.*†

The right to call ex parte councils has been con-

---

* *Eccl. Hist.* Vol. I. p. 142, 144. See also, an important note to the same purport by *Dr. Murdock*, p. 142, n. 2.

† *Mather's Ratio Disciplinæ*, Art. IX.; *Upham's Ratio*, ch. 17.

sidered an objectionable feature in our system. But in reality, it is far otherwise. This right furnishes an effectual check to the exertion of arbitrary power by the majority of a church. These councils are courts of errors, to which the humblest member of a congregational church may appeal. This appeal cannot, however, be made until a mutual reference has been refused: and this will rarely occur, unless there be a measure of unchristian obstinacy and self-will in the refusing party. An ex parte council should in no case act until assured that a mutual council has been refused.

Some persons seem to think, that one ex parte council may be arrayed against another, almost *ad infinitum*. But, if the above doctrine be regarded, this cannot take place — one ex parte council cannot be arrayed against another. For illustration: if the majority of a church should propose to call a council, to consider the expediency of dissolving the pastoral connection; and the pastor and the minority should refuse to join them, and they (the majority) should proceed to call an ex parte council, the pastor and the minority would have no right to call another ex parte council. And, for an ex parte council to assemble, and proceed to act upon the doings of the church and a previous council, without being assured that the party calling them had, in their turn, proposed to the other party a mutual council — would be to violate good usage and sound doctrine.

Nay, more, it is, in my view, very doubtful whether those who have once refused the offer of a mutual council, and thus compelled their brethren to call an ex parte, have any further claim to the advice of a council; least of all, to that of an ex parte council of their own choosing. If upon reflection, the minority should consent to refer all their difficulties to the consideration of a mutual council — though they had previously refused so to do, and by their refusal had constrained their brethren to call an ex parte council — it would be an act of Christian kindness and condescension, and perhaps of *duty*, for the majority to consent to such an arrangement. But, under other circumstances, the majority of a church are authorized to act finally on the advice of an ex parte council, when called regularly; and the minority have no ground of complaint, that all reasonable measures have not been employed to adjust their difficulties on christian and Congregational principles.*

AUTHORITY FOR COUNCILS.

If the question be asked: "On what grounds do Congregationalists rest their opinions respecting

* The decisions of such a council, resulting in the removal of a pastor, would, doubtless, in the eye of the law exonerate a church or parish from the payment of the pastor's salary after the date of such decision. See a *Report of Avery vs. Inhabitants of Tyringham*, in Mass. Reports for Sept. Term, 1807. The inhabitants voted that they would no longer consider the plaintiff minister of said town. The minister sued for his salary; and the court gave it to him; on the ground, that in cases of disagreement between a pastor and a people, *a mutual council* should be proposed, and on this being refused, an *ex parte* should be called, whose decisions would have equal force in dissolving the connection between the contending parties.

synods and councils?"* The answer is twofold: First, on the sisterly relations which our churches sustain to each other. We regard ourselves as branches of one family; each of which, though settled apart and competent to manage all its ordinary affairs, has a family interest in every other branch. And, inasmuch as every branch of the family will feel a special interest in preserving every member of the family circle from mistakes and errors, there is a peculiar propriety in asking counsel of each other in cases of unusual difficulty. We call our churches *sisters*, because we have "one Lord, one faith, one baptism; one God and Father of all" . . . (Eph. 4: 1–6;) and endeavor to "walk by the same rule," and to "mind the same thing," Phil. 3: 16. If such be our relation to each other, how suitable that we should advise with each other in all cases of unusual difficulty relating to our common faith and order!

Secondly, on the ground of Scripture injunction and example. The Scriptures inculcate the duty, in general terms, of asking advice, and seeking counsel in cases of doubt and difficulty. See Prov. 11: 4. 12: 15. 13: 10. 15: 22. And, that the general principle here recognized — that wisdom and safety require men in cases of doubt and difficulty to seek counsel and take advice — is applicable to churches, is evident from the example recorded in the fifteenth

* The chief, if not the only difference between synods and councils is, that synods are *general* councils, in their attendance and objects; councils are limited to a few churches, and are called for private and specific purposes. These purposes are specified in the Letter Missive; beyond which the members of the council are not authorized to go in their deliberations.

chapter of Acts: whence it appears, that a very difficult question had arisen in the church at Antioch, which could not be satisfactorily adjusted by the church itself, even with the aid of Paul and Barnabas; who, having no special revelation respecting the question, could not speak authoritatively, as upon many other points. After much dissension and disputation, the church determined that Paul and Barnabas, with certain brethren of the church, should go up to Jerusalem, and ask counsel of the apostles and elders, and, as the result shows, of the whole church likewise. The question having been submitted to the consideration of the church at Jerusalem, including the apostles, elders, and brethren, it was resolved, after mature deliberation, and an assurance that they had "the mind of the Spirit," to embody their result in a letter, written in the name of the "apostles, elders, and brethren," and by the authority of the Holy Ghost,"* and to send this by the hands of "chosen men" of the church at Jerusalem, together with Paul and Barnabas, to the church at Antioch, and elsewhere.

Now, though this transaction has in it few of the circumstances of a modern ecclesiastical council; and though the decisions of the apostles, elders, and brethren, acting under the special direction and impulse of the Holy Ghost (v. 28), may have had an authority which a modern council cannot

---

* Neander renders the clause — "It seemed good to *the Holy Ghost* and to us" — thus: "For it seemed good to us, *under the guidance of the Holy Spirit.*" — *History of the Planting*, etc., of *Chris. Chh. by the Apostles*, Vol. I. p. 145, 3d ed.

have* — yet, we see in this transaction a very clear warranty for one church to ask counsel of another in cases of difficulty: and, inasmuch as the pastors and some chosen men from several churches would ordinarily be better qualified to investigate a matter of difficulty, and to give sound and scriptural advice, than the pastor and brethren of a single church — therefore the plan of councils, composed of the pastors and delegates of a number of churches, has been adopted by us, in conformity with the general principle recognized in this fifteenth chapter of Acts and the dictates of sound discretion.

And the same general principles which authorize *any* councils, equally authorize *ex parte* councils. For, if it be agreeable to reason and revelation that counsel should be sought by churches of one another in cases of difficulty, and some members of a church, who equally need this counsel, refuse to ask it, their refusal should not deprive others in the same church of that advice and assistance which they need, and are disposed to seek.

The above are believed to be, for substance, the views of Congregationalists on the subject of councils, mutual and ex parte.

---

* It ought perhaps to be noted, that all the suppositions in the text are by no means universally admitted truths. Thomas Hooker contends, that this conference at Jerusalem was purely deliberative, and unattended by any special divine revelation; and that the authority of the "Holy Ghost," to which reference is made in the 28th verse, was simply that authority which was clearly deducible from the Sacred Scriptures. He further insists, that the decrees of this council had only the weight of good advice, which was consonant with God's Word. — *Survey*, P. iv. ch. 1.

IV. Another doctrine of Congregationalism, is, that *the equality and completeness of the several churches adopting this system do not free them from all accountability to each other.*

Samuel Mather maintains this doctrine distinctly; and, among other authorities, quotes the testimony of Jeremiah Burroughs, as follows: "Those in the Congregational way acknowledge, 1. That they are bound in conscience to give account of their ways to churches about them, or to any other who shall require it. This not in any arbitrary way, but as a duty which they owe to God and man." * John Cotton taught the same doctrine. † Congregational doctrine in regard to church accountability is this: If a Congregational church is believed to have swerved from the truth, a sister church may call the offender to an account; and if necessary, withdraw fellowship from the erring and obstinate church. ‡ But, in doing this, it is necessary for the complainant to take, as nearly as possible, the regular steps enjoined in Matt. 18: 15–18. The inquiring party having failed, by a private interview, to obtain satisfaction from her erring sister, should next call for the assistance of one or more of the neighboring churches; and if unsuccessful in this second step, may either withdraw fellowship immediately, or call a council of neighboring churches, to advise in the case.§

---

* *Burroughs' Irenicum*, p. 43, 44–47, in Mather's Apology, App.—Part II.

† *Keyes of the Kingdom of Heaven*, p. 101–108.

‡ *Mather's Ratio Disciplinæ*, Art. 9, § 1, 4.

§ *Cambridge Platf.* ch. 15; *Mather's Ratio*, p. 172. Also *Upham's "Ratio Disciplinæ,"* p. 174, 206.

Upon this general subject, the Cambridge Platform (Chap. 15) says: "Although churches be distinct, and therefore, may not be confounded one with another, and equal, and therefore, have no dominion one over another; yet, all the churches ought to preserve church communion one with another, because they are all united unto Christ, not only as a mystical, but a political head, whence is derived a communion suitable thereunto. The communion of churches is exercised sundry ways. 1. By way of mutual care, in taking thought for one another's welfare. . . . 2. By way of consultation one with another, when we have occasion to require the judgment and council of other churches. . . . 3. By way of admonition, when a church neglects discipline or becomes corrupt. . . . 4. By admitting members of sister churches to occasional communion with one another. 5. By letters of recommendation or dismission from one church to another. . . . 6. By affording relief and succor one unto another, either of able members to furnish them with officers, or of outward support to the necessities of poorer churches, as did the churches of the *Gentiles* contribute liberally to the poor saints at *Jerusalem*."

The mutual relation and the fellowship of the churches were strenuously maintained by the fathers of New England.* They abhorred any such independency as excused a church from giving account of itself—its doctrines and its practice—to all in fellowship with it. This feature of the system has

---

* *Hooker's Survey*, Part II. ch. 3, p. 80; *Cotton's Way Cleared*, ch. 3, sec. 1.

been tenaciously held by all consistent Congregationalists to the present time.

I have now finished an enumeration and brief explanation of the most essential Principles and Doctrines of the Orthodox Congregationalists of New England. Such is the system of Church polity which the fathers of New England fondly loved and cherished; and in the maintenance of which they endured persecution in their native land, the perils of the ocean, and the hardships of the wilderness.

It was not, however, their love of rites, and forms, and ceremonies, in the worship of God; it was not their attachment to any one mode, in itself considered, that made them so willing to sacrifice the endearments of home, and the enjoyments of cultivated society; but it was their love for the Church of Christ, the welfare of which they considered identified with the maintenance of Congregationalism:— it was this that brought them hither. They loved pure religion; and regarding Congregationalism as best adapted to propagate and maintain the institutions of religion in their purity, they cherished this system with self-denying, self-sacrificing fondness. It was not the casket itself which they so much valued; but the casket, as a necessary protection to the pearl of great price which it contained. It was not the form of godliness, which they so much admired; but the power which accompanied this form. In a word, it was not Congregationalism in itself considered, which our fathers so devotedly loved and cherished; but Congregationalism, as that form of church government which Christ had fixed upon, as best adapted to promote the interests of His kingdom and the glory of His name. While, therefore, we approve and admire the fair model of a christian church which our fathers reared in the New World, let us not forget the spirit which of old dwelt in the New England churches. And while we rejoice in the valued inheritance which our fathers have bequeathed us, let us never forget, that it will be in vain that we cry, "The temple of the Lord, The temple of the Lord are these!" if the presence of the Lord dwell not in our churches. It should never be forgotten, that Congregationalism is a spiritual system of church government. It is designed for, and adapted to spiritual persons—those who have been taught, and are now led by the Spirit. Its strength and permanence depend on the spirituality of those who adopt it. It controls them by no other power than that which is moral; it inflicts no other pains and penalties. It can live and prosper only in the smiles of heaven. Without the Divine presence our churches cannot be governed. Without this, they must fall to pieces, or dwindle away and die. Of all denominations we are most entirely cast upon Providence. Without Christ we can do nothing.

These facts, while they furnish strong presumptive evidence of the correctness of our principles and doctrines, at the same time suggest a powerful argument to the mind of every Congregationalist, why he himself should be holy, and why he should labor to promote the holiness of all about him.

PART III.

ECCLESIASTICAL HISTORY.

It will be seen from the preceding pages, that Congregationalists derive their principles and doctrines from the Sacred Scriptures; that Jesus Christ is regarded by them as the author of their church polity; and the Apostles, as the builders of the first Congregational churches. In this belief, they feel themselves fully sustained by the passages already quoted from the Evangelists and the Apostles, who wrote as they were moved by the Holy Ghost, and whose movements in organizing the first christian churches had the sanction of the Great Head of the Church. Although our chief dependence is upon these inspired guides, and nothing is received by us as truth which is contrary to these, still it is pleasant to find the correctness of our interpretation of the Scriptures sustained by the testimony of the most ancient Fathers of the Church, and by the judgment of many of the most learned and impartial modern writers on Ecclesiastical History. To their testimony we will now attend.

THE FATHERS.*

Clement. — Among the earliest and most valued pieces of antiquity is the epistle of Clement, written in the name of the church at Rome, to the church at Corinth, somewhere about A. D. 64–70.†

The main design of this epistle seems to be, to set before the Corinthian church the inconsistency and sin of suffering a few "ringleaders" — "foolish and inconsiderate men" — so far to influence the church, as to induce them to disregard their spiritual guides and rulers; and even to "cast off those from their ministry, or bishopric, who had holily, and without blame, fulfilled the duties of it." I will arrange under distinct heads the testimony of this venerable and admired writer respecting the primitive order and discipline of the churches.

1. The first point established by this epistle is, that in Clement's time (as late at least as A. D. 64–70), the churches retained their *independent congregational* organization.

The address or salutation of the epistle goes to

---

* The *Apostolic Fathers*, or those who were contemporary with the apostles or their immediate disciples, were Barnabas, Clement of Rome, Hermas, Ignatius, and Polycarp. *The Fathers of the Church*, include all the Christian writers between the second and the sixth century — some say, *twelfth* century.

† Historians differ widely respecting the date of this epistle. — *Lardner* places it about A. D. 95. — *Waddington* supposes this to be about the true date. — *Dr. Campbell* has some valuable remarks upon this epistle, in his 4th Lec. on Ecc. Hist.

show this. It runs thus: "The church of God which is (or which sojourneth) at Rome, to the church of God which is at Corinth, elect, sanctified by the will of God through Jesus Christ our Lord: grace and peace," etc. Here we have two distinct and complete churches spoken of; the one *at*, or sojourning at, Rome; the other at Corinth. The language employed is precisely such as one Congregational church in these days might use when addressing another.

Clement also speaks of the church "being conscientiously *gathered together*, in concord with one another." — § 34. Which goes to show that the church consisted of a single congregation only, which was accustomed to assemble together for church purposes.

2. Another point established by this epistle is, that *the churches were composed of professed saints.*

The church at Corinth is called — "the church of God," "elect, sanctified by the will of God, through Jesus Christ, our Lord." Mention is made of "the firmness of their faith, and its fruitfulness, in all good works;" of their "religion in Christ," and "certain knowledge of the Gospel:" they are said to have "walked according to the laws of God," etc. § 1; they are called "the flock of Christ," § 54; and "the sheepfold of Christ." — § 57. And if such was the character of the *Corinthian* church, we may reasonably infer, that of such materials were *all* the churches of that time composed.

3. Clement speaks of the *disciplinary power of the churches.*

"Beloved, the reproof and the correction which we

exercise towards one another, is good and exceeding profitable: for it unites us more closely to the will of God." — § 56. He admits, as we shall presently see, that the church had authority to discipline, even its ministers.

4. Other points in the order of the primitive churches, to which this epistle bears testimony, respect the number and character of church officers; the authority which they posessed; and the part which a primitive church had in the institution of its own officers.

The officers of the churches are thus spoken of by the venerable Clement: "The apostles have preached to us from our Lord Jesus Christ; Jesus Christ, from God. Christ, therefore, was sent by God, the apostles by Christ; so both were orderly sent according to the will of God. For having received their command, and being thoroughly assured by the resurrection of our Lord Jesus Christ (1 Thess. 1: 5), and convinced by the Word of God, with the fulness of the Holy Spirit, they went abroad, publishing, 'that the kingdom of God was at hand.' And thus preaching through countries and cities, they appointed the first-fruits of their conversions [that is, the first converts, and consequently the most experienced Christians] to be BISHOPS and DEACONS, over such as should afterwards believe, having first proved them by the Spirit. Nor was this any new thing, seeing that long before, it was written concerning bishops and deacons. For thus saith the Scripture in a certain place: 'I will appoint their *overseers* [bishops] in righteousness, and their *ministers* [deacons] in faith.'" Isa. 60: 17. — § 42. "And what wonder if they to whom such a work was committed by God in Christ, established such officers as we before mentioned; when even that blessed and faithful servant in all his house, Moses, set down in the Holy Scriptures all things that were commanded him." — § 43.

In another place, referring to the disorders which had prevailed in the church, he says: "Who is there among you that is generous? who that is compassionate? who that has any charity? let him say, if this sedition, this contention, and these schisms, be upon my account, I am ready to depart; to go away whithersoever ye please; and do whatsoever ye shall command me: only let the flock of Christ be in peace, with the elders that are set over it." . . . — § 54. A clear intimation that the church of Corinth remained as the apostles left it; "*with elders* (not a bishop and elders) set over it."

But, does not Clement elsewhere say: "The chief priest has his proper services; and to the priests their proper place is appointed; and to the Levites appertain their proper ministries; and the layman is confined within the bounds of what is commanded to laymen?" Yes, he does: but for what purpose? not to inculcate the doctrine that the christian church should have the same grades in their ministers which the Jewish church had; this was a discovery of a much later period: but simply to enforce on the Corinthians the duty of order and regularity in their religious services. So he himself tells us, in the very next sentence; "Let every one of you, therefore, brethren, bless God in his proper station, with a good conscience, and with all gravity, not exceeding the rule of his service which is appointed to him," (§ 40, 41); a sort of paraphrase of the apostle's words: 'Let all things be done decently and in order.'

The argument of Clement is this: As under the ancient Jewish Dispensation God assigned to the high priest, the priests, Levites, and all the people their appropriate parts in His service, that nothing might be done "rashly and disorderly;" so, under the Christian Dispensation, it becomes both ministers and people to observe their proper stations, and do their appropriate work in the service and worship of God.—Compare § 37, 38.

After alluding to the "emulation among the tribes concerning the priesthood," and the measures adopted by Moses to quell the rising strife, by referring the matter to God, who caused Aaron's rod, of all the twelve, to blossom—Clement proceeds: "What think you, beloved? did not Moses before know what should happen? Yes, verily; but to the end there might be no division, nor tumult in Israel, he did in this manner, that the name of the true and only God might be glorified: to him be honor forever and ever—Amen. So, likewise, our apostles knew by our Lord Jesus Christ, that there should contentions arise upon the account of the ministry, or the name of the bishopric, [or, as Dr. Owen renders it—'about the name of episcopacy,' that is, episcopacy itself]. And therefore, having a perfect foreknowledge of this, they appointed persons, as we have before said, and then gave direction how, when they should die, other chosen and approved men should succeed in the ministry. Wherefore we cannot think that those may be justly thrown out of their ministry, who were either appointed by them, or afterwards chosen by other eminent men, *with the consent* [or choice] *of the whole church* (συνεδοκησάσης τῆς ἐκκλησιάς πάσης); and who have with all lowliness and innocency ministered to the flock of Christ in peace, and without self-interest; and were for a long time commended by all. For it would be no small sin in us, should we cast off those from their ministry, (or bishopric,) who holily, and without blame, *fulfil the duties of it.* Blessed are those priests [πρεσβύτερους, *elders*] who, having finished their course before those times, [when churches are so fastidious and contentious] have obtained a fruitful and perfect dissolution; for they have no fear lest any should turn them out of the place [heaven], which is now appointed for them. But we see how you have put out some who lived reputably among you, from the ministry, [ἀπο τῆς ἐπίσκοπης, *from their bishoprics*] which by their innocence they had adorned." — § 44.

This most interesting and remarkable passage establishes several points: (1) That *bishops*, or *elders* as he calls them § 54, and *deacons* were the only officers known in the churches of Christ in the days of Clement — thirty or forty years after Christ. For surely, if there had been any others known to those primitive churches, Clement would scarcely have written as he did. (2) That "*the consent of the whole church*" was obtained to the appointment of these officers. (3) That the apostles, foreseeing that contentions would arise respecting the ministerial office, left particular directions "how, when they" — that is, the elders or bishops which were ordained over the churches during the lifetime of the apostles — "should die, other chosen and approved men should succeed in the ministry." These directions, we have in their sacred writings and in the example of the churches founded by them. From both of which sources we learn, that approved men were to be chosen and set apart to the ministry, "*with the consent of the whole church.*" (4) That the apostolic and primitive churches had the power to discipline, and even *to cast off* their ministers — their bishops. This the Corinthians had done. And Clement nowhere intimates that they had not a perfect right so to do; but only complains that they had not exercised their authority in a judicious and christian manner — that they had exercised it upon men who deserved their confidence and love, and not their censure. Such is the testimony of Clement, the disciple of Peter, the "*almost-apostle*" of the Primitive Church; the man of whom Paul makes mention (Phil. 4: 3), as one whose name is written in the "Book of Life." Such is Clement's testimony to the order and discipline of the apostolic churches.

Dr. Campbell says of this epistle: "Nothing that is not Scripture can be of greater authority in determining a point of fact, as is the question about the constitution of the apostolic church." — Lec. iv. p. 72. Waddington, himself an Episcopalian, speaking of this Epistle, says: "The Episcopal form of government was clearly not yet here [at Corinth] established, probably as being adverse to the republican spirit of Greece." — p. 35.

Polycarp. — The epistle of Polycarp stands next in order. This was written probably some time between

A. D. 108 and 117,* and is addressed: "To the church which is at Philippi," or, which *sojourneth at* Philippi, τῇ περοικούσῃ Φιλίπποις). The church is addressed as consisting of persons who had "the root of faith" remaining firm in them. — § 1.

Polycarp speaks not as one having authority; but apologizes for writing to the Philippians, by alluding to the fact that they had desired it: "These things, my brethren, I took not the liberty to write unto you concerning righteousness, but you yourselves before encouraged me to it." — § 3.

He then goes on to speak of the duties of the whole church. After this follows: "Also the *deacons* must be blameless before him, as the ministers [or servants] of God in Christ, and not of men." He tells the church that it is their duty to be "subject to the *priests* [or elders] and *deacons*, as unto God and Christ;" — that is, to obey them who, by the consent of the whole church, have the rule over them and admonish them. He then tells the elders how they must conduct in the church. "Let the *elders* be compassionate and merciful towards all; turning them from their errors; . . . . being zealous of what is good," etc. — § 6. He speaks of the defection of "Valens, who was once a presbyter [or elder] among" them; and exhorts the church in their discipline of him: "be ye also moderate upon this occasion; and look not upon such as enemies, but call

* Owen and Waddington and Lardner place it about A. D. 108; Wake, A. D. 116–117. Campbell says, it must certainly have been within "a considerable time before the middle of the second century." — *Lec.* iv. p. 72.

them back as suffering and erring members, that ye may save your whole body: for by so doing, ye shall edify your own selves." — § 11.

In this epistle there is nothing to lead us to suppose that the churches had undergone any material change in their order and discipline since Clement wrote — between forty and fifty years earlier. The churches are still spoken of as separate, independent, congregational bodies; as composed of visible saints; as not subject to the authoritative direction or instruction of any one out of their own body; and to their own officers, only "as the ministers of God in Christ;" and these officers we learn were elders and deacons, who, in common with the other brethren, were subject to the discipline of their respective churches.

Ignatius. — We have seen that there were at first in most, if not all of the apostolic churches, several elders, of equal rank and authority.* We have now — if we may trust to these epistles — arrived at that period in the history of the churches, when it was thought necessary to appoint one of the elders of each church to be a sort of president, — a *princeps inter pares* — a presiding officer among equals in rank. To distinguish him from the other elders, he was called ἐπίσκοπος, the superintendent, overseer, bishop. To this arrangement in the churches, the next apostolic father from whom we shall quote, often alludes.

---

* *Ante*, p. 91, 92.

Ignatius wrote near A. D. 116.* There has been much dispute about his writings. Many have questioned whether any of his genuine epistles are extant. Dr. Campbell regards these epistles as interpolated and corrupted: "I say not that these epistles ought to be rejected in the lump, but that undue freedoms have been used even with the purest of them, by some overzealous partisans of the priesthood." . . . . "The style, in many places, is not suited to the simplicity of the times immediately succeeding the times of the apostles." . . . . "It abounds with inflated epithets." . . . . "But it is not the style only, which has raised suspicion, it is chiefly the sentiments." — *Lec.* 5, p. 99, 100, 101. Prof. Norton rejects these epistles as manifest forgeries: "I doubt," says he, "whether any book, in its general tone of sentiment and language, ever betrayed itself as a forgery more clearly, than do these pretended epistles of Ignatius." Prof. Pond says: "After an impartial view of the whole case, I accord with the sentiment of Prof. Norton, as expressed in his very learned work on the 'Genuineness of the Gospels.'" — "*The Church*," p. 126. Gibbon says: "We cannot receive with entire confidence either the Epistles or the Acts of Ignatius." — *Dec. and Fall of Rom. Emp.* Vol. I. ch. 16, note 70. Mosheim says: "The whole subject of the Ignatian Epistles in general, is involved in much obscurity and perplexity." — Vol. I. p. 76, 2d Ed. Dr. Murdock, in his note (No. 31) upon this remark

---

* Authorities vary about the *date* of these epistles, as they do about every thing which concerns them. Dr. Lardner dates them about A. D. 107.

of Mosheim, says: "Moderate men, of various sects, and especially Lutherans, are disposed to admit the genuineness of the epistles in their shorter form; but to regard them as *interpolated* and *altered*." Waddington speaks of "the interpolations with which the party zealots of after-times have disfigured them." — p. 31. Lardner, speaking of the genuineness of even the smaller epistles of Ignatius, says: "Whatever positiveness some may have shown on either side, I must own, I have found it a very difficult question." — *Credibility Gosp. Hist.* Vol. I. ch. 5.

I pretend not to be competent to decide this question. This, however, I will venture to say — and every man of common sense will say the same on examination — that the reputed epistles of Ignatius are extremely unlike those attributed to his contemporaries, Clement and Polycarp. These latter abound with simple Bible truths, and contain almost entire pages of quotations from the Scriptures; they urge reverence to God and obedience to his commands as the whole duty of man; very little is said of the officers of the church, and nothing of any but bishops, or elders, and deacons. But the burden of Ignatius' epistles is — "love your excellent bishop." But, as these epistles of Ignatius are greatly relied upon by Episcopalians to prove the early existence of three orders of christian ministers, and as he is the first christian father who mentions them, I have thought his testimony upon other points, of considerable importance.

Archbishop Wake, from whose translation I generally quote, regards seven epistles as unquestionably the genuine and authentic writings of Ignatius.

These are addressed — "To the church which is at Ephesus in Asia" — "To the church which is at Magnesia, near the Meander" — "To the holy church which is at Tralles in Asia" — "To the church which also presides in the place of the region of the Romans" — "To the church of God, etc., which is at Philadelphia, in Asia" — "To the church which is at Smyrna, in Asia," and "to Polycarp, bishop of the church which is at Smyrna; their overseer, but rather himself, overlooked by God the Father, and the Lord Jesus Christ."

1. *In these epistles the distinct, independent, complete, and congregational character of the churches is very fully recognized.*

The titles, or salutations of the several epistles, go to show this. In every instance in which a church is addressed, it is, "*the* church which *sojourneth*," etc. in such a city. He exhorts the church at Ephesus, "to come more fully together." "For," says he, "when ye meet fully together in one place, the powers of the devil are destroyed," etc. — § 13. To the Magnesian church, he says: "Being come together into the same place, have one common prayer." . . . And again, "Come ye all together, as unto one temple of God, as to one altar," . . . — § 7. He speaks of the Romans being "gathered together in love," (§ 2,) and of the Philadelphians coming "all together into the same place." — § 6. Now, these expressions all indicate that a church in Ignatius' day consisted of no more persons than could conveniently assemble together in one place, for prayer and the worship of God. This is what we understand by a *congregational* church, in distinction from a national, provincial, or diocesan church, or a church embracing several congregations of believers.

2. The churches are represented as "holy" — as "blessed through the greatness and fulness of God the Father, and predestinated before the world began" — "much beloved of God" — "of well ordered love and charity in God" — persons of "blameless and constant disposition through patience" — as those who had "obtained mercy from the majesty of the most high God and his only begotten Son Jesus Christ, beloved and illuminated." All these expressions denote that the churches were composed only of visible saints — professed Christians.

3. The language of these epistles is, indeed, somewhat different from that of Clement or Polycarp, respecting the ministry of the churches. Mention is frequently made of the president, or superintendent, who after a while engrossed the title of bishop, or overseer, to the exclusion of his fellow-elders.

Ignatius exhorts the Ephesians to be subject to their "Bishop and the Presbytery," — § 3; again, he speaks of their "famous Presbytery," worthy of God, "being fitted as exactly to the Bishop as the strings are to the harp." — § 4. To the Magnesians he says: "I exhort you that ye study to do all things in a divine concord: your Bishop presiding in the place of God, your Presbyters in the place of the council of the apostles; and your deacons most dear to me, being intrusted with the ministry of Jesus Christ." — § 6. To the Trallians he says:

"without your Bishop you should do nothing: also, be ye subject to your Presbyters, as to the Apostles of Jesus Christ our hope. . . . The Deacons, also, as being the ministers of the mysteries of Jesus Christ must by all means please all." To the Smyrneans he writes: "See that ye all follow your Bishop as Jesus Christ, the Father: and the Presbytery, as the apostles. And reverence the Deacons, as the command of God," etc. — § 8.

If these passages may be relied upon as genuine, they fully authorize the assertion of Mosheim, that a change was introduced into the government of the church during the second century. These quotations, however, by no means countenance the opinion that diocesan Episcopacy, having bishops, priests, and deacons, all different grades in the ministry, and occupying different stations among the congregations of the Church, had any existence in the second century.

The kind of bishop of which Ignatius speaks was associated with the presbyters and deacons in the management of one and the same church; and this, not a diocesan church, but a congregational — one that could "meet together in one place" — which could worship in "one temple of God" — which could follow its bishop, or pastor, as sheep their shepherd. Thus he addresses the Magnesians: "Seeing then I have been judged worthy to see you, by Damas, your most excellent Bishop; and by your most worthy Presbyters, Bassus and Apollonius; and by my fellow-servant Sotio, the deacon, in whom I rejoice, forasmuch as he is subject unto his Bishop as to the grace of God, and to the Presbytery as to the law of Jesus Christ; I determined to write unto you." — § 2.

4. *There is not the slightest intimation in these epistles that bishops had the least authority beyond the limits of their own particular congregational churches.** And so far are these epistles from encouraging the notion that the bishops were the sole representatives of the apostles, and were for this reason a distinct and superior order in the ministry, that Ignatius repeatedly speaks of the *presbyters*, or the *presbytery*, as the representatives of the apostles. Thus he says: "Your presbyters, in the place of the council of the apostles" — "Be ye subject to your presbyters, as to the apostles of Jesus Christ our hope." — Trall. sec-

---

* Dr. Campbell says: "The great patrons of the hierarchy, who found so much on the testimony of Ignatius, will not deny, that on this article [the independency of the churches, and the limited extent of the bishop's power] he is quite explicit." "The bishop's charge is, in the primitive writers, invariably denominated *ἐκκλησία, a church, or congregation,* in the singular number, never *ἐκκλησίας, churches, or congregations,* in the plural." — *Lect.* vi. p. 105. — Dr. C. discusses the merit of these epistles of Ignatius in this Lecture.

Stillingfleet, in his *Irenicum*, (p. 309,) though an Episcopalian, says of the support derived from these epistles: "In all those thirty-five testimonies produced out of Ignatius, his epistle for Episcopacy, I can meet but with one which is brought to prove the least resemblance of an Institution of Christ for Episcopacy; and if I be not much deceived, the sense of that place is clearly mistaken too. The place is Ep. ad Ephesios: He is exhorting the Ephesians *συντρέχειν τῇ γνώμῃ τοῦ Θεοῦ*, which I suppose may be rendered, *to fulfil the will of God,*" etc. — Stillingfleet afterwards modified his opinions in some particulars and became a bishop; but, whether he ever saw reason to alter his translation of Ignatius, or his opinion of his doctrine, I know not.

tion 2. "Reverence . . . the presbyters as the Sanhedrim of God, and college of the apostles." — Ib. § 3. And so in other passages.

5. *These epistles distinctly recognize the authority of the churches to elect, and set apart to their service, such servants as they needed.*

To the Philadelphians, Ignatius writes: "Now as concerning the church at Antioch which is in Syria, seeing I am told that through your prayers and the bowels which ye have towards it in Jesus Christ, it is in peace; it will become you as the church of God [*πρέπον ἐστιν ὑμῖν ὡς ἐκκλησία Θεοῦ* — it is proper for you as a church of God] to ordain some deacon [*χειροτονῆσαι** *ἐπίσκοπον*, to choose or appoint by vote a bishop] to go to them thither, as the ambassador of God; that he may rejoice with them when they meet together [*ἐπὶ τὸ αὐτὸ* in the same place]; . . . other neighboring churches have sent them [i. e. to the church at Antioch] some bishops, some priests, [*πρεσβυτέροις, elders*] and deacons." — § 10. Ignatius urges the same duty upon the Smyrneans: "It will be fitting, and for the honor of God, that your church appoint some worthy delegate, who being come as far as Syria, may rejoice together with them that they are in peace," etc. — § 11.

Now, for whatever purpose these bishops, priests, and deacons were to be chosen and sent abroad by the churches, one thing is evident, namely — the

---

* It is observable that this is the very word which is used in Acts 14: 23; "*ordained* them elders in every church." — One is at a loss to know why *ἐπίσκοπον* should be translated *deacon*, as it is by Archbishop Wake; or *πρεσβυτέροις*, *priests.*

churches in the time of Ignatius possessed the right to elect their own representatives. This right constitutes a distinctive peculiarity of the Congregational system of church government.

From this cursory survey of the epistles of Ignatius, it appears, that, although some changes had been made in the government of the churches since Clement wrote, still they remained, A. D. 108–17, independent, congregational bodies, subject to no human authority except that of their own overseers and guides.

The Epistle of Barnabas — is of somewhat doubtful authority, though very ancient.* Its spirit is, however, totally unlike the epistles attributed to Ignatius. It more nearly resembles Clement's. He says nothing about the three orders, on which Ignatius is made to harp so much; and nowise contradicts the general impression made by Clement — that the churches remained at the close of the first century in their organization and government very nearly as the apostles left them.

Hermas, — another reputed contemporary of Ignatius, furnishes but little matter to our purpose. In his Dreams, Visions, and Similitudes, we discover nothing to contradict Clement's testimony and that of Polycarp — nothing to support the Ignatian doctrine of three orders in the ministry. In the second

---

* Dr. Lardner says: "I shall quote it as being *probably* Barnabas's" (the Barnabas spoken of Acts 4: 36, 37, and 15: 36,) and certainly ancient, written soon after the destruction of Jerusalem by Titus; most likely in the year of our Lord 71 or 72." — *Cred. Gosp. Hist.* Part II. ch. 1.

Book, eleventh Command, there is a passage, which speaks of the congregational character of the churches: "When, therefore, a man who hath the spirit of God shall come into the church of the righteous, who have the faith of God, and they pray unto the Lord, then the holy angel of God fills that man with the blessed spirit, and he speaks in the congregation as he is moved of God." — § 2. In the second Vision mention is made of "the *elders* of the church." — § 4. In his ninth Similitude there is a passage which seems to imply that bishops and deacons, such as the apostles ordained, still remained in the churches: "For what concerns the tenth mountain, in which were the trees covering the cattle, they are such as have believed, and some of them been *bishops*, that is governors of the churches: others, are such stones as have not feignedly, but with a cheerful mind entertained the servants of God: then such as have been set over *inferior ministries*, and have protected the poor and the widows, and have always kept a chaste conversation, therefore they also are protected by the Lord." — § 27. These "inferior ministries" are so described as to leave little doubt but that *deacons* are meant. Here, then, we have only *bishops* and *deacons*, in the churches.

I transcribe these passages, not because I think any great stress should be laid on them, but simply to show that the Ignatian epistles stand alone, among the reputed writings of the Apostolic Fathers, in support of the doctrine of three orders in the ministry.

If from the most ancient Fathers of the church,

we come down to those of a somewhat later period — to those who lived in the second, and the first half of the third century, we shall find that the churches still retained many of their Apostolical and Congregational peculiarities.

Justin Martyr — wrote an Apology for the Christians, addressed to Antoninus Pius, the Roman Emperor, and his two sons, about A. D. 150. In this apology he gives the following account of their manner of receiving members to the churches, and of their public religious services: "Whoever are convinced, and believe to be true the things which are declared and taught by us, and take upon themselves to live in accordance with our instructions, are taught to seek of God by fasting and prayer, the remission of their former sins, we uniting with them in prayers and fasting. Afterwards they are led by us where there is water, and regenerated [or baptized] in the same way as we ourselves are regenerated: — For in the name of God, the parent and lord of all, and of Jesus Christ, our Saviour, and of the Holy Spirit, they are then washed in water. . . . . After we have thus baptized the person who is a believer and agreed with us in doctrine, we conduct him to the brethren, as they are called, where they are assembled together offering earnestly their united prayers and supplications for themselves, for the illuminated [or baptized person] and for all others, of all nations. . . . . Prayers being ended, we salute each other with a kiss. Then is brought to him who presides over the brethren, bread, and a cup of wine and water. Which being received, he offers praise and glory to the Father of all, through the Son and the Holy Spirit. . . . . And when he has finished the prayers and thanksgivings, all the people present proclaim their approval, by saying—Amen. . . . . Then those whom we call *deacons* distribute to each one present, the bread, and the wine and water, that each may partake of that for which thanks are given; and then carry it to those who are absent. This aliment is called by us the *eucharist;* of which it is not lawful for any one to partake except those who believe our doctrine to be truth, and have been washed in the laver for the remission of sins, and regeneration, and live as Christ has required. . . . . . . On the day called Sunday, there is an assembly of all who live in the cities or in country towns, in one place (ἐπι το αὐτὸ), and the commentaries of the apostles and the writings of the prophets are read as time permits. The reading being over, the president makes an oration [preaches a sermon], in which he instructs the people, and exhorts them to the practice of good works. After this, we all rise up and pour forth our prayers: And as we have before related, prayers being ended, the bread, and the wine and water are brought forward. And the president [προεστώς, the elder presiding over the church] according to his best ability, offers up prayers and thanksgiving, and the people signify their approbation, by saying—Amen. And distribution and communication is then made of those things for which thanks are given, to each one present, and sent to the absent, by the hands of the deacons. Those who are rich and willing, contribute each one according to his pleasure; and what is collected, is deposited with the president; and he from thence relieves the orphans and widows, and those who, through disease or any other cause, are in want, and those also who are in prison, and those foreigners who happen to be our guests; and, as we may in a word say — He is the provider for all the indigent. We all assemble on Sunday, because this is the first day on which God, dispelling the darkness and forming matter, made the world; and also, because, on this day, Jesus Christ our Saviour rose from the dead; for the day before Saturday he was crucified, and the day after it, which is Sunday, he appeared to his disciples, and taught them those things which we have now related for your consideration." *

The above extracts teach us, (1) That in the days of Justin Martyr, apparent piety was essential to church membership. (2) That an open profession of this was required, and an engagement to walk in accordance with the instructions of Christ. (3) That after such a profession, baptism and the Lord's supper were administered to the initiated. (4) That the church, to whose communion the believing and baptized person was thus admitted, was a *congregational* church, composed of no more brethren than could conveniently assemble together for fasting and prayer, to hear the Scriptures read and the truth preached, and to celebrate the Lord's supper. (5) That in this church there were but two kinds of officers — a *president*, or presiding officer, and *deacons*. (6) That the work assigned to the president was

* *Apology*, II. p. 93–99, Ed. Gr. et Lat. 1686.

very nearly what every Congregational pastor is now expected to do, namely: To preach and pray in the assemblies of the church, to administer the ordinances of baptism and the Lord's supper, and to take the general oversight of the church. (7) That the deacons, as among us, distributed the elements used at the Lord's supper, to the communicants. A christian church, in the days of Justin Martyr, A. D. 150, was, then, substantially, a congregational church in its constitution, discipline, worship, and officers.

Passing by intermediate writers, we will next consider the testimony of a very distinguished father of the Church, who lived a hundred years after Justin Martyr.

Cyprian — lived, and wrote the epistles which we shall now examine, somewhere about A. D. 250. In one of these, he furnishes the following evidence that the original rights and divinely invested authority of the brethren of the several churches were not utterly destroyed, even after the lapse of more than two centuries from the death of Christ.

"For this cause," says Cyprian, "the people, obedient to the commands of our Lord, and fearing God, ought to separate themselves from a wicked bishop, nor take part with the worship of a sacrilegious priest, *since they especially have the power of choosing the worthy priests, and of rejecting the unworthy.* Which power we see comes from Divine authority, that a priest should be chosen in the presence of the people, and before the eyes of all, and approved by the public judgment and testimony, as a fit and worthy person: as God commanded Moses in Numbers (20: 23–27) saying:" [here follows an account of the consecration of Eleazar, as high-priest, in the sight of the whole congregation of Israel]. "God orders that the priest should be constituted in the presence of the whole congregation; that is, he teaches, and by example shows, that priestly ordinations should not take place except by the concurrence (conscientia) and assistance of the people. So that by the presence of the people, the crimes of the wicked may be exposed, or the merits of the good proclaimed, and that the ordination may be just and lawful which has been approved by the suffrage and judgment of all."

In proof of these positions, Cyprian then refers to the election of Matthias to supply the place of Judas, recorded in Acts 1: 15–26; and to the popular election of deacons, given in Acts 6: 2–6. The very examples which Congregationalists quote in proof of their right to choose and ordain their own church officers.

A little further on in this epistle, Cyprian speaks of "*the vote of all the brethren*" being had in the ordination of his colleague, Sabinus.* Indeed, he often speaks of "the *suffrages of the people*," as among the things which are essential to a rightly constituted, divinely sanctioned bishop. This Father also distinctly acknowledges the right of the people to take part in the discipline of the church. In one of his letters to his church, he says of certain lapsed brethren whose cases were then under consideration: "Every thing shall be examined, *you being present* and

* *Epistola* LXXVIII. p. 117-120. Paris, 1726.

judging of it." — *Epist. ad Plebem.* XI. In another place, he tells his people of his purpose to examine these matters pertaining to the lapsed, in a convocation of his associates and in their (the people's) presence, and *with their aid.* — *Ib.* p. 22.

From this entire epistle, according to Cyprian's Annotator, is to be gathered that not the clergy alone, but also the laity, took part with the bishop and clergy in judging of all matters of serious import. — *See Notae*, p. 398.

In an epistle to his presbyters and deacons, he says, in regard to certain matters about which they had desired his opinion: " I cannot reply to it alone, since, from the very commencement of my ministry, I have resolved to do nothing privately, of my own mind, without your advice, and the consent of the people." — *Ep.* V. p. 11.

Other quotations to the same effect might be given were it necessary.

This testimony to the rights of the primitive churches is the more valuable, because it comes from " the most bold and strenuous defender of episcopal power that had then [about A. D. 250] arisen in the church," and the principal author of important innovations upon the government and rights of the churches, which were developed in the course of the third century.*

Such is the testimony borne by the Fathers of the Church to the Congregational character of the Apos-

---

* See *Mosheim*, *Cent.* III. B. I. P. 2, ch. 2, § 3; *Barrow's Theol. Works*, Vol. VII. p. 302. 12mo.

tolic Churches. And it is certainly sufficiently explicit, to authorize us in claiming the weight of their authority, even, in our favor.

MODERN WRITERS.

From the most ancient writers, we will pass to the consideration of several modern divines and writers on ecclesiastical antiquities. Their testimony will be adduced simply to show, that "crude and absurd" as some wise men have professed to regard our views, yet many writers, distinguished alike for their learning and impartiality, and not themselves Congregationalists, have freely admitted, that the Apostolic churches were organized and governed substantially as our modern Congregational churches are.

Mosheim. — Many quotations from Mosheim's Ecclesiastical History have been already given. For the information of such of my readers as have not access to his works, and for the convenience of others, I shall make some further extracts from this learned and impartial historian. Mosheim's statements are the more valuable, since, being himself a *Lutheran*, he had no partialities for Congregationalism. His *opinions* respecting what is now best, must go for what they are worth; his *facts*, alone, are authoritative.

Under the general head of "History of the Teachers, and of the Government of the Church" in the *first century*, Mosheim says: "As to the external *form* of the church, and the mode of governing it, neither Christ himself, nor his apostles gave any express precepts. We are, therefore, to understand, that this matter is left chiefly to be regulated as circumstances may from time to time require, and as the discretion of civil and ecclesiastical rulers shall judge expedient. If, however, what no Christian can doubt, the apostles of Jesus Christ acted by divine command and guidance, then that form of the primitive churches which was derived from the church at Jerusalem, erected and organized by the apostles themselves, must be accounted divine; yet it will not follow, that this form of the church was to be perpetual and unalterable.*

"In these primitive times each christian church was composed of the *people*, the *presiding officers*, and the *assistants* or *deacons.* These must be the component parts of every society. *The highest authority was in* THE PEOPLE, OR THE WHOLE BODY OF CHRISTIANS; for even the apostles themselves inculcated by their example, that nothing of any moment was to be done or determined on, but with the knowledge and consent of the brotherhood. — Acts 1: 15. 6: 3. 15: 4. 21: 22. And this mode of proceeding, both prudence and necessity required, in those early times. The assembled people, therefore, elected their own rulers and teachers; or, by their authoritative counsel, received them, when nominated to them. They also by their suffrages, rejected or confirmed the laws that were proposed by their rulers, in their assemblies; they excluded profligate and lapsed brethren, and restored them; they decided the controversies and disputes that arose; they heard

* The dissent of Congregationalists from these views has been noticed, p. 19–27.

and determined the causes of presbyters and deacons; in a word, THE PEOPLE DID EVERY THING THAT IS PROPER FOR THOSE IN WHOM THE SUPREME POWER OF THE COMMUNITY IS VESTED. All their rights the people paid for, by supplying the funds necessary for the support of the teachers, the deacons, and the poor, the public exigencies, and unforeseen emergencies.

"The rulers of the church were denominated, sometimes *presbyters* or *elders;* — a designation borrowed from the Jews, and indicative, rather of the wisdom, than the age of the persons; and sometimes, also, *bishops;* for it is most manifest, that both terms are promiscuously used in the New Testament of one and the same class of persons. — Acts 20: 17, 28. Phil. 1: 1. Tit. 1: 5, 7. 1 Tim. 3: 1. These were men of gravity, and distinguished for their reputation, influence, and sanctity. — 1 Tim. 3: 1, etc. Tit. 1: 5, etc. From the words of Saint Paul (1 Tim. 5: 17) it has been inferred that some elders *instructed* the people, while others served the church in some other ways. But this distinction between *teaching* and *ruling* elders, if it ever existed (which I will neither affirm nor deny) was certainly not of long continuance; for St. Paul makes it a qualification requisite in *all* presbyters, or bishops, that they be able to teach and instruct others. — 1 Tim. 3: 2, etc."

"In this manner," continues Mosheim, "Christians managed ecclesiastical affairs, so long as their congregations were small, or not very numerous. Three or four presbyters, men of gravity and holiness, placed over those little societies, could easily proceed with harmony, and needed no head or president. But, when the churches became larger, and the number of presbyters and deacons, as well as the amount of duties to be performed increased, it became necessary that the council of presbyters should have a *president;* a man of distinguished gravity and prudence, who should distribute among his colleagues their several tasks, and be, as it were, the central point of the whole society. He was at first denominated *the Angel* (Rev. 2: 3); but afterwards, *the Bishop;* a title of Grecian derivation, and indicative of his principal business, (that is, of an *overseer*). It would seem, that the church of Jerusalem when grown very numerous, after the dispersion of the apostles among foreign nations, was the first to elect such a president; and, that other churches, in process of time, followed the example. But, whoever supposes that the bishops of the first and golden age of the church, corresponded with the bishops of the following centuries, must blend and confound characters that are very different. *For in this century and the next, a bishop had charge of a single church which might, ordinarily, be contained in a private house; nor was he its head, but was in reality its minister or servant;* he instructed the people, conducted all parts of public worship, attended on the sick and necessitous, in person; and what he was unable thus to perform, he committed to the care of the presbyters; but without power to ordain or determine any thing, except with the concurrence of the presbyters and the brotherhood. It was not long, however, before the extent of the Episcopal jurisdiction was enlarged. For the bishops who lived in the cities, either by their own labors or by those of their presbyters, gathered new churches in the neighboring villages and hamlets; and these churches continuing under the protection and care of the bishops by whose ministry or procurement they received Christianity, ecclesiastical provinces were gradually formed, which the Greeks afterwards called *dioceses.** The persons to whom the city bishops committed the government and instruction of these village and rural churches, were called *rural bishops* or *chorepiscopi* (τῆς χώρας ἐπίσκοποι, episcopi rurales, seu villani), that is, bishops of the suburbs and fields. They were an intermediate class between the bishops and presbyters; being inferior to the former [because subject to them] and superior to the latter [because intrusted with discretionary and perpetual power, and performing nearly all the functions of bishops].† All the churches in those primitive times were independent bodies; or

---

* *Dr. Bloomfield*, in his note on Eph. 4: 11, seems to admit the correctness of this account. "It is thought," says he, "that the ποιμένες [pastors] were those who had the more important pastoral charges in cities and large towns: the διδάσκαλοι [teachers], the smaller ones. . . . Thus it would happen, that *the city* ποιμένες would have an *influence* with, and then an *authority* over the *country* pastors. Hence, gradually, their offices would vary and become distinct; the ποιμένες [or city pastors] first discharging all the ordinary pastoral duties; and afterwards, when they became regarded as *superintendents*—and were then styled ἐπίσκοποι [that is, overseers, superintendents, or bishops]—they discharged them or not, according to circumstances."

Dr. Campbell, in his learned Lectures on Ecclesiastical History, gives substantially the same account.—*Lect.* viii. p. 130–136. Phil. ed. 1807.

† See Dr. Owen's account of this matter, in which he agrees with Mosheim.—*Complete Works*, Vol. XX. Pref. p. 29 seq. Also *Barrow*, ut sup. p. 302 seq.

none of them subject to the jurisdiction of any other. For, though the churches which were founded by the apostles themselves, frequently had the honor shown them to be consulted in difficult and doubtful cases; yet, they had no judicial authority, no control, no power of giving laws. On the contrary, *it is clear as the noonday, that all christian churches had equal rights, and were, in all respects, on a footing of equality.*" *

In giving an account of the government of the church during the second century, Mosheim remarks: "The form of church government which began to exist in the preceding century, was, in this, more industriously established and confirmed in all parts. One president, or bishop, presided over each church. *He was created by the common suffrage of the whole people.* . . . During a great part of this century, all the churches continued to be, as at first, *independent* of each other; or, were connected by no consociations or confederations." — Vol. I. p. 142.

The preceding testimony of Mosheim goes to sustain the following positions, namely: (1) The apostolic churches were *single congregations of Christians*, with their appropriate officers. (2) The government of these churches was essentially *democratical.* Each church elected its own officers, determined by what particular regulations it would be governed, exercised discipline upon its members; in a word, *did every*

---

* *Murdock's Mosheim*, Vol. I. p. 80–86, 1st ed. The several points touched upon by Mosheim in the above extracts, will be found more particularly stated and argued in his *Larger History of the First Three Centuries.* — Vol. I. p. 193–267.

thing that those possessing the supreme power were authorized to do. (3) Their officers at first consisted simply of *presbyters* (who were also called bishops, or overseers, and elders) and of *deacons;* and when, for prudential reasons, a president was chosen from among the elders of a single church, and the title of *bishop*, or overseer, was given to him, to distinguish him from his coequal elders, his authority was confined to *a single church* or religious society, and was essentially unlike a modern diocesan bishop. (4) That all the churches in those primitive times, though bound together by a common faith and order, were *equal and independent bodies*, subject to no earthly power nor authoritative control beyond themselves. Such, briefly, is Mosheim's testimony respecting the order of the churches of Christ during the first, and a part of the second century.

Before the close of the second century, this simple and beautiful form of church order and government lost something of its fair proportions. In the third century, "although the ancient mode of church government seemed, in general, to remain unaltered, yet there was a gradual deflection from its rules, and an approximation towards the form of a monarchy. For the bishops claimed much higher authority and power than before, and encroached more and more upon the rights, not only of the brotherhood, but also of the presbyters. . . . . This change in the form of ecclesiastical government, was followed by a corrupt state of the clergy."

This deflection from apostolic church order, and this corruption of the clergy, prepared the way for the fatal union of Church and State, under Constantine the Great, in the early part of the fourth century. This Emperor, after assuming the supreme power over the Church, proceeded to model its outward form and to adapt its government to the peculiarities of the Roman State. The Emperor governed the bishops; the bishops the churches; and the poor churches, by the hands of these governors, were gradually stripped of their ancient rights and privileges, until, at the close of the fourth century, they retained little else that was apostolic than the mere name of Christian Churches. It is not, however, my present purpose to trace the progress of declension in the ancient churches; * but rather to mark out their earliest order and government. What these were, in the judgment of Mosheim, we have just read.

Admitting, now, the competency and honesty of this witness, must we not conclude that the apostolic churches were essentially the same in their order and discipline as our modern Congregational churches?

But Mosheim stands not alone. Other writers of distinguished learning maintain essentially the same positions:—

(1) In relation to the *congregational* character of the apostolic, and earliest christian churches.

Lord King, in his learned "Inquiry into the Constitution, Discipline, etc., of the Primitive Church," says: "The usual and common acceptation of the word [ἐκκλησία, church], and of which we must chiefly

---

* I have attempted to do this briefly in the *History of Congregationalism*, particularly in the Introduction.

treat, is that of a particular church; that is, a society of Christians meeting together in one place under their proper pastors, for the performance of religious worship and the exercising of Christian discipline." — Chap. I. § 2.*

Zuinglius's definition of a christian church is very nearly the same. — See *Jacob's* "*Attestation*," p. 215.

Neander says: In the apostolic age "the word

* In quoting from the work of Lord Chancellor King, I am aware that it is asserted by Episcopalians, who are greatly annoyed by the "Inquiry," that Mr. Slater's review of the work converted the Chancellor from the opinions expressed therein. But what proof do they bring of this conversion? Why, that Lord King never replied to Mr. Slater; and that he presented him with a lucrative benefice, which was at the disposal of the Lord High Chancellor.

The fact that his Lordship never replied to Mr. Slater, to my mind is an evidence that he was *not* converted, rather than the contrary. For surely, a man of Lord King's integrity, modesty, impartiality, and earnest desire for truth, could hardly have satisfied his conscience without retracting his opinions and assertions, if convinced that they were erroneous. But, instead of doing this, he suffered a second edition of his Inquiry to be published without any such retraction. — See Dr. Vaughan, on "Religious Parties in England." And, though it has been asserted that he did not authorize the publication of this second edition — of which, however, no satisfactory proof is furnished — yet, knowing that it was published, if he had "given up his book," as it is said he had, at that time, it was incumbent on him to publish to the world his recantation. But this he never did; and until better vouchers for its truth are furnished, we are not authorized to believe this story, that Mr. Slater's book convinced his Lordship that he was in error.

As it respects the benefice: It can hardly be accounted strange that a man of Lord King's character and standing — an Episco-

ἐκκλησία [church] signifies either the whole christian church, the total number of believers forming one body, under one head; or a single church or christian society." — *Apostolic Chh.* Vol. I. p. 169, note. 3d Edition, Edinb.

Dr. Campbell's definition of a church is the same as Neander's. — *Lect. Ecc. Hist.* L. ii. p. 26, see also Lec. vi, p. 105, supra, p. 148.

Augusti says: "The term ἐκκλησία, in the New Testament, and by the ancient fathers, primarily denoted an assembly of Christians, i. e. believers in the christian religion, in distinction from all others." — *Coleman's Antiquities*, p. 47; also p. 57. See Locke's definition of a church, supra, p. 28, note.

(2) Regarding the right of individual churches to *choose their own officers and discipline offending mem-*

---

palian of the Erastian school, and Lord High Chancellor of a kingdom in which Episcopacy was the established religion — should give a valuable benefice to a clergyman of Mr. Slater's learning and ability, though he had written a book against him.

That Lord King would have publicly recanted, had he been convinced of his errors, seems wellnigh certain from his preface to the "Inquiry." After modestly requesting any one to point out his errors, he says; "And then *I promise, if my mistakes are fairly shown, I will not pertinaciously and obstinately defend, but most willingly and thankfully renounce them,* since my design is not to defend a party, but to search out the truth." Now, that his Lordship did never "renounce" the statements and opinions contained in his "Inquiry," is very strong presumptive evidence that he never considered them errors; and consequently, that Mr. Slater's review did not convert him.

bers, etc., we may add to Mosheim's testimony, the following:—

Barrow.—"In ancient times, there was not any small church which had not a suffrage in the choice of its pastor."—*Barrow on the Pope's Supremacy*, Supposition 5th, § 12. Also, Supp. 6th, Argument 6th, § 4.

Beza.—"I find nowhere in any christian church built up, that any is promoted either to the ministry of the word, or the deaconship, or eldership, any other way than by a *public and free election.*"—*Jacob's Attestation*, p. 23, London. 16mo.

Augusti.—"That the church, i. e. the united body of believers, has had a part in the election of their pastor, from the earliest period downward, *is certain;* not merely from the testimony of Scripture, but also from the most ancient of the Fathers." . . .—*Coleman's Antiquities of the Christian Chh.* p. 60, 61.

Waddington, an Episcopal historian, agrees with Mosheim. His words are: "It is also true that in the earliest government of the first christian society, that of Jerusalem, *not the elders only, but 'the whole church,' were associated with the apostles;*" . . . In a note he adds: "still, of course, with some degree of subjection to apostolic authority. This, according to Mosheim, was the model of all the primitive churches."—*Ecc. Hist.* p. 41.

Dr. Neander, a Lutheran, in his learned and elaborate work on the History of the Planting and Progress of the Christian Church under the Apostles, Vol. I. ch. 5, distinctly maintains this doctrine — that the whole church took part in the government of the same: "It is consequently certain, that each church was governed by a union of church elders or of church overseers, out of its own midst. . . . But their government by no means excluded the participation of the whole church in the management of the common concerns." — *Vol.* I. p. 169, 170.

Dr. Campbell, a Presbyterian divine, takes the same ground, in his Lectures on Ecclesiastical History. — *Lect.* iii. p. 31–33.

Lord King maintains essentially the same opinion of primitive church government. He tells us, that "every church," [that is, "every single parish, every particular church" or congregation of believers] was, in this sense, independent; that is, without the concurrence and authority of any other church; it had a sufficient right and power in itself to punish and chastise all its delinquent and offending members. — *Inquiry*, ch. 8, § 1, compared with ch. 1, § 2. See, also, ch. 7th, throughout.

Barrow says: "Each church was vested with a power of excommunication, or of excluding heretics, schismatics, disorderly and scandalous people." — *Unity of the Chh.* Vol. VII. of his Theol. Works, p. 497 and 259. 12mo. Edinb.

Augusti says: . . . "As a member of the church, each communicant had that important right of taking part in all the transactions of that body, especially *in the choice of the clergy and in the discipline of the church*," etc. — *Coleman's Antiquities*, p. 60, 61.

Dr. Campbell tells us, that in the apostolic age, "Not only were such private offences [as are particularly referred to in Matt. 18: 15–18] then judged by the church, that is, by the congregation, but also those scandals which affected the whole Christian fraternity." . . . "Now, though in after-times the charge of this matter also came to be devolved, first on the bishop and presbyters, and afterwards solely on the bishop, yet that the people, as well as the presbyters, as far down at least as to the middle of the third century, retained some share in the decision of questions wherein morals were immediately concerned, is manifest from Cyprian's letters still extant." — *Lect.* 3d, p. 31, 32.

Cranmer, Leyghton, Coren, and Oglethorp, the leading Reformers in the days of Henry VIII. and Edward VI., all agreed, that the Scriptures gave to the churches (i. e. to the people — the congregations) the right to elect their own officers, and to excommunicate offending members. — See *Burnet's Hist. Reformation*, passim; or, *Hist. Congregationalism*, A. D. 1509–47.

(3) With Mosheim's declarations respecting *the officers of the apostolic churches*, coincide the following authorities: —

Waddington, and others, as given at page 91 of

this work . . . "Such is the plain interpretation of the Scripture passages." — *Hist. Chh.* p. 41 and note.

Milner, even, is compelled, though with apparent reluctance, to admit, that "at first indeed, or for some time, at least in some instances, church governors were only of two ranks, presbyters and deacons." — *Chh. Hist.* Cent. II. ch. 1.

The identity of scriptural bishops and presbyters was admitted very generally by the Reformers.

The "King's Book," published in 1543, asserted, that there was "no real distinction between bishops and priests;" and taught essentially the same doctrine respecting the deacon of the primitive church, as is now held by Congregationalists. It further declared, that the Scripture made no mention of any other church officers but these two, priests, or elders, and deacons. — *Hist. Cong.* ut sup. — *Dwight's Theol.* Serm. 151.

Neander's account of the officers and government of the Gentile churches during the apostolic age, is as follows: "It is, therefore, certain that every church was governed by a union of the elders or overseers chosen from among themselves; and we find no individual distinguished above the rest, who presided as a *primus inter pares* [a chief among equals], though, probably, in the age immediately succeeding the apostolic, of which we have, unfortunately, so few authentic memorials, the practice was introduced of applying to such an one the name of ἐπίσκοπος, [bishop, overseer] by way of distinction." — *Hist. Apost. Chh.* Vol. I. p. 168, 169.

The correctness of Mosheim's account of the humble character and limited authority of the primitive bishop, is admitted by *Waddington;* who says: "The government of a *single person* protected *each society* from internal dissension — the *electiveness* of that governor rendered probable his merit." — *Hist. Chh.* p. 44.

Lord King's representation is: "There was but one bishop, strictly so called, in a church at a time, who was related to his flock as a pastor to his sheep, and a parent to his children." — *Inquiry*, ch. 1, § 5. And again: "There was but one church to a bishop:" And this church, he tells us, was "a single congregation." — *Ch.* 2, § 1. "The bishop's diocese exceeded not the bounds of a modern parish, and was the same, as in name, so also in thing." . . . *Ib.* § 2.

Dr. Campbell gives the following account of the bishop's relation to his church, in the third century: —

"The bishop, who was properly the pastor, had the charge of no more than one parish, one church or congregation, the parishioners all assembling in the same place with him for the purposes of public worship, religious instruction, and the solemn commemoration of the death of Christ." . . . *Lec.* viii. p. 128.

Gieseler's account of the apostolic churches is this: "The new churches everywhere formed themselves on the model of the mother church at Jerusalem. At the head of each were the *elders*, πρεσβύτεροι, ἐπίσκοποι, [elders, bishops] all officially of equal rank, though in several instances a peculiar authority seems to have been conceded to some one individual from personal considerations. After the death of the apostles and the pupils of the apostles, to whom the general direction of the churches had always been conceded, some one amongst the presbyters of each church was suffered gradually to take the lead in its affairs. In the same irregular way the title of ἐπίσκοπος, *bishop*, was appropriated to the first presbyter."— *Coleman's Antiq.* p. 101–103.

(4) Respecting the *independency* of the primitive churches.

Dr. Campbell agrees with Mosheim when he says: "The different congregations, with their ministers, seemed, in a great measure, *independent of one another*. Every thing regarding their own procedure in worship, as well as discipline, was settled among themselves. But it is extremely plain, that a total independency was not adapted to the more general character that belonged to all as members of the commonwealth of Christ."— *Lect.* ix, p. 142.

The reader will not fail to remark, that this is precisely what Congregationalists maintain. Each Congregational church is complete, and independent, "regarding its own procedure in worship, as well as discipline," while it maintains a sisterly relation to other members of the Congregational family. We abhor all such independency as would lead us to refuse to give account of our faith and practice to our sister churches. So said our fathers, and so say we. Dr. Campbell refers to the first council at Jerusalem, about circumcision and other Jewish ceremonies, to illustrate the nature of "the correspondence and intercourse with one another," which the early christian churches maintained. This is the very case to which the framers of the Cambridge Platform refer. — *Chap.* 15, § 2.

Barrow, speaking of "the primitive state of the Church," says: "Each church separately did order its own affairs, without recourse to others, except for charitable advice or relief in cases of extraordinary difficulty or urgent need. Each church was endowed with a perfect liberty, and a full authority, without dependence or subordination to others, to govern its own members, manage its own affairs, to decide controversies and causes incident among themselves, without allowing appeals, or rendering accounts to others. This appeareth by the apostolical writings of St. Paul and St. John to single churches; wherein they are supposed able to exercise spiritual power for establishing decency, removing disorders, correcting offences, deciding causes, etc." — *Unity of the Chh.* Vol. VII. p. 486.

Dr. Barrow in his celebrated work on the Pope's Supremacy, further says: "At first, each church was settled apart under its own bishop and presbyters; so as independently and separately to manage its own concernments: each was *αὐτοκέφαλος*, and *αὐτονόμος*, governed by its own head, and had its own laws. Every bishop, as a prince in his own church, did act freely according to his will and discretion, with the advice of his ecclesiastical senate, and with the consent of his people, (the which he did use to consult,) without being controllable by any other, or accountable to any, further than his obligation to uphold the verity of Christian profession, and to maintain fraternal communion in charity and peace with neighboring churches did require; in which regard if he were notably peccant, he was liable to be disclaimed by them and rejected from communion, together with his church, if it did adhere to him in his misdemeanors. This may be collected from the remainders of state in the times of St. Cyprian:" [which would be as late as the middle of the third century: for Cyprian suffered martyrdom, A. D. 258.] *Supposition* 5th, Arg. 10, Theol. Works, Vol. VII. p. 302.

Dr. Campbell, speaking of the character, etc. — of the churches during the first and second centuries, says: "Every church had its own pastors, and its own presbytery, [i. e. council of church officers], *independently of every other church.* And when one of the presbyters came to be considered as *the pastor*, by way of eminence, while the rest were regarded as his assistants, vicars, or curates, who acted under his direction; as then every church or congregation had but one who was called bishop, so *every bishop had but one congregation or church.* This is a remark which deserves your particular notice, as it regards an essential point in the constitution of the primitive church, a point which is generally admitted by those who can make any pretensions to the knowledge of Christian Antiquities." — *Lec.* vi. p. 104: also 7th *Lec.* See, also, quotations from Lord King, ch. 8, § 1, supra, p. 169.

The Magdeburg Centuriators, in their celebrated

work, published in 1559–1574, in describing the constitution and discipline of the churches of the first and second centuries, furnish the following testimony in our favor: "A visible church was an assembly, or congregation, of persons who believed and followed the writings of the prophets and apostles; which should be composed of persons regenerated by the word and sacraments, though there might be in this assembly, many persons, who, though they agreed with the regenerate in doctrine, were nevertheless, not sanctified in heart. Clemens [of Alexandria] says: I call not a place, but a congregation of the elect, a church." — *Century* II. ch. 4, p. 39, Ed. Basil. 1624.

Of excommunication, they say: "the right of excommunication was committed to the hands of the church and its ministers." — *Cent.* I. *Lib.* 2, ch. 3, p. 274.

"The power of announcing the remission of the sins of penitent offenders was also in the hands of the church; though, for the sake of order, except in cases of necessity, it was exercised by the ministers of the church." — *Ib.* p. 276.

"The whole assembly, or church in any particular place — including laymen and clergy — had power to elect, call, and ordain suitable ministers; and to depose and avoid false teachers, or those whose evil lives threatened injury to the church. These things appear from the testimony of the Scriptures concerning the power of the keys; for the keys were given to the whole church. But the church if she calls her ministers to act, does nothing else than commit to them the keys. That power, therefore, pertains to the whole of the church. Moreover, the examples in the New Testament teach the same thing: for, in the first of Acts, it appears that not by the apostles alone, but by the whole church, Matthias was put in the place of Judas; and in Acts sixth chapter, the deacons were chosen, called, and ordained, not by the apostles alone, but also by the rest of the church. In Acts thirteenth chapter, the whole church of Antioch gathered together by command of God, and sent forth Paul and Barnabas to teach the Gospel to the Gentiles." — *Ib.* p. 299.

The following summary view of the constitution, government, and rights of the churches of the second century is given by these learned ecclesiastial historians: —

"If any one examines the approved writers of this century, [the second,] he will see, that the form of church government was *very like a democracy* (δημοκρατίας). For each church had equal power of preaching the pure word of God, of administering the sacraments, of absolving and excommunicating heretics and wicked persons, of observing the ceremonies received from the apostles, or, even, for the sake of edification, of instituting new ones; of choosing ministers, of calling, of ordaining, and for just causes, of deposing them again; of assembling councils and synods; of instituting and supporting schools; and, in matters of doubt or controversy, of demanding the opinion of others; of judging and deciding." — *Cent.* II. ch. 7, p. 102–103.

Father Paul of Venice (Fra Paolo Sarpi) a learned and distinguished Romanist of the sixteenth century, author of the celebrated "History of the Council of Trent" and many other learned works, bears the most unequivocal testimony to the democratic and congregational character of the apostolic and primitive churches. In his profound "Treatise of Ecclesiastical Benefices and Revenues," he says: "*It is plain the government of the Church in its beginning was entirely democratical*, all the faithful having a share in all deliberations of moment. Thus we find them all assisting at the election of Matthias to the apostleship (Acts i.), and of the seven deacons (Acts vi.), and when St. Peter had received the Centurion Cornelius, who was a Gentile (Acts iii.) into the number of believers, he gave an account of it to the whole church (Acts xi.). Thus the famous council of Jerusalem was composed of the Apostles, the Priests, and other Brethren in the Faith; and the letters which were writ from the assembly, went in the name of those three Orders (Acts xv.). But as the church increased in numbers, the Faithful neglecting to assist any longer at those public assemblies, and withdrawing themselves to the cares of their own families, the government rested solely in the Ministers of the Church, and so insensibly became aristocratical; which brought all affairs to have their determinations by Councils, excepting as to elections, which continued popular still." *

Neander says: "The view we are led to form of

---

* *Treatise of Ecclesiastical Benefices and Revenues*, Ch. XVI. Westminster Edition, 1736, p. 52, 53. See, also, in confirmation of these general statements, p. 5, and 6, Ch. III.; p. 16, Ch. VI.; p. 19 and 20, Ch. VII.; Ch. IX.; p. 157 and 158, Ch. XXXV.

the original constitution of the churches among Gentile Christians as they existed in the apostolic age — *that it was entirely democratic* — is also one of the distinguishing marks between the churches of Gentile and those of Jewish origin. The case appears to be thus: All the affairs of the churches were still transacted in an entirely public manner, so that every deliberative meeting of the church resembled a *strictly popular assembly*." — *Planting and Training of the Christian Church by the Apostles*, Vol. I. p. 165, note, 3d Ed.

Not to enlarge by quotations from other writers on Christian antiquities, in illustration of the several points under consideration, I will finish, by transcribing the allegation of the learned and pious *John Owen;* who, after a labored investigation of this whole matter, lays down and successfully proves this proposition: "*That in no approved writers for the space of two hundred years after Christ, is there any mention made of any other organical, visibly professing church, but that only which is parochial, or congregational.*" "A church of any other form, state, or order, papal or oecumenical, patriarchal, metropolitical, diocesan, or classical, they [the writers of the first two centuries] know not, neither name nor thing, nor any of them appear in any of their writings." — Vol. XX. p. 132. By which he means: that all the churches during the first two centuries were distinct, independent bodies; no one of them so numerous as to prevent them from assembling together for public worship and the transaction of church business; and that each one was invested with sufficient and complete authority for all the purposes of church organization.

Every one who is acquainted with the character of John Owen, well knows that he did not deal in rash assertions. Every one who has examined his works on church order and discipline, must be aware that in these, neither sound argument nor extensive learning are wanting. His conclusions are those of an eminently pious and learned man, who, after a careful examination of the arguments of Congregationalists, *for the purpose of refuting them*,* became himself a decided friend to their views of church order, and, for nearly forty years, was a leader among the English Congregationalists. The work from which I have extracted, was written near the close of his life, and contains, with his maturest thoughts, his dying testimony to the principles of church government which he advocated. It well deserves the careful study of every one who would fully understand the foundation on which rest our principles and doctrines.†

Thus, I conceive, it has been shown, from the testimony of numerous and distinguished ecclesiastical

---

* The book of which Owen undertook "the examination and confutation," was John Cotton's work "On the Keys." — See *Owen's Memoirs*, p. 55, 56.

† In these remarks, I would not be understood to express an unqualified approval and adoption of all his views of church order and discipline. There are some points on which modern, and especially New England Congregationalists, would slightly differ from Owen; but his writings, as a whole, are almost incomparably excellent, sound, and learned upon this subject.

historians — none of whom except Dr. Owen were Congregationalists, and who, consequently, were without any inducement to misunderstand or misinterpret facts in our favor — that the leading principles and doctrines of the Congregational system were developed in the constitution and discipline of the Apostolic Churches; that this organization, for substance, was retained during the first two centuries of the christian church; and that corruption and error followed the abandonment of the apostolic models. The correctness of their opinions is not made to rest on the bare assertions of these historians, however learned and impartial they are acknowledged to be; but, numerous extracts from the Apostolical and Christian Fathers have been introduced, to prove the statements made and the opinions advanced.

And now, though the strength of our cause lies not in the testimony of the Fathers, nor the opinions of eminent men — the Scriptures being our only infallible guide — must it not be conceded by all parties, that the correctness of our interpretation of the Scriptures, or, the scriptural character of our system, receives strong confirmation from the testimony of the earliest uninspired writers of the christian church, and the concurrent voice of many modern authors, alike distinguished for their profound learning and their sound and impartial judgment?

PART IV.

ECCLESIASTICAL PRACTICE.

THE principles and doctrines embraced by Congregationalists have induced certain ecclesiastical practices, which have become a sort of common law to the denomination. A knowledge of these is necessary to a perfect understanding of Congregationalism. There may be slight deviations among us from what will now be specified as agreeable to good usage; but it is believed that the denomination will agree substantially in what follows: —

I. ORGANIZATION OF CHURCHES.

If in any place a sufficient number * of persons wish to be organized into a Congregational church, an orderly procedure would be the following: —

---

* The number is not fixed: it may be more or less, according to circumstances. Under ordinary circumstances, it should not be less than *seven;* because a less number cannot conveniently discharge the duties enjoined by Christ in the xviii. of Matt. When, however, there is a reasonable prospect of a speedy addition to

After a season of fasting and prayer, the brethren would appoint a committee to advise with one or more of the neighboring Congregational pastors and churches; to draw up a Confession of Faith and a Covenant, with articles of government and practice; and, to send "Letters Missive,"* as they are called — that is, letters of invitation — to so many of the neighboring churches as should be agreed upon, soliciting their attendance by pastor and delegate, at an appointed time, to take into consideration the question — Whether the interests of religion required the organization of a Congregational church in that place?

At the time and place specified for the meeting of the council, the several persons proposing to unite in church fellowship would be present, with the record of their previous doings, a copy of their covenant and articles, and, so many of them as had been connected with christian churches, with their letters of dismission and recommendation; and prepared to give to the council any information which would be necessary to a perfect understanding of the merits of the question before them. If the associated brethren

---

their number, if *two* or *three* should covenant together in the name of Christ, they may expect his presence and blessing. Tertullian says: "Where there are three persons, though they are laymen, there is a church." — *De Exh. Castitatis*, p. 668, Ed. 1634.

Cotton Mather says: "*Seven* is the least number that has been allowed among us, as capable to form a church state for the enjoyment of all special ordinances; but usually there is a larger number expected." — *Ratio*, Article I. § 1. So, for substance, said Richard Mather, in his answer to Herle, 1644.

* See form of this letter, *Appendix*, No. 1.

had already selected their future pastor, it is agreeable to ancient usage that he should be present, to be embodied in the church as one of its members, and immediately afterwards ordained as its pastor.*

The pastors and delegates of the churches being assembled, they are called to order by the reading of the Letter Missive, which is the warrant for their meeting. The council is then organized, by choosing a moderator and scribe; and proceeds, after prayer for Divine direction, to examine the papers laid before them by the committee of the brethren at whose request they have assembled, and to hear statements from them respecting the peculiarities of their situation, etc., which, in their opinion, render the organization of a Congregational church desirable. If satisfied with these statements, etc., and with the covenant and articles agreed upon by the brethren, and of their christian character and standing,† the council vote — to proceed to the organization of a Congregational church; and fix upon the time and place for the public exercises. The parts are then assigned, as: Invocation and Reading of suitable portions of Scripture — Introductory Prayer — Sermon — Reading of the Covenant — Recognition of the Church and Consecrating Prayer, (usually assigned to the moderator,) — The Fellowship of the

---

* *Mather's Ratio*, Art. I. § 3.

† This satisfaction is obtained either by a personal examination of the candidates, if they have never been connected with a christian church; or by letters of recommendation and dismission from the church or churches of which they have been members. — For a form, see *Appendix*, No. 12.

Churches — The Concluding Prayer, and the Benediction.

At the appointed time and place, these services are publicly attended, and the associated brethren recognized as a Congregational church.*

II. CHOICE AND CONSECRATION OF OFFICERS.

The church thus organized, as soon as convenient meet together; and, after appointing a moderator and clerk, proceed to choose their officers; namely, a pastor, if previous arrangements admit of it, and two, or more deacons, according to the size and circumstances of the church.†

Choice of a Pastor.

The orderly course in choosing a pastor is substantially this: The church, having enjoyed a sufficient opportunity of hearing a minister preach and of becoming acquainted with his religious character, his literary attainments, his personal habits, etc.; ‡

---

* Mather gives a detailed and particular account of all the proceedings in organizing a church, in his *Ratio Disciplinæ*, Art. 1. Mr. Upham's third chapter is devoted to this subject. It is full and valuable.

† When it can be done, it is desirable that this meeting should take place in season to have the same council which organizes the church, assist in the consecration of the pastor. And, when this is intended, it should be mentioned in the letters missive; and the necessary preliminary arrangements should be made.

‡ There is reason to fear that our churches are not all as particular upon these points as they ought to be; they are certainly far less so than were our fathers. It was once thought necessary

after a season of fasting and prayer for Divine direction, vote to give him a call to become their pastor.* It is usual, though not strictly necessary upon Congregational principles, to invite the religious society which statedly worships with the church, to concur in this call and to fix the salary to be offered to the candidate.†

These preliminary steps being taken, the call of the church and the concurrence of the society are forwarded to the pastor elect, signed by the moderators and clerks of the respective bodies, or by committees appointed for this purpose. The call being accepted by the candidate, a committee of the church, after consultation with the pastor elect, agree upon the churches which shall compose the ordaining council. Letters Missive are then prepared,‡ signed by the committee, and sent, agreeably to previous arrangements.§

At the appointed time and place, the pastors and

---

for a candidate for settlement, to spend months among the people of his prospective charge; but now, some churches are satisfied with an acquaintance of a few days only; and some, are ready to call a pastor without having had any personal acquaintance with him. This, undoubtedly, is one reason why there is now so little permanency in the pastoral relation. Are we not verifying the maxim — To innovate is not necessarily to improve.

* See a form, *Appendix No.* 2.

† *Mather's Ratio*, Art. II.; *Upham's Ratio*, ch. 6, § 58–65.

‡ See *Appendix No.* 3.

§ It is common to intimate in these letters the wishes of the committee respecting the particular part in the ordination services which each pastor is desired to take: and the ordaining council usually regard the wishes thus expressed, in the assignment of the several parts.

delegates assemble and organize, and after prayer, proceed to business.

The record of the doings of the church and society is first laid before the council; then, the call of the church, the concurrence of the society, the provision made for the support of a pastor, and the acceptance of the same by the candidate, are all made known. These being satisfactory, the council vote — to proceed to the examination of the candidate for ordination.

A certificate of his church membership is first presented, or evidence that he has become a member of the church over which it is proposed to ordain him; * then his license to preach the gospel. These papers being satisfactory, the council next examine the candidate respecting his religious experience, his motives for entering the ministry, his theological views, and his literary acquisitions. This examination is usually conducted by the moderator of the council, each member being allowed the privilege of proposing any additional questions.†

The council being satisfied upon these several points, vote — to proceed to assign the parts in the ordination services. These are, generally, Invocation and Reading of the Scriptures — Introductory Prayer, Sermon — Ordaining Prayer, accompanied with the

---

* This, as it seems to me, is most agreeable to Congregational principles and early usage. Every pastor should be a member of his own church. The reader will find this matter discussed in the *Appendix, No.* 13.

† The lay delegates have the same privilege as the pastors; and should never hesitate to use it. This examination is open to the members of the church and society.

Imposition of Hands — Charge to the Pastor — The Fellowship of the Churches — Address to the People * — Concluding Prayer, and Benediction.†

INSTALLATION.

In case the pastor elect has been previously ordained, the proceedings of the council vary from those first described in two particulars: First, in requiring a certified copy of the proceedings of the

---

* This is rather a modern innovation; whether an *improvement*, I pretend not to decide. But one thing is certain — that the Address to the people is generally little better than a twice told tale; the appropriate topics of it being generally regarded as common property by the other speakers. And the people themselves are weary enough by the time the Address begins, to wish to be left to their own reflections. If, however, every man would keep within the bounds of his own appointment, both as to matter and time, an address, or charge to the people, might be an appropriate and profitable part of every ordination service. From Mather's Ratio Discip. it would seem that an address to the people was anciently included in the Right Hand of Fellowship. — Art. II. p. 33–40.

† The churches of our denomination in Great Britain invite neighboring ministers to assist in ordaining their pastors, but do not call ecclesiastical councils for this purpose. "The Right Hand of Fellowship" does not enter into their ordination or installation services. In England, laying on of hands does not *always* form a part of the ordination services. — MS. letters from Rev. Mr. Robinson and Rev. Mr. Buckham; the former a Scotch Congregationalist, the latter an English.

Thomas Hooker says: "The church of Scotland is so far from conceiving laying on of hands necessary in ordination, that they do not only not use it, but judge it unlawful to be used, unless some special considerations be attended." — This was said in 1648. — *Survey*, P. II. p. 60.

council which ordained him; or, if he has been a pastor, of the council which dismissed him from his previous charge; and their recommendation of him, as a worthy minister of the Lord Jesus: Secondly, in not imposing hands upon him at the time of the installing prayer. In all other respects, the proceedings of the council are the same in ordination and installation.*

Choice and Consecration of Deacons.

Deacons are chosen by a vote of the church. They should be men of wisdom and integrity, of good, practical common sense, well rooted and grounded in the faith, and eminent for piety; and, whenever it is possible, men of mature years, and considerable religious experience. It is judged proper that the choice should not be made until opportunities have been enjoyed by the brethren to consult together freely, and perhaps repeatedly, and to become united in opinion respecting the most suitable persons for the office.

When the choice has been made, it is proper to give the deacons elect some time to consider the question of acceptance. Their acceptance being signified it is consistent with the ancient usage of our denomination to set them apart to their work by

---

* The first planters of N. E. imposed hands, on the settlement of a pastor, even though he had been previously ordained. — See *Magnalia*, Vol. II. p. 209, Hartford ed. Some account of the sentiments of our fathers respecting ordination may be found in *Appendix*, No. 13.

prayer and imposition of the hands of the pastor. Our churches have not, however, been very uniform or particular in the practice of ordaining deacons, for more than a hundred years past. Cotton Mather tells us, that even in his day (1726) 'in many of these churches this rite of confirmation is fallen into a desuetude.' So at the present time, some of our churches ordain their deacons by the imposition of hands; others do not, perhaps from the apprehension that false impressions may be received respecting the design of the rite, and the nature of the office. But, if it be distinctly explained, that this ceremony is simply the act of designating, and setting apart in a solemn manner, these men to the appropriate work of the deaconship, I can see no sufficient reason for disregarding ancient, and what appears to have been, apostolic usage.*

---

* *Mather's Ratio*, p. 130–133; *Upham's Ratio*, § 40–43. Upon Congregational principles, the right and power to ordain church officers — whether deacons or elders — is undoubtedly in the churches. And when ordination is performed by ministers, they act not by any inherent right or power in themselves, as ministers, but as the representatives of their respective churches, and as the agents of the particular church over which the pastor is placed. Thus, Thomas Hooker says: "Though the *act* of ordination belong to the presbytery [i. e. the elders of a church] yet the *jus et potestas ordinandi* [the right and power of ordination] is conferred firstly, upon *the church*, by Christ, and resides in her. It is in them [the elders] *instrumentaliter;* in her, *originaliter;*" — in them as instruments, in her as the original source. — *Survey*, P. II. Ch. 2, p. 76. See, also, p. 73–77. — See *Ante*, p. 158, seq. — In regard to the ordination of Deacons, see *Appendix*, No. 16.

There is, however, a propriety in calling upon neighboring churches to assist in the ordination of *ministers*, which does not exist in the case of *deacons*. A minister may be called to officiate

III. CHURCH MEETINGS FOR BUSINESS.

Every well regulated Congregational church has occasional meetings for the transaction of business.

---

to other churches, in the administration of the gospel and the ordinances of the church. But the work of a deacon is confined to the particular church which chooses and ordains him, and the fellowship of other churches is not, therefore, needed.

In several instances, the fathers of the New England churches ordained their *pastors* even, without the aid of other ministers. *Trumbull*, in his History of Connecticut, mentions several cases, Vol. I. p. 298, 299. See also *Winthrop*, Vol. II. p. 18. Hutchinson mentions one instance in which this was done when two clergymen were present.—*Hist. Mass.* Vol. I. p. 425. This is according to the *Platform;* ch. 9, sect. 4. The synod of 1680 questioned the propriety of lay-ordination.— See *Magnalia*, Vol. II. p. 218, 219. Few Congregationalists would now approve of lay-ordination; and I am not sure but that some would consider it invalid. Yet, upon Congregational principles, the church is the depositary of all ecclesiastical authority, under Jesus Christ: and if so, then must it have the right and authority to ordain its own pastor, with its own hands. I do by no means, however, advocate lay-ordination. I think that it is manifestly proper, for reasons already assigned, that the pastors of neighboring churches should be employed as agents in this work: but still, I must regard it as the abstract right of every duly organized church, to ordain its pastor without the aid of neighboring ministers. No body of believers can be considered an entire, complete church, which has not the power and right to do all that is essential to its personal well-being and usefulness. But, if a church must be absolutely dependent on ordained clergymen to institute its pastor, it surely is not that complete body which our principles suppose.

The opinions advanced in this note, are maintained with great ability and earnestness by Samuel Mather, in his *Apology for the*

In our cities these are more frequent than in the country. Many city churches meet weekly, and business may be transacted at every meeting, if necessary; though the special object of most of these meetings is religious improvement. Some churches devote one meeting a month to business; while the other meetings are for devotional purposes.

In a Congregational church the pastor is, *ex officio* — as overseer, ruler, and guide of the church — moderator of the meeting; he puts all motions, and gives advice and instruction respecting the proper method of adjusting all matters under consideration.*

This is believed to be in accordance with the doctrine and practice of our churches generally.

In many of our churches the pastor keeps the records of the church, and makes all the entries of

---

Liberties of the Churches in N. E. He devotes an entire chapter to "The Right of these churches to ordain their Ministers." — *Chap.* 2. This also was the opinion of those learned and famous English Independents, Goodwin, Nye, Burroughs, Simson, Bridge, Greenhill, and Carter. — See account of Westminster Assembly Debates, in *Neal's Puritans*, Vol. III. p. 283. — The distinguished English Baptist, Andrew Fuller, was of the same opinion. — See Vol. II. p. 661, Complete Works. "As for ordination," says John Milton, "what is it but the laying on of hands; an outward sign or symbol of admission? . . . It is but an orderly form of receiving a man already fitted, and committing to him a particular charge." . . — *Hanbury*, Vol. I. p. 191, 2, note. Richard Mather maintains essentially the same view of ordination, and of the right of churches to ordain their own pastors, in his Answer to Herle's 4th Arg. and Ans. to Rutherford, Chaps. 24th and 25th. So does John Cotton, in his *Way of the Cong. Chhs.* p. 26.

* See 1 Thess. 5: 12. Heb. 13: 7, 17. And *Doddridge's* remarks on the same.

votes, etc. Others have a church clerk for this purpose, who makes the needful records under the pastor's direction.

If at any time the church should be destitute of a pastor, or, if the pastor should be unavoidably absent from a church meeting, the senior deacon may act as moderator of the church, or one may be chosen for the occasion.

At all church meetings, every brother has entire liberty to express his views and feelings upon every subject which is brought before the church; and all questions are decided by the votes of the brethren.* It is not common, however, to settle questions of great importance, by a bare majority vote. A greater degree of unanimity is generally sought and usually obtained.† Very few ministers would feel justified in accepting the call of a mere majority of a church, unless the circumstances of the case were very peculiar.

It is generally thought desirable that the female members of a church should be present at the transaction of all ordinary business, for their satisfaction and instruction; but, it is utterly inconsistent with established usage for females to take any part in

---

* In the Appendix, No. 15, the reader will find 'A Manual for Church Meetings;' or, brief rules for transacting business in church meetings.

† The churches of our denomination in Ireland seem to consider *entire* unanimity indispensable. "If there be but *one* member of a different mind from the rest, it is the same as if there were the *one half*."—"Rev. A. Carson's Reasons for Separating from the Synod of Ulster," p. 12.

business transactions. Their views and wishes are to be expressed privately to their pastor or their brethren. We suffer not a woman to speak in the church, agreeable to apostolic injunction. — 1 Cor. 14: 34, 35. 1 Tim. 2: 11, 12.*

IV. ADMISSION OF MEMBERS.

Congregational principles require that every candidate for church membership should give to the church satisfactory evidence of his personal piety and his soundness in the faith.† In some instances the

---

* I would not be understood to say that no Congregational church pursues a different course. I have had occasion to know of one, at least, which has followed a different practice to its cost. All deviations from the course described in the text are spots upon the fair and scriptural practice of our churches. The apostolic prohibitions do not, as we suppose, exclude women from answering questions, or giving testimony when desired; or from relating their religious experience when under examination for church membership; or from making confession of particular sins by which their covenant engagements have been broken, and dishonor brought on the cause of Christ. — See *Cotton's Keys*, p. 86.

† *Camb. Platf.* ch. 12; *Magnalia*, Vol. II. bk. 5, p. 209–212. It seems more consistent with our principles, and with early and good usage, that this account should be given, orally or in writing, before the whole church. I am aware that this is considered a fiery ordeal for a timid person; but it should not be so regarded. Every church is a Christian family, having similar views and feelings, a common object, and like hopes and fears. The candidate for admission professes to be one with the church in all these particulars. In communicating with the church, he speaks to the family of which he is to become a member, to persons who can sympathize with him, and who are prepared to receive him with open arms, as soon as they are assured of his worthiness.

After more than thirteen years' experience of the course here

relation of his religious experience is given verbally; in others, in writing. In both cases, the candidate

---

recommended, in the admission of some two hundred members, I am constrained to believe that the difficulties in the way of this practice are rather imaginary than real. The examination of candidates is always interesting and often highly useful to the church; it gives the members a knowledge of God's dealings with his children, and furnishes encouragement to labor and pray for the conversion of sinners. Furthermore, the self-denying decision which it requires to submit to a public examination — by public, I mean before the whole church — is often of essential advantage to the candidate himself. It no doubt prevents, too, some proud and hypocritical persons from entering the church. Few such persons would care to submit to the scrutiny of a whole church, though they might venture upon a more private examination.

Besides, it seems to me to throw too much responsibility upon the pastor and a few brethren of the church, to make them judges of the fitness of every candidate for church membership. The whole church are called upon to vote in the admission of a member; is it not proper, then, that they should have an opportunity to form their judgment by personal examination of the candidate? Should they trust wholly to others? The admission of a member is now the act of the *whole church;* and not of a *committee* of the church. But if our churches are induced to yield their right to *examine* candidates for their fellowship, to *a committee*, is there no reason to fear that they may, erelong, be called upon to yield, to a committee, their right to *admit* members? And would not this be to renounce Congregationalism?

It is proper to add, that the question considered in this note is by no means a settled one; nor have our churches been uniform in their practice for a long period past. Cotton Mather (ut sup.) gives the different views entertained by the churches in his day; and they are not materially altered by the lapse of a century. Samuel Mather, who wrote about twelve years later than his father, C. Mather, warns the New England churches not to give up the business of examining candidates, to the elders, nor to be negligent of their duty; but to insist on an *open profession* from

is expected to answer any questions which the pastor or brethren may propose; and to remove, by explanation, etc., any difficulties which may exist in the mind of any member of the church. After the church have satisfied themselves of the sincerity, religious knowledge, and piety of the candidate, they vote to have him "propounded for admission."

A week or more previous to the approaching communion season, his name is publicly announced, as a candidate for church membership; and any person knowing aught against him, or any good reason why he should not be received to church fellowship, is desired to make known the same to the pastor. Whether this wish be expressed in words or not, such is the meaning and intention of the act of "propounding a person for admission to the church."

If, after being propounded, no objection appears to the admission of the candidate, on the next sacramental occasion — which, in most churches occurs as often as once in two months, in many monthly, though in some country churches less frequently — he publicly assents to the church covenant, articles of faith, government, and practice, and solemnly promises to walk with the church in accordance with these, and in the observance of all the duties of a religious life. He is then received into the church, by a vote or by tacit consent, and declared entitled to all its ordinances and privileges.* Thus strict and

all candidates for church fellowship, and to except against all whom they think to be disqualified for communion with them. — *Apology*, ch. 5th.

* Many of our churches have their Covenant and Articles printed, with copious references to Scripture. A copy is placed

cautious are Congregational churches in the admission of members.

V. DISMISSION OF MEMBERS.

If, for any good reason, a church member wishes to remove his relation to another church, he applies for a letter of dismission and recommendation.* If

---

in the hands of candidates for church membership, that they may know what the church professes to believe, and the reasons for their faith, and what will be required of those who unite with the church.

The Congregational churches in Scotland, with few exceptions, practise " weekly communion," at the Lord's supper. In the admission of members, the work of examination is intrusted to the pastor and " two visitors," who are appointed by the church. After satisfying themselves of the piety, and other qualifications of the candidate for church fellowship, they report accordingly to the church; and the candidate " is admitted, after exhortation to duties, etc., and prayer."

I quote from a manuscript letter of Rev. Mr. Robertson, for thirty years pastor of a Congregational church in Scotland. I am greatly indebted to this gentleman, and to Rev. Mr. Buckham, already referred to, for valuable information, respecting Congregationalism in Great Britain.

* It is believed to be contrary to regular Congregational usage, to dismiss a member, and recommend him " to any church with which he may please to unite." The church should be *specified*, and be known to be in fellowship with the dismissing church. If a member is about to leave the neighborhood of the church to which he belongs, and does not know with what church he shall wish to connect himself, he may take from the pastor or the clerk of the church, a certificate of his regular standing, and a letter of general introduction (see Appendix, No. 4); which will secure for him the privilege of occasional communion with any church which acknowledges *that* from which he goes, as a church of Christ.

This, however, will not supersede the necessity of a letter of

the two churches are in fellowship — that is, if they recognize each other as churches of Christ — the church vote to dismiss their brother, and recommend him to the church specified. — See Acts 18: 27. Rom. 16: 1. 2 Cor. 3: 1.

Until this letter is presented, and the individual is received by the church to which the letter is addressed, he remains a member of the church from which the letter is taken, and is subject to the watch and discipline of the same.* Any disregard of this authorized practice of our churches is considered an irregularity, alike injurious to the churches and to the individuals concerned.

It may be proper to remark in this connection, that we suppose Christ has given his churches no authority to dismiss any of their members to the world. Church members have been known to apply to their pastor for "a dismission from the church;" assigning as a reason, perhaps, their personal unfitness for church fellowship; or, their dissatisfaction with the sentiments or doings of the church. Now, every person about to unite with a Congregational church ought distinctly to understand, that there are only two ways by which a member may become permanently separated from one of our churches; one is, by dismission and recommendation to a sister church; the other is, by exclusion from church fellowship.†

---

dismission and recommendation to some particular church. — This is the doctrine of the Cambridge Platform, ch. 13. — *Mather's Ratio*, Art. 8, § 2.

* See *Appendix*, No. 5.

† Chauncey in his *Divine Institution of Congregational Churches*, says: "In such a dismission these things are to be observed: —

There are no private ways to get in or out of our churches.*

VI. DISMISSION OF A PASTOR.

If, for any sufficient reason, it is deemed expedient to dissolve the connection between a pastor and his church, the regular course is as follows: The pastor lays before the church a statement of his wishes and his reasons for the same, and requests the church to unite with him in calling a council to advise in the premises. If the church are unwilling to dissolve the pastoral connection, they vote to that effect; and appoint a committee to confer with their pastor, and to dissuade him if possible from his pur-

---

(1) That the said brother dismissed be not under the censure or dealing of the church dismissing him. (2) That the letter of dismission may be either with or without commendation, as the case may require or the carriage of said member hath been, though he hath not been under the dealing of the church for any censurable action — many a *good man* proving an *ill* church member (as such an one may be an ill husband) not carrying himself orderly and duly in his relation. (3) That a dismission be granted either upon good reason alleged by him, or upon his peremptory insisting upon it, for the peace of the church. (4) A church member is not to be dismissed at large, to join what church he pleases; for this is to dismiss him to himself and not to a church, the church to which he is dismissed being not specified. . . . A church may not dismiss a member to them that it hath no church communion with, and therefore not to the wide world," etc. etc. — See *Chap.* XIII. § 4.

By "exclusion from church fellowship," is meant both excommunication and withdrawing of fellowship; between which acts I make a distinction, as may be seen a few pages over.

* See *Platf. ch.* 13, § 7.

pose. If, however, the church consider it expedient to comply with the pastor's request, they so vote, and appoint a committee to assist in the selection and call of a mutual council.*

When the council assemble, all the proceedings of the parties are laid before them. They examine the reasons assigned by the pastor for wishing a dismission from his church, and the grounds of concurrence on the part of the church. If, in view of all the circumstances, it is judged proper that the pastor's request should be granted, the council so vote, and advise the church to dismiss him. If the council should deem the reasons in favor of a dismission insufficient, they advise the church and pastor accordingly.

A church may vote upon a pastor's request for dismission — that they will grant it, *provided a mutual council shall advise thereto;* and thus supersede the necessity of any further action of theirs after the decision of the council.†

---

* For the form of a Letter Missive, see *App.* No. 6.

† It is proper to apprise the reader that many churches and ministers advocate and pursue a course somewhat different from that pointed out in the text. They say, that in cases where there are no difficulties to be adjusted, and where a church and its pastor agree on the expediency of dissolving the pastoral connection, and on the terms upon which it shall be done, there is really no occasion for an advisory council; that the church and the pastor (the contracting parties) are entirely competent to annul the contract and to judge of the sufficiency of the reasons for so doing, and that the only work for a council in such cases is, to examine the proceedings of the parties sufficiently to satisfy the council that the retiring pastor is entitled to a letter of commen-

If a church should think the removal of their pastor desirable, a regular procedure would be, for the deacons, or some of the older members of the church, to converse freely and frankly with him, state their convictions, and suggest to him the expediency of asking a dismission from the church. If the pastor should decline so to do; they might then desire him to call a meeting of the church, for the purpose of conferring together, and acting, should it be judged expedient, in reference to the matter. The pastor would, of course, absent himself from such a meeting, unless he had some special communication to make to the church; or, he would retire after having opened it in the usual form and stated the object of the meeting. The church being left by themselves, would proceed to discuss the subject before them: if agreed in opinion, they would appoint a committee to lay before the pastor their reasons for wishing a dissolution of the pastoral connection; and request him to unite with them in calling a council to consider the matter and advise in the premises. Should he decline their offer of a *mutual* council, the church would then be entitled to the advice of an *ex parte*

---

dation to the churches, as a faithful minister of the gospel, and deserving their confidence.

Such I understand to be the views and practice of some of our churches and ministers.

It may be proper further to remark, that as councils are *merely* advisory, there is an obvious impropriety in their pronouncing the final decision, that "he (the pastor) be, and hereby is, dismissed." The council should merely *advise* to the dismission, and leave the final act with the church, where the power belongs, unless, as in the case supposed in the text, the church has already voted the dismission on condition that the council advise thereto.

council. The way would thus be prepared for an orderly adjustment of the business, upon Christian and Congregational principles.*

VII. CHURCH DISCIPLINE.

It is a settled conviction of Congregationalists, that purity of faith and practice cannot be secured to the churches except by the maintenance of strict and faithful christian discipline. The members of our churches are therefore pledged to watch over, to admonish, to reprove, and to discipline each other, as necessity may require. A church that neglects this care of its members is liable to be dealt with by its sister churches as a "disorderly walker." We regard the eighteenth chapter of Matthew 15–18 verses, as a general directory respecting all church discipline: "If thy brother shall trespass against thee, go and

---

* I regret to say, that our churches are not always so observant of the course pointed out in the text as they should be. Neither Congregationalism nor any other *ism* but *barbarism*, countenances the practice of starving, or driving a minister from his pastoral charge.

The practice of the English and Scotch Congregationalists — I call them by this name, though, in respect to all such matters as we are now considering they are *Independents* — differs somewhat from that described in the text. Councils are unknown to them, either in the settlement or dismission of their pastors. A pastor wishing to leave his field of labor, resigns his office; the church accepts his resignation, and thus the business begins and ends. It is, however, a thing of very rare occurrence for a Congregational pastor in those countries to leave his church unless called to another sphere of usefulness. "For a minister to be 'unsettled' for any considerable time, would be injurious to his ministerial reputation." — *MS. Letters.*

tell him his fault between him and thee alone; if he shall hear thee, thou hast gained thy brother. But if he will not hear thee, then take with thee one or two more, that in the mouth of two or three witnesses every word may be established. And, if he shall neglect to hear them, tell it unto the church; but if he neglect to hear the church, let him be unto thee as an heathen man and a publican. Verily I say unto you, whatsoever ye shall bind on earth, shall be bound in heaven; and whatsoever ye shall loose on earth, shall be loosed in heaven."

Agreeably to these Divine directions, the regular course of procedure, when a church member is believed to be chargeable with unchristian conduct or heretical sentiments, is substantially this: A brother who is acquainted with the circumstances of the case, immediately — and without conference with any one — seeks a private interview with the trespasser; he tells him plainly, but with gentleness and kindness (Gal. 6: 1), what he has seen or known offensive and unchristian in his conduct. If the trespasser acknowledges his fault and makes christian satisfaction, here the matter may end, nothing more need be said or done. What shall constitute christian satisfaction, must depend upon circumstances. If the offence be strictly private — known only to the complaining brother — a private acknowledgment of it and a promise of reformation would be deemed satisfactory. If known only to a few individuals, and not liable to greater notoriety, a confession to these persons might be deemed sufficient. But if the cause of complaint should be extensively known; the confession must be public. This may be regarded as a general rule — Confession and satisfaction should be as public as the offence. So said John Robinson; so say we.

But, if the offender refuses to give such satisfaction, the complainant then selects one or two judicious and intelligent brethren, to assist him in his efforts to convince and reclaim the erring brother. If their united efforts prove unavailing, a regular complaint is laid before the church — generally, if not always, in writing — specifying the particular charges against the offending brother, and the persons by whom, or the means by which it can be proved; and stating, also, the attempts which have been made to adjust the difficulty privately. It is considered entirely out of order for a church to receive a complaint against one of its members until assured that "the private steps" — as these preceding measures are called — have been taken.* The church being satisfied that

* Many churches make an exception to this rule, in cases of open and notorious scandal, etc., and receive a complaint before private means have been tried to reclaim the offender. *The Cambridge Platform* admits of this summary mode of proceeding in offences "of a more heinous and criminal nature, namely, such as are condemned by the light of nature." — Ch. 14, § 3; see, also, *Mather's Apology*, p. 97; *Calvin's Inst.* B. IV. Ch. 12, § 3, 6; and *Cotton's Keys*, p. 85. The course pointed out in the text seems to me, however, preferable, as a general rule, in cases of *public* as well as of *private* scandal; for one prominent reason, if for no more, namely: that it is better adapted to secure one great end of all church discipline — *the reformation of the offender*. Almost any one will be more likely to be convinced of error and brought to repentance by the kind and faithful efforts of a friend in private, than by a public arraignment, in the first instance, before the whole church.

this has been done, vote to examine the charges. Evidence of the truth of these is then called for. Witnesses may be introduced who are not professors of religion, if necessary. If by the testimony adduced, the church are convinced of the guilt of the accused, they, by their pastor or a committee — not excluding others — labor to convince the offender of his sin, and to induce him to make christian satisfaction for his offence. These efforts being successful, he is restored to good standing. But if unsuccessful, the church, after suitable delay, proceed to excommunicate, and cut him off from all relation to, or connection with the church — to cast him out, as "a heathen man and a publican." * The decision

---

* Suspension and admonition, which are advocated by some persons, may be proper, as steps preparatory to excommunication, in order to furnish the offender longer space for reflection and repentance; but never, I conceive, as punishments, which being endured, offset — so to speak — the offence, and entitle the sufferer to a restoration to church privileges, and to favor with his brethren. Christ's direction: "If he neglect to hear *the church*, let him be unto thee as an heathen man and a publican" — requires the excommunication of every obstinate offender.

Mather devotes sixteen pages to church discipline, giving the forms used in admonition, excommunication, etc. He teaches the doctrine above detailed. — *Ratio, Art.* 8, § 2, 3. Such, too, is the doctrine of the *Platform.* — Ch. 14. Cotton's description of this process of church discipline in his day (1645) agrees substantially with the above. — *Way of the Chhs.* p. 89–94.

Chauncey says: "Some speak much of, and practise a censure of suspension, when an offending brother is forbid by the church to come to its communion in the Lord's Supper, till it appears whether he be guilty or no of the sin charged on him. Our Lord Jesus Christ hath given no such rule to churches to walk by," etc. *Divine Inst.*, Ch. XIII. § 18.

of the church should be announced to the offender by the pastor; either by an address to him — recapitulating the circumstances of the case, and then solemnly pronouncing his excision from the visible body of Christ, and exhorting him to repentance, and assuring him of the readiness of Christ to forgive him, and of the church to receive him — or by a letter of the same general import, written in the name of the church.

If at any future time the excommunicated person should give evidence of repentance, he may be restored to the fellowship of the church by making a public confession and giving the church satisfactory evidence of a thorough reformation.

If the question be asked: What do Congregational churches regard as offences which render one liable to excommunication as "a heathen man and publican?" It may be answered, in general terms, Whatever in doctrine, practice, or general spirit is plainly inconsistent with the character of a Christian. A fundamental principle in the organization of our churches is, that "none but good people" should be members of them. Reputed piety and visible conformity to the laws of Christ's house are indispensable qualifications for church membership. Whatever, therefore, destroys the evidence of one's piety, or is inconsistent with such conformity, unfits, of course, that person for church fellowship.

Besides such offences as affect a church member's moral or christian character, and which are to be treated as above; there are certain other irregularities which demand the notice, and if not corrected, the disciplinary labors of the church. Among these may be classed, all breaches of covenant in relation to matters not fundamental. If a member, under the plea of having changed his views of duty, should leave the church with which he had covenanted to walk, and absenting himself from the assemblies of his christian brethren, should associate with persons, who, though not fundamentally erroneous, yet did not recognize the body which he had left as a christian church; or which so varied from what that church deemed orderly and correct in sentiment and practice that it could not fully recognize them as a church of Christ — it would be the duty of the church to call their brother to account; and, if he persisted in his course without exhibiting an unchristian spirit, it would be necessary for the church to "*withdraw*" from him, as one who "*walketh disorderly*" (ἀτάκτως, out of his rank, or place — in an irregular manner), agreeably to 2 Thess. 3: 6, 14, 15. — "Now we command you brethren, in the name of our Lord Jesus Christ, that ye *withdraw yourselves from every brother that walketh disorderly*, and not after the tradition which ye received of us. . . . . If any man obey not our word by this epistle, *note that man, and have no company with him*, that he may be ashamed. Yet, count him not as an enemy, but admonish him as a brother." *

In the same way should those church members be treated, who, though not heretical or profane, yet leave the communion and fellowship of the churches

---

* For additional remarks on this topic — the difference between excommunication and the act of withdrawing fellowship — see *Appendix*, No. 14.

with which they have covenanted to walk, and wander about to different places of public worship, or attach themselves to one place of worship, but persist in neglecting to ask a letter of dismission from the church with which they are in covenant. The church, after reasonable efforts to reclaim them, should withdraw from them; for, though their lives may not be scandalous, their conduct is irregular, disorderly, and very evil and disorganizing in its tendency, and should not be countenanced.

VIII. DISCIPLINE OF PASTORS

Sound Congregational principles subject every pastor to the watch and discipline of his church. This seems to be taught by Paul's direction to the Colossian church: "Say to Archippus, Take heed to the ministry which thou hast received in the Lord, that thou fulfil it." — Col. 4: 17. If a pastor becomes heretical in doctrine or corrupt in practice, we believe that he should be dealt with as any other member of the church would be; "only with such special terms of respect, and repetition of address, as the relation of a father may call for." *

Our churches, however, uniformly call for the advice of a council, before they proceed to excommunicate a pastor. All the preparatory steps should be taken as in the case of a private member; the charges

* *Cotton Mather's Ratio Discip.* Art. IX. § 2, p. 162. See, also, *Samuel Mather's Apology*, p. 80–85; *John Cotton's Keys of the Kingdom*, p. 31, 32, 41–43; and *Chauncey's Divine Inst. of Cong. Chhs.* Ch. XII. § 8. The reader will find this matter discussed, at some length, in the *Appendix*, No. 13.

should be proved before the church, and the church should vote — That they are convinced of the criminality of their pastor, but, in view of the peculiar importance and solemnity of the business, will take the advice of the neighboring churches before proceeding further. The pastor is then invited to unite with the church in calling a mutual council. If he refuses, the church call an ex parte council. This council — mutual or ex parte, as the case may be — examines all the doings of the church, and hears all the evidence in the case; if satisfied with the measures pursued, and convinced of the guilt of the pastor, they vote accordingly. They then proceed to depose the unworthy man from the ministry, and advise the church to excommunicate him. The church follow the advice of council, and thus terminates the melancholy business.

It is no doubt true, as the Platform maintains (Chap. 10, § 6), that the "church have *power* according to order" — that is, according to the general principles on which a Congregational church is organized — to remove a pastor from office, without the advice and direction of a council; though it distinctly speaks of the propriety of "the council of other churches, where it may be had, directing thereto." But the reason why "the council of other churches" should direct thereto, is not because a church has not sufficient power to perform this act of necessary discipline, as well as every other; but because, having invited "the council of other churches" to advise and assist in putting their pastor *into* office, and thus declared their wish to be recognized as a member of the Congregational family and to maintain fellowship and communion with sister churches — consistency and decorum require that the same sort of advice and assistance should be sought in removing their pastor *from* office. And furthermore, this course is proper, because sister churches have an interest and concern in the removal from office of one who has sustained a sort of official relationship to them all.* Another reason for the course pointed out, is, that as the business of licensing to preach the gospel, and thus introducing into the ministerial office, is committed to the hands of the ministry, it is evidently proper that the same hands should be concerned in taking away a license to preach, and deposing from the ministry. If it should be said, that the same body is not, after all, employed in deposing from the ministry which introduced into the ministry — the latter being an association of clergymen, and the former, a council of churches — the answer is obvious: every *Association* acts in the name of the whole ministry and on behalf of all the churches, in giving licenses to preach the gospel; so that a council, composed of ministers and lay delegates, represents both the ministry and the churches; and is, therefore, manifestly the most suitable body to act under the circumstances supposed. The propriety of the course now urged, will appear from this consideration, among others: If the council did not first act decisively in the business, by deposing the unworthy man from the ministry, it might happen, that a minister would be an excommunicated person and still be an authorized preacher of the

---

* See Note, p. 191–193.

gospel. But on the other hand, if a council should be called previously to any action of the church in relation to charges preferred against their pastor, it might appear on examination, that there were not sufficient grounds for complaint against the pastor. For these reasons, regular practice requires the adoption of the course prescribed.

IX. WHO SHALL COMPLAIN OF OFFENDERS.

If an offence be *private*, or known only to a very few individuals, it has already been remarked, that Congregational usage requires that one of the persons privy to the offence should go privately to his trespassing brother. It is a great irregularity to communicate the affair to any one previously unacquainted with the circumstances, unless it be a case of such difficulty as requires advice. This course we conceive to be required by Christ's directions, Matt. 5: 23, 24; "If thou bring thy gift to the altar, and there rememberest that thy brother hath aught against thee, leave there thy gift before the altar, and go thy way; first be reconciled to thy brother, and then come and offer thy gift." By parity of reasoning—If thou bring thy gift to the altar, and there rememberest that *thou* hast aught *against thy brother*, leave there thy gift before the altar and go thy way; first be reconciled to thy brother, etc.

But, suppose the offence be one of public notoriety; who then shall take the first step? Generally, one of the deacons of the church, or some one of the more aged and experienced brethren. There may be prudential reasons for preferring one brother to another in a given case, as the person to take the first step with an offender. These reasons should be allowed their full weight. But, if the *most* suitable person will not commence this important work, this will not excuse another from undertaking it — yea, the *least* suitable person in the church. All are equally bound by their own covenant engagements to discharge this duty; and if one, or ten, or one hundred neglect it, this will not cancel the obligations of the others. The business must be attended to, or the whole church are made partakers of the sin of the offender.

It is deemed important, generally, that some time should elapse between the several steps of discipline, in order that the offender may have opportunity for reflection, before the ultimate appeal is made to the church. It may be proper in some cases to repeat the private steps; perhaps even several times, before the complaint is lodged with the church. Every case that can be adjusted without telling it to the church, should be; and many cases may be, if judicious and persevering and christian efforts are made for this purpose.

X. DISCIPLINE OF SISTER CHURCHES.

It has already been remarked, that though Congregational churches are independent of each other in respect to all their internal arrangements and management, yet, every church regards itself as a part of a great family, each member of which has a common interest in the welfare of every other branch, and holds itself bound to give account of its doings to the family whenever desired. A prominent design in changing the name of our denomination, from *Independents* to *Congregationalists*,* was to avoid the imputation, that our churches were united by no common bond, and that they refused to give to each other any account of their faith or practice. Hence the Platform says: "The term *independent* we approve not;" † and makes provision for the discipline of *churches* as well as individual members.‡

An orderly procedure in case a church has reason to think a sister church unsound in doctrine, lax in discipline, or corrupt in practice, would be — to choose a committee to visit and converse with the officers of the suspected church. If they could satisfy the visiting committee that their fears were groundless, the state of the case would be reported to the inquiring church, and there the matter would rest. But if the committee could not obtain satisfaction, on reporting this to the brethren, the church would vote to call on one or more neighboring churches to unite in the labor. These united committees failing to obtain satisfaction, the several churches to which they belonged would propose a council of churches (not including themselves), to whom the whole business should be submitted. This mutual council having heard the statements of the churches complaining, and that complained of, would give their opinion, whether there was sufficient ground of complaint

---

* John Cotton, probably gave us this name. He, at least, is the first writer, so far as my reading goes, who used the term.

† *Chap.* 2, § 5.

‡ See *Platf.* ch. 15, also *Mather's Ratio*, Art. IX.

against the accused church, to warrant sister churches in withdrawing fellowship from it. If they believed that there was, they would vote to that effect; and recommend to all Congregational churches to withdraw fellowship from the erring member of the family, lest they should become partakers in other men's sins. It would then be in order for individual churches to act upon the advice of the council. This being accepted and adopted, the offending church would no longer be regarded as a sister of the great family of Congregational churches; its pastor would not be recognized as a minister of the Lord Jesus; its members would not be received to permanent, or even occasional communion; and any church recognizing them as a church of Christ, would be considered as walking disorderly — as countenancing the errors and sins of the offending member — and would expose itself to be dealt with accordingly.

But, in case the pastor or any members of the offending church should satisfy the council, or the committees of the churches, that they did not approve of, or countenance the conduct of the majority of the church with which they were connected, such pastor or dissenting members would not be included in the act of exclusion from fellowship to which the majority of the church were subjected; though they would be expected to use their utmost endeavors to reclaim their erring brethren, and if, after due trial, they failed in their efforts, to renounce all connection with them, and to unite with some other Congregational church. The remarks in the preface to the Platform upon this topic — the removal of individuals from corrupt churches — deserve careful consideration.

In all this, however, Congregational churches assume no authority nor power to disband and dissolve churches, or to interfere with the right and privilege of churches to order their affairs as may seem to them most accordant with the truth. They simply assert their own right to say with whom they will hold communion, and with whom they can walk as sister churches. The body from which they have thus withdrawn fellowship still remains, for aught that the withdrawing churches can say or do — a *church*, if any are disposed so to regard it. The churches withdrawing, wash their hands of the errors and corruption complained of. To their own master the erring are left to stand or fall.*

XI. MISCELLANEOUS MATTERS.

Under this general head, I shall mention several matters which are of a mixed character, scarcely belonging to the Ecclesiastical practice of Congregationalists, and yet illustrative of the peculiarities of the denomination.

---

* S. Mather gives a particular account of these matters, and defends this method of proceeding. — *Apology*, p. 133, 134. So does Mr. Upham, in his XX Chap. The reader will find the usages of our churches more fully detailed by Prof. Upham, in his Ratio Discip. than the plan of this work allows. Mr. Mitchell, in his Guide to the N. E. Chhs. has an excellent chapter on church discipline. Though constrained to differ from this brother on some points of church polity, yet I esteem his " Guide " a work of much practical excellence.

The "way of Congregational churches," in relation to the more important matters of Ecclesiastical usage, has now been considered. Those points only have been touched upon, in which there is a very general, if not uniform agreement among consistent and intelligent Congregationalists. In respect to various other things of minor importance, there is some diversity of practice in the denomination: as, for example, respecting

The Method of Raising the Salary of Ministers.

Some societies do this by levying a tax on property; others, by taxing pews; some, by weekly contributions from the congregation; others, by voluntary subscriptions, running indefinitely, or for a term of years; others still, by voluntary contributions of provisions, and clothing, and fuel, to a fixed amount. Some churches are the owners, in common, of their meeting-house,* and raise a part, at least, of their pastor's salary, by the yearly sale or lease of the pews. Some few, to their injury, have funds sufficient to support their pastors. A multitude are so poor that they feel unable to do more than raise a part of their pastor's salary, depending on yearly grants from our Home Missionary Societies to make up the deficiency.†

But in all cases a Congregational pastor has a stip-

---

* Mather, in his *Ratio Disciplinæ*, takes pains to tell his readers that, "A Meeting-house is the term most commonly used by the *New English* Christians."

† A diversity of practice and opinion respecting the best method

ulated salary; and this is generally fixed at the lowest sum that will afford him a respectable maintenance. The practice of our churches is believed to be nearly uniform in this last particular. If it be not a fundamental doctrine of the denomination — as it is said

---

of raising a minister's salary seems anciently to have prevailed. Some of the fathers of the New England churches maintained, that the pastor's salary should be raised by voluntary contributions, "*laid by*," if not *contributed* "on the first day of the week;" agreeably to 1 Cor. 16: 2; "Upon the first day of the week let every one of you lay by him in store, as God hath prospered him," etc. The famous John Cotton insisted that this was the only proper way to raise a minister's salary.

Thomas Hooker, in his "Survey of the Summe of Church Discipline," devotes several pages to the discussion of this question. See Part II. p. 27–32. The differing views of good men in his day are thus summarily expressed by Hooker: —

"Some conceive (the Lord's treasury being committed to the deacons, for the supply of all tables of officers and the tables of the poor, both its own and others,) that this treasury should be furnished every Lord's day, by the freewill offerings of the assembly, every one casting into [it] as God hath blessed him. — 1 Cor. 16: 1, 2, 3. They also conceive this rule of Gal. 6: 6, may be attended in this way, every one bringing in all of the good things in *a proportional value*, as may suit the occasion of the church. Others, again, conceive that the maintenance mentioned in the foregoing plan cannot be fully raised by a treasury common to the poor and to ministers, nor can it be gathered upon the Sabbath day."

To this plan of raising the minister's support by contributions on the Sabbath, etc., Hooker mentions several objections. And it is not unlikely that these, and like objections, induced a gradual discontinuance of the method; for, when Cotton Mather published his *Ratio Disciplinæ Fratrum Nov-Anglorum* (1726), the salary of our ministers was generally raised by a tax on all the inhabitants of a parish. — See *Ratio*, p. 20, 21. *Hooker's Survey of Chh. Discip.* was published in London in 1648.

to have been of some of the early dissenters from the Papal Hierarchy — that their pastors shall be poor; certain it is, that the general practice of Congregational churches very effectually accomplishes this end. It is presumed that in New England, the salaries of the Congregational clergy will not average five hundred dollars a year; multitudes of them do not receive the value of three hundred dollars in money. That minister cannot be considered a bad economist, who can support a family, keep "a bishop's table," and meet the numerous calls for charity, with a yearly stipend of five hundred dollars.*

The provision made for the support of the early Congregational ministers of New England, was nominally less than the average of modern salaries; but really much better. In nearly every country parish — and there were few others in those days — every pastor was furnished with "a lot of land," which, with tolerable husbandry, provided a support for his family. His salary, whether much or little, was generally an *addition* to what was indispensable to his comfortable maintenance, and went for the purchase of books, the education of his children, and in

---

* This estimate of the salaries of Congregational ministers was made in 1843. Since that time, there has been a very considerable advance in the prices of all the necessaries of life, and a pretty general advance in the salaries of clergymen; but not, certainly, greater than in the cost of living. New England Congregational ministers have still, it is believed, harder work and poorer pay than any class of professional and educated men in the community.

some instances, became an accumulating fund for his family after his decease.*

---

* I must be allowed to say a few words, in this connection, upon the prevalent notion, that whatever is paid for the support of a minister is a *gratuity*—something for which he has no claim, and which, being a work of supererogation, entitles the parishioner to special commendation, and lays the minister under special obligations. If the eye of such a reasoner should ever look upon this note, I would ask him: Do you consider what you pay the mechanic or day-laborer whom you employ, *a gratuity?* Do you think that the lawyer, the physician, the schoolmaster, who serve you in their respective callings, have no claim on you for services rendered? Or, that the care of your property, health, and mind, are more important than the care of your soul? Is it more necessary that your field should be ploughed, or your house or your furniture repaired, than that you should be taught the way of salvation; and in the hour of sickness and death, have some one to instruct you and your family, and administer to you the consolations of the Gospel, and the rites of religion? If you and your family wish to live and die as do the heathen; so be it. If you never, in any way, claim or enjoy the services of a clergyman, he certainly will not set up any claim upon you. But if you regard the observance of the Sabbath, and the maintenance of the public and social rites of religion as necessary to the comfort and welfare of yourself and family and the community at large, upon what principle can you refuse your aid in supporting a minister? If he, after years of laborious and expensive preparation for his duties, devotes his whole time to the labors which you and others require at his hands, there is no principle of law or equity on which you can refuse your proportion of his support. And what you pay him is no more a *gift* than what you pay your physician, or your schoolmaster, your mechanics, or your day-laborers.

To such persons as are disposed to plead *the freeness* of salvation, and the example of Christ and his Apostles, as reasons for not contributing towards the support of those who preach the Gospel, I would commend a careful examination of the following passages of Scripture:—Numb. 35: 1–8, compared with Lev. 25:

Continuance of the Pastoral Connection.

The *theoretical practice* of our churches (if I may be allowed such an expression) is now, as of old, to ordain a pastor for life; but, the understanding has come to be very general, that the connection between a pastor and his flock will be short-lived. The denomination, however, are beginning to feel the evils of these temporary arrangements; and are more disposed of late, to return to the good old way in which their fathers walked, and to give greater permanency to the connection between a pastor and his church.

Solemnization of Marriage.

The first settlers of New England, in their hatred of Popery and Prelacy, were disposed to commit the work of solemnizing marriages exclusively to the civil magistrate.* At first, the magistrate performed

---

32–34; Deut. 12: 19. 14: 27. 16: 16, 17. 18: 1–8; 2 Chron. 31: 1–10; Neh. 13: 10, 11; Ezek. 44: 15–31.

The above references will show what care was taken of the ministers of religion under the Law. The following will show that the Gospel is no less explicit in recognizing the principle, that they who labor about holy things should be supported by those for whom they labor; or, that "the workman is worthy of his meat." Matt. 10: 9, 10; Luke 8: 1–3; 1 Cor. 9: 1–14; Gal. 6: 6; Phil. 4: 10–18. 1 Tim. 5: 17, 18.

* John Robinson, in his "Apology," says "of the celebration of marriage" — "we cannot assent to the received opinion and practice answerable in the Reformed churches, by which the pastors

all — even the devotional parts of the service. After a while, the pastor of the church, when present at the marriage, was called upon to offer one or both of the prayers. And finally, the business of solemnizing marriages was left chiefly with the pastors. So it remains to this day.

We have no prescribed form for solemnizing marriage. Every pastor consults his own taste and judgment. The ceremony commences generally with prayer; in which God — the Former of our bodies and the Father of our spirits, who in the beginning created man male and female — is adored, and his presence and assistance invoked. The parties are then directed to join hands. This being done, the minister addresses, first the man, to this effect:—

"The person whom you now take by the hand, you take to be your wedded wife; depending on the grace of Heaven, you promise to love her, to honor her, to support her, . . . so long as you live both together in this world. This promise you make as in the presence of God, and before these witnesses."

And then the woman:—

"The person whom you now take by the hand, you take to be your wedded husband; with dependence on the grace of heaven, you promise to love him, to honor him, to obey him, . . . so long as you both live together in this world. This promise you

---

do celebrate marriage publicly and by virtue of their office." He adds, that the pastor's office ought not "to be stretched to any other acts than those of religion, and such as are peculiar to Christians, amongst which marriage, common to the Gentiles as well as to them, hath no place." — See also *Mather's Ratio*, p. 111–117.

make as in the presence of the great God and these witnesses." *

A consent to this covenant being in some way signified, the minister adds: —

"I then declare you to be husband and wife; married according to the laws of this State; and, so far as I know, in accordance with the will of God."

Then follows either a nuptial benediction, or a set prayer, invoking the blessing of God upon the newly married pair — upon their basket and their store, upon their outgoings and their incomings, upon their bodies and their souls, for time and eternity.

Thus were marriages celebrated among Congregationalists in the days of Cotton Mather, and thus are they now.

Funerals.

The same may be said of funerals, as of marriages: we have no set form of service. Our religious rites vary according to circumstances, and in different sections of the country.

In our cities and large towns, where funerals are frequent, a single prayer often constitutes the whole burial-service. In our country parishes, an address to the company collected is common. And in some sections, a sermon is almost uniformly preached on the occasion, accompanied with prayer and singing.

---

* I quote from the formula given by Cotton Mather, in 1726. — *Ratio Discip.*, p. 114–116.

Public Worship.

Having no Liturgy, our method of conducting public worship has never been entirely uniform. John Cotton describes the usual services of the Sabbath in his day, (1645,) thus: "First, we make 'prayers, and intercessions, and thanksgivings for ourselves and for all men.' . . . . After prayer, either the pastor or teacher readeth a chapter in the Bible and expoundeth it, giving the sense, to cause 'the people to understand the reading.' And in sundry churches, the other — whether pastor or teacher — who expoundeth not, he preacheth the Word. . . . . Before sermon, and many times after, we sing a psalm. . . . . In the afternoon, after public prayer, ... and the Word read and expounded by them who preached in the morning, ... and the sacrament of baptism administered, if any of the church do offer their children thereunto; the deacons . . . . do call upon the people, that as God hath prospered them and made their hearts willing, there is now time left for contribution. . . . . After the contribution is ended, the time is taken up, in sundry churches, in the trial and admission of . . . . members into the church: . . . . and so, after a psalm of praise to God, with thanksgiving, and prayer to God for a blessing upon all the ordinances administered that day, and a blessing pronounced upon the people, the assembly is dismissed." *

---

* *Way of the Congregational Churches*, p. 66–70.

In the days of Cotton Mather, (1726,) the services of the morning of the Lord's day were generally commenced — after reading the "bills," or requests for prayers from the sick, afflicted, etc. etc. — with a long prayer; then followed singing; next came the sermon, — "*generally limited unto about an hour;*" this was followed by a short, concluding prayer. In some congregations singing followed the last prayer, "at least in the afternoon." "And in some of the congregations they [had] also in the afternoon . . . . a *collection*, according to apostolic direction, 1 Cor. 16 : 2." "The pastor dismissed the congregation with pronouncing a benediction." *

Modern practice varies a little from the above.

The more common method, perhaps, of conducting public worship among us now, is, to begin the morning exercises with a short prayer, or invocation; followed by the reading of the Scriptures, sometimes accompanied with brief explanatory remarks; then follows singing; then come the requests for prayers, and the long prayer; then singing again; then sermon — not quite so long as of yore — followed by a short prayer and the benediction. In the afternoon, the services are introduced by singing; after this, prayer — singing again — sermon — prayer — singing — and the benediction. Some pastors read the Scriptures both forenoon and afternoon.

Our fathers were not entirely agreed about the propriety of reading the Scriptures, as a part of

---

* *Mather's Ratio*, Art. III.

public worship, unless accompanied with exposition; some calling simple reading — "*dumb reading*." Others, however, approved of it, and practised accordingly; prefacing the reading, as in these days, with a short prayer or invocation. John Cotton approved, and pursued this latter course.

In their general method of conducting public worship, our churches are believed to conform essentially to the primitive practice.* As to the slight variations in different churches, we regard them as nowise objectionable. In the early ages of the Christian Church, even after the introduction of Liturgies — which occurred "after the decay of the gifts of the first Primitive Church," † — each bishop seems to have been left to form such an order of public service as appeared best in his own eyes and that of his church. And even the English Church knew nothing of strict and entire uniformity in the order of her worship, until after the Reformation: and well would it have been for her if her Reformers had been as wise in this particular as the Pope.‡

Associations of Ministers.

It has long been the practice of Congregational ministers residing within convenient distances of each other, to associate together, for personal im-

---

* See extract from *Justin Martyr*, in this work, *ante*, p. 152–154.

† *Stillingfleet's Irenicum*, p. 238.

‡ See *Neal's Hist. Puritans*, Vol. I. p. 96, 97; *Mosheim*, Vol. I. p. 86, 413, n. 1, 2d ed.; *Hist. Congregationalism*, p. 205–208.

provement, for the cultivation of brotherly kindness, and to assist each other by council and advice in discharging parochial and ministerial duties. These Associations are mentioned by Cotton Mather, as things "proposed," though "not yet" [in 1726] in all regards universally complied withal.* "The Heads of Agreement" between the Congregational and Presbyterian churches in England, (1692,) recognize the importance of such associations. — Ch. IV. Art. 1.

It is now believed to be nearly or quite *universal* for our ministers to meet together, as often as once in three months, for the purposes above specified. And these meetings are regarded as most important helps to pastoral usefulness and ministerial improvement. On such occasions exegetical and critical essays on difficult passages of Scripture are exhibited; recitations from the Greek and Hebrew text are attended to; sermons and plans of sermons are submitted for criticism; and questions of practical importance respecting church discipline, pastoral duties, and the best means for promoting the religious improvement of the people under their care are discussed. The exercises which require preparation are assigned at a previous meeting. The advantages of such associations are manifold and obvious.

County Conferences.

These are usually composed of the pastors and delegates of all the Congregational churches of a

---

* *Ratio Disciplinæ*, p. 179–181.

county, if not too large. They meet once or twice a year, in different parts of the county, to hear accounts of the state of religion in each church and society, to consult together for the general good, and to stir up each other's minds "by way of remembrance." They afford seasons of great religious interest and improvement. They are generally attended by large numbers of the brethren of the different churches, and also by delegates from corresponding bodies in other counties, and by the representatives of the different benevolent Societies.

General Meetings of Pastors and Churches.

As a bond of christian union, and as a means of religious encouragement and improvement, our denomination have long practised the holding of stated general meetings of pastors, or of pastors and delegates from the churches. These bodies, though designed for the same general purposes, and essentially alike, are known by different names: as, Conferences, Associations, Conventions, Consociations. They usually include either all the pastors of a State, or their representatives. They sometimes embrace, with the pastors, lay representatives of the churches; a plan most perfectly in accordance with the spirit of Congregationalism. These meetings are attended by representatives from corresponding bodies in other States, by delegates from the General Assemblies of the Presbyterian churches, and by the agents of the great charitable and benevolent Institutions of the country.

At these meetings the statistics of each Congregational church in the State are given; e. g. the additions — removals, by death, dismission, or excommunication — baptisms — charitable contributions, etc.; also any facts of interest connected with the religious history of any of the churches. Thus a complete view is obtained of the condition and prospects of the entire denomination throughout the State.

From the representatives of corresponding bodies, a general view of the churches within their respective bounds is expected. From the agents of the various benevolent societies, and from the annual reports, etc., of the secretaries of the several State Societies which hold their anniversaries in connection with the meeting of the General Conference, Association, or Convention, — we are able to learn the condition, wants, and prospects of our country at large, and of the world.

These general associations, etc., claim no legislative nor judicial authority. The end of their existence is, to promote vital godliness in the denomination, and to preserve unbroken the ties of religious and denominational sympathy and union among all the branches of the Congregational family.

Licensure of Pastors.

For some time after the settlement of New England, our churches were supplied with pastors from the mother country, most of whom had been educated at the Universities and had been preachers in England, and many of them, to the very people among whom they settled in this country. But, anticipating the time when they should be deprived of their venerable pastors, — most of whom, on their removal to this country, being advanced to the meridian of life, or beyond that period, — the churches early made provision for the education of ministers in New England. To this end Harvard College was founded and nurtured by the contributions and prayers and affections of the Pilgrims. From this source came a considerable proportion of the ministers who occupied the New England pulpits during the next century after the landing of the Pilgrims.

For more than half a century after the settlement of this country, (until 1692–1708,) there seems not to have been any provision made, or plan devised for the examination and licensure of candidates for the sacred ministry. "Any well-disposed young men of a liberal education [were] brought into the pulpits by any of the pastors, as soon as they pleased; and, if the people approved of them, they were at liberty, *without any more ado*, to proceed unto an election of them for the work of the ministry, and the pastoral charge in any vacancy." *

The first suggestion on this subject, so far as I have discovered, came from the "United brethren" — Congregational and Presbyterian — in England, 1692. See Heads of Agreement, Ch. II. Art. VII. The next, from the Saybrook Synod, Conn., 1708, Art. XII. †

The state of things at present is materially different from what it was in Mather's day. It is believed

---

* *Mather's Ratio Discip.*, p. 117.

† *Trumbull's Hist. Conn.*, Vol. I. p. 506, 507, 508–513; "*Congregational Order*," p. 236, 279.

to be now the uniform practice of our churches, to commit the work of examining and licensing candidates for the ministry, to the local Associations of pastors. The approbation of an Association is necessary, even after a candidate has passed through a three years' training in one of our theological seminaries. At these examinations, personal piety and church standing are usually the first subjects of inquiry; and, unless a candidate can satisfy the Association upon these heads, there is an end to all hopes of a license to preach the gospel. Another part of the examination relates to systematic theology; recitations from the Hebrew and Greek Scriptures are expected of all who have had an opportunity of studying them, — and very few enter the ministry among us now who have not some acquaintance with these languages; the candidate is also examined respecting his general intelligence — literary, historical, and scientific. The examination proving satisfactory upon these several points, the applicant is furnished with a certificate, signed by the moderator and scribe of the Association, certifying their approbation of him, and recommending him to the churches, as suitably qualified and furnished to preach the gospel.

If in any instance, there should be some doubt respecting the propriety of a full license, and yet not enough to exclude the applicant entirely, Associations sometimes give a permit to preach for a limited time; at the expiration of which the permission is withdrawn, or, on further examination, renewed. Some Associations, ordinarily, give licenses for a term of years only, at the end of which the license may be rescinded or renewed, at the pleasure of the Association.

I have dwelt somewhat minutely on the usages of Congregational churches; but I could not otherwise exhibit the practical operation of the principles and doctrines of the system which I am attempting to develop, nor make my little book a faithful guide to such as would walk in conformity with this system. But little use has been made of arguments to prove the correctness of the practices which have been detailed; for most of these practices are deductions and inferences from principles and doctrines presumed to have been established by previous testimony and arguments, and must, consequently, stand or fall with the foundations on which they rest. And, so far as our practice is merely *prudential*, it is sufficient for our purpose that it is not unscriptural nor unlawful, and that the wisdom and experience of ages have sanctioned it.

And now, what shall we say of Congregationalism in *practice?* Is it not as fair in practice as in theory? Does it allow of any disorder or irregularity in the churches? Is there in it any lack of energy and efficiency? Can any churches show a purer or more blameless practice? or one better adapted to effect the great purposes of church organization? If not, what more can we ask or expect of any system of church government?

PART V.

ADVANTAGES OF CONGREGATIONALISM.

Having, in the preceding pages, discussed the principles and doctrines of the Congregational system, and described with some minuteness the ecclesiastical usages of the denomination, I know not that I can more suitably conclude my labors, than by summing up, and placing distinctly before the reader in a connected view, a few of the more prominent advantages which Congregationalism is supposed to possess over all other systems of church government. And this I shall do, not that I may rail at other systems, but, that I may more fully and faithfully exhibit my own.

Every man who has fixed principles or settled opinions on any controverted subject, has arrived at them by a process of *comparison* as well as investigation. And there is no way in which we can more effectually aid an inquirer in settling a disputed point, than by placing fairly before him the contending theories or systems between which he must judge. This is emphatically true in respect to the question now before us. It is only by seeing the system advocated in these pages, in contrast with opposing systems, that we shall be made fully sensible of its superior advantages.

And why may not this comparison be made without subjecting the author to the imputation of invidious feelings or unworthy motives? All systems and published opinions of church order and discipline are fairly open to examination, and comparison with other systems and opinions, and to animadversion, if occasion is discovered. And, if this be done with fairness and christian courtesy, no one has any right to complain. We may number among our personal and cherished friends — as the writer is most happy to do — persons who embrace almost every form of church government; and yet we may, and ought, as conscientious men, to claim for ourselves, what we cheerfully yield to others, the right of private judgment, and the liberty to express with entire freedom our convictions, without being charged with unworthy or unchristian motives and feelings. We may even go further, and say with a controversialist of some distinction: "We are not to be afraid to contend firmly against what we conceive to be error, even at the hazard of deeply offending those by whom it is embraced." * In what may now be said of other ecclesiastical systems, I will not, knowingly, deviate in the smallest particular from the truth. But the best intentions will not always preserve a man from error. And I beg, that my mistakes, if any I make, may be

---

* *Dr. How's Vindication of the Prot. Episcopal Chh.* quoted by Smyth, in his Lecs. on Apostolical Succession.

attributed to misapprehension, not to design. With these prefatory remarks — which the language of some who have noticed my humble labors seemed to demand — let us proceed to the inquiry: —

WHAT ARE SOME OF THE MORE PROMINENT ADVANTAGES WHICH CONGREGATIONALISM IS SUPPOSED TO POSSESS OVER OTHER SYSTEMS OF CHURCH ORDER AND GOVERNMENT?

1. *We regard Congregationalism as the most scriptural system of church government.**

We do not assert that all other systems are totally destitute of scriptural authority; nor, that this is exactly conformed to the polity of the apostolic churches; but we do assert, that the order and discipline of our churches is more nearly in accordance with the model furnished by the New Testament than that of any other denomination. This consideration may be addressed equally to those who deny that the Scriptures furnish *any* model of church government, and to those who admit that the *great outlines*, if not the minor particulars of church polity, are given therein.

Those who deny that the word of God furnishes any pattern for church building, will, it is presumed, admit, that the church which has *most* of scriptural architecture about it, best deserves their regard. Dr. Stillingfleet, though he considered "the form of church government a mere matter of prudence, regu-

---

* When I speak of the *Scriptures* furnishing a model of church polity for us, I would be understood to refer exclusively to the *New Testament.*

lated by the word of God," yet admits: "That form of government [to be] the best, according to principles of christian prudence, which comes the nearest to Apostolic practice, and tends most to the advancing the peace and unity of the Church of God." * And Dr. Campbell, though he could "see no reason why a Church may not subsist under different forms, as well as a State;" yet owns, "that one form may be more favorable than another to the spirit and design of the constitution." †

I beg leave to put it to any such person: If that form of church government may not be reasonably regarded as most agreeable to the principles of christian prudence, and most favorable to the constitution of Christianity, which most nearly resembles the one selected and established by the Founder of Christianity?

If, now, it has been shown in the preceding pages, as I trust it has, that all the fundamental principles and the important doctrines of Congregationalism have the sanction of scriptural precept or apostolic usage; and that the authorized practice of this denomination is nowise inconsistent with the same precepts and example,—then certainly, Congregationalism is *scriptural;* the word of God *allows,* if it does not require the adoption of it. And, if Congregationalism is scriptural, then it is *more* scriptural than any other system, in just so much as any other system differs from this in its fundamental prin-

---

* *Irenicum,* p. 414, 415, 2d Ed.

† *Lecs. Ecc. Hist.* L. iv. p. 50, and L. 8, p. 128.

ciples and doctrines; unless it can be proved — which it cannot be — that the Scriptures equally countenance different systems.

But, in what particulars do other systems of church government differ from this?

All governments may be classed under three general heads: Monarchical, Aristocratical, or Democratical. The distinctive peculiarities of these three forms may be, to some extent, intermixed in any given system; but all governments, ecclesiastical as well as civil, may be classed under one of these heads.

The Episcopal form of church government may be regarded as monarchical, the Presbyterian as aristocratical, and the Congregational as democratical. The predominating characteristics of these three forms of government are sufficiently, if not exactly expressed by these titles.

Episcopacy is the government of the church by bishops. Each bishop is the sovereign of his diocese. His power may be that of a despot, or of a limited monarch, according as the people are allowed more or less influence in the government. Romish Episcopacy may be considered a despotism. The Pope is the supreme, infallible head of the Church on earth. English Episcopacy is less despotic than Roman, though derived from it; and American Episcopacy is a modification of English Episcopacy, presenting a still milder form of monarchical church government.

THE CHURCH OF ENGLAND.

Suppose, in order to test the question, Which is the more scriptural system of church government? we compare Congregational church order and government, with that adopted by the Church of England.

1. The first objection which presents itself against the hierarchal government of the Church of England, is the intimate union which subsists between it and the State. By the act of supremacy, Henry VIII. became head of the Church of England, as really as he was before, head of the State; and as truly so, as the Pope had previously been. With the *Crown*, the successors of Henry have inherited the supreme headship of the *Church* of England. And now a woman rules the Church of England; the government of the church being virtually committed to the sovereign, as its temporal head, and to Parliament, as the monarch's council. She convenes, prorogues, restrains, regulates, and dissolves all synods and ecclesiastical convocations; appoints the archbishops, bishops, deans, and a considerable portion of the clergy;"* or at least nominates them, simply because she is the Head of the State; though Christ, the Great Head of the Church, has emphatically declared, that his disciples and his kingdom, are not of this world.—John 17: 14, 16. 18: 36.

---

* Nearly one tenth of all the benefices in England and Wales, in 1853, were in the gift of the Crown.—See *Census of Great Britain*—Religious Worship, p. 37.

2. We object to the existence and authority of the dignitaries and officials of the Church of England.

Next to the Queen, in ecclesiastical dignity, are the archbishops; who, appointed by her authority, rule in her name. There are two of these dignitaries; and between them, the kingdom is divided; each being supreme in his own province, and in addition, having a diocese of his own, in which he exercises episcopal jurisdiction. Next to the archbishops, rank the Bishops; of whom there are twenty-six; each one of whom is a sovereign in his own diocese. Each diocese is divided into Archdeaconries; of which there are about seventy in the kingdom; each archdeaconry is divided into Deaneries; and each deanery into Parishes. The archdeacon is the bishop's vicar, or vicegerent; and is authorized to examine candidates for "holy orders," to make parochial circuits, and oversee the clergy within his jurisdiction; and also to hold ecclesiastical courts, in order to inflict censures, suspend or excommunicate persons, prove wills, hear ecclesiastical causes, etc.; subject to an appeal to the bishop. The deans, and canons or prebendaries, are supposed to be the bishop's counsellors. Rural Deans are assistants to the bishops in smaller spheres. Anciently ten parishes constituted a Rural Deanery; but now they are diverse in extent, and the whole number in England and Wales amounts to about 463.

I have now named the dignitaries of the Church of England. The working clergy are styled Rectors, Vicars, Perpetual Curates, and Curates. The title of *rector* is given to those ministers who have the charge and care of a parish and are entitled to *all* the tithes; that of *vicar*, to those who act as deputies to others, and are entitled to only *a portion* of the tithes, or to a stipulated salary.*

A *perpetual curate*, is quite like a vicar, in that he is appointed for life, and as the delegate of the tithe-impropriator, is entitled to a portion of the tithes during life.

A *curate* is the lowest grade of clergyman in the Church of England, and is generally employed by a rector to do the laborious work of a parish, at a moderate salary.

---

* The usual form of inducting a person into a benefice, who may be either a rector or vicar, is as follows: "The inductor takes the clerk [i. e. the person to be inducted] by the hand, and placing it on the key of the church, which must be then in the door, says: 'By virtue of this instrument, I induct you in the real, actual, and corporeal possession of the rectory or vicarage of A—, with all its fruits, profits, members, and appurtenances.' This done, he opens the door, puts the clerk in possession of the church, and shuts the door upon him; who, after he has tolled the bell (if there be any) to give the parishioners due notice of their new minister, comes out, and desires the inductor to indorse a certificate of his induction, on the archdeacon's warrant, and all persons present signify it under their hands."

Such is the process by which a man becomes the pastor of a flock in the Church of England. The people are made acquainted with the important fact that they have a spiritual guide provided for them, by hearing the bell toll, "if there be any!"

If a benefice is in the hands of a bishop, Institution and Induction only, are requisite: these are called *collative* benefices. There are, also, what are called *donative* benefices; which are obtained by the donation of the patron in writing, without presentation, institution, or induction. — *London Encyclopedia*, Art. Induction.

These are the official persons who have in their hands the government of the Church of England, and the care of souls; and yet, so far as I have been able to discover, the people who constitute the Church of England, have no voice in the election of these men to office; church-wardens and parish clerks, alone, being chosen by the people; and even these, are sometimes appointed by the minister of the parish. I need not say to any one who has read the authorities cited in this work, that this exclusion of the people from the government of the church is contrary to the usage of the apostolic and primitive churches, who held the supreme power, under Christ, and elected all their officers, governors, and teachers. In fact, the entire government and discipline of the Church of England is as unlike that of the apostolic churches as well can be.

4. The Ecclesiastical Courts of the Church of England suggest another most serious objection to this Hierarchy.

Instead of recognizing the right of individual churches to "open and shut," to "bind and loose," agreeably to the words of Christ in Matt. 18: 18, the framers and governors of the Church of England have placed all disciplinary power in a series of Ecclesiastical Courts.

First on this list of courts stands the *Court of Delegates*, which is the sovereign's court, where, as Supreme Head of the Church, the King or Queen of England, represented by the Privy Council, tries and settles all cases of appeal from all inferior tribunals. The *Provincial Courts*, are the archbishops' courts, and take cognizance of all ecclesiastical business within their jurisdictions respectively. The *Diocesan Courts* are held in each diocese, in the name and by the authority of the respective bishops, and take cognizance of all matters of discipline within their several dioceses. There is an appeal from these to the archbishop's court. The *Archdeacon's Court* inflicts censures, suspends or excommunicates persons, and transacts other business, subject to an appeal generally to the Bishop's Court. Besides these, there are *Courts of Peculiars*, so called, and *Manorial Courts*. These, though numerous, are of circumscribed authority, though in these a portion of the business usually done in the Archdeacon's or Bishop's courts, may be transacted.

To manage this disciplinary machinery of the Church of England, particularly in its higher departments, a distinct and peculiar class of professional men has been raised up, called Doctors of Law, and Proctors. From the former of these, the archbishops select the judges of their archiepiscopal courts. The Proctors are the solicitors and attorneys of these spiritual tribunals.

I have now enumerated and very briefly described the dignitaries by whom, and the Ecclesiastical Courts by which the Church of England is ordered and disciplined. The question recurs: Did Jesus Christ intend to have his Church governed by such instrumentalities? Is it in this way that his disciples are to prove to the world that Christ's kingdom is not of this world?

May not the wayfaring man, though a fool, discern

the utter dissimilarity between this pompous and complicated hierarchal establishment and the simple organization and government which Christ sanctioned, and his apostles developed in the primitive churches of Christendom? And yet, this very Hierarchy is pronounced by its friends and advocates — "the most *scriptural church* in Christendom" — "*the sanctuary of scriptural piety*" — "the wonder and glory of Christendom." *

5. The enormous income deemed necessary to support the pomp and dignity of the English Hierarchy affords another serious objection to the entire Establishment

Revenue of the Church of England.

In order to estimate more accurately the value of such praise as has just been quoted, it may be well to inquire the cost of such a "*sanctuary*," as the Church of England provides. My limits will not allow me to go into many particulars. Look, however, at the following items: To support a single dignitary of this "Scriptural church" — the Archbishop of Canterbury — a net, yearly revenue is allowed, of £19,182, or 85,168 dollars; and for the Archbishop of York, £12,629, or 56,072 dollars; making a sum total of *one hundred and forty-one thousand two hundred and forty* dollars annually for these two ornamental dignitaries!

And what does it cost yearly to support some

* *British Review*, No. 48, 1825, Review of James' Church Member's Guide.

seven and twenty bishops, who claim to be the direct successors of the apostles, and to receive their authority and dignity from him who had not where to lay his head? No less than *five hundred and seventy thousand, four hundred and fifty-five* dollars!*

* The following was the return of the Commissioners of Ecclesiastical Inquiry, of the net annual revenue of the different sees, at an average of three years, ending with 1831.

		Net annual income.
Bishopric of	St. Asaph	£6,301
"	Bangor	4,464
"	Bath and Wells	5,946
"	Bristol	2,351
"	Canterbury	
"	Carlisle	2,213
"	Chester	3,261
"	Chichester	4,229
"	St. David's	1,897
"	Durham	19,066
"	Ely	11,105
"	Exeter	2,713
"	Gloucester	2,282
"	Hereford	2,516
"	Llandaff	924
"	Lichfield and Coventry	3,923
"	Lincoln	4,542
"	London	13,929
"	Manchester	
"	Norwich	5,395
"	Oxford	2,648
"	Peterborough	3,103
"	Ripon	
"	Rochester	1,459
"	Salisbury	3,939
"	Sodor and Man	2,555
"	Winchester	11,151
"	Worcester	6,569
"	York	
	Total net annual income,	£128,481 or $570,455.

I reckon the English pound (£) at $4.44, only; whereas the

The total gross annual revenue of the twenty-eight Deans and Chapters in 1831, was estimated at £284,241, or *one million, two hundred and sixty-two thousand and thirty dollars.* This sum, added to the income of the archbishops and bishops, gives us a total of NEARLY TWO MILLIONS OF DOLLARS expended yearly on the *dignitaries* of the Church of England. This church should certainly be styled — "*the* WONDER *of Christendom!*"

The whole number of benefices in England and Wales in 1851, was 11,728. The number of parishes somewhat exceeded this number. The total gross annual income of these benefices is about £3,251,-159, or, *fourteen million, four hundred and thirty-five thousand, one hundred and forty-five dollars!* This would give an average annual income to each incumbent, of £303, or *one thousand, three hundred and forty-five dollars.*

Here, then, we find an annual sum total appropriated to the support of the dignitaries and the clergy of this establishment, of nearly SIXTEEN AND A HALF MIL-

---

pound sterling is now worth about $4.84; and I make no account of the odd cents.

Since the report of the Commissioners was made in 1831, some changes have been made in the bishoprics; two new sees have been erected — Ripon and Manchester — and the boundaries of some of the other sees arranged with reference to an equalization of the inhabitants in them respectively; but the total income of the several bishoprics has not been diminished; for according to the Census Report of Great Britain for 1851, "no fewer than 2,029 new churches have been built, and the value of church property has much increased" since 1831.—*Religious Worship, Report and Tables*, p. 37, 38, compared with p. 166, Table 24.

LIONS OF DOLLARS. If we add to this, the revenue of the Irish Protestant Episcopal Church, £865,535, or *three million, eight hundred and forty-two thousand, nine hundred and seventy-five dollars* — we shall find the annual cost of the established churches in England, Wales, and Ireland, to be more than TWENTY MILLIONS OF DOLLARS!!

And, let no one suppose that these estimates are extravagant; for they are much below what has been generally believed to be the truth. Good authority has set down the revenue of the Episcopal Hierarchies of England, Wales, and Ireland, as greater, by nearly two hundred thousand dollars, than that of all the other churches in the world.*

I need not dwell on the points of difference between this splendid, complicated, expensive hierarchal establishment, and the unostentatious, simple, economical, and yet effective polity of the Congregational churches of this country and of Great Britain. A cursory view of the Church of England is sufficient to explain the rapid increase of Dissent in England and Wales. Already the Dissenting congregations are numbered by tens of thousands; and nearly

---

* The Catholic Miscellany, as quoted in American Encyclopedia, Art. Church, estimates the revenue of the Churches of England, Ireland, and Wales, at £8,896,000, or $39,498,240; and the revenue of all other Churches in Christendom, at £8,852,000; which is £44,000, or, $195,360 less than that of the above establishments.

In the outline which has been given of the Chh. of Eng. etc., I have relied chiefly on *McCulloch's Statistics of the British Empire*, — Vol. II.; the *London Encyclopedia*, passim; and the *Census of Great Britain* for 1851 — Religious Worship.

or quite one half of the inhabitants of England and Wales are Dissenters from the State Church.*

But we must leave England and her Hierarchal Church Establishment, to consider Episcopacy under a less objectionable form.

---

* See *Census Report* — Religious Worship, 1851.

According to this Report, the Congregationalists, alone, had, in 1851, no less than 3,244 places of public worship, with sittings for 1,067,760 persons, and an actual attendance on public worship of more than one fifth as many persons as attend worship in the State Churches of England and Wales; while the Methodists — of whom there are no less than nine different kinds enumerated in the Census — had 11,944 places of worship, (937 of which belonged to Calvinistic Methodists), capable of seating 2,443,976 persons; the Baptists — of whom there are six different kinds, and all of whom are believed to be essentially Congregational in their church government — had 2,789 places of worship, with sittings for 752,343 persons; the Friends, 371 places of worship, and sittings for 91,599 persons; the Unitarians, 229 places of worship, and 68,554 sittings; the Latter Day Saints, 222 places of worship, and 30,783 sittings; the Presbyterians, 161 places of worship, and 86,812 sittings; various other sects and isolated congregations, — including 53 Jewish synagogues, 32 congregations of the "Catholic and Apostolic Church," 50 New Church congregations, and 32 Moravians — 859 places of public worship, and 163,710 sittings; and finally, 570 places of worship, with 186,111 sittings, belonging to the Roman Catholic Church.

Thus it appears, that in 1851 the various religious bodies not in connection with the Church of England, in England and Wales, had no less than 20,330 places of worship, with accommodations for 4,851,288 persons! while the Church of England, with all the patronage of the State and the aristocracy to back her, had but 14,077 places of worship, capable of seating 5,317,915 persons!

And, notwithstanding that the provision by the State Church, for the accommodation of worshippers, was somewhat larger than that furnished by *all other* denominations and sects together, it

THE PROTESTANT EPISCOPAL CHURCH OF THE U. S.

The Episcopacy of this country is a scion from the mother land — a continuation of the Church of England under a new name. The first Episcopal bishops of America were consecrated by the archbishops of Canterbury and York;* but not until those functionaries were assured that no material deviation from the English Hierarchy, in doctrine or practice, would be admitted by the American Episcopal Church. This assurance seems to have been remembered by American Episcopalians; for, in the Preface to the Book of Common Prayer, published by the Protestant Episcopal Church in the United

---

is a most noticeable circumstance, that by actual count, the Protestant Dissenting Congregations, on a given Sabbath, were more numerous than those of the Church of England by 159,529 persons! and, adding the attendants on Roman Catholic worship (249,389), and some other bodies, the State Church had actually fewer worshippers by 433,711, than were found in the various other places of public worship in the kingdom!

The statistics on this head stand thus: — The whole population of England and Wales in 1851, was 17,927,609; the whole number present at the most numerously attended services on Sunday, March 30, 1851, by actual count, was 6,356,222; and of these 2,971,258 were in places of worship controlled by the Church of England, 3,110,782 in Protestant Dissenters' places of worship, 249,389 in Roman Catholic chapels, and 24,793 in other places of worship. — See *Census Report*, 1851, — Religious Worship, Table A, Supplement 1, p. 181, and Table N, p. 300.

* One American bishop had been previously consecrated by the *non-juring* bishops of Scotland.

States, speaking of the alterations made in it from the Book of Common Prayer of the Church of England, it is said: "In which it will also appear, that this church is far from intending to depart from the Church of England, in any essential point of doctrine, discipline, or worship; or *further than local circumstances require.*"

(1) We are constrained, then, to object to "The Protestant Episcopal Church in the United States of America" first, that it is essentially a *National Church:* "the jurisdiction of this Church extending in *right*, though not always in *form* to all persons belonging to it within the United States."* For such a church we find no authority in the New Testament.

(2) We further object, that in the general government of this church, the rights and privileges of particular churches are not duly recognized, and that unauthorized power is given to the bishops and clergy.

The members of a parish are allowed to elect a parish clerk, church-wardens, vestry-men, and deputies to the State, or Diocesan Convention. These persons, with their minister, represent the parish, and act for it in things temporal and spiritual. Each Diocese — embracing usually a single State — holds a yearly Convention, composed of all the clergy, and of lay delegates from each parish, with the Bishop as president. The members of this convention choose their own bishop or bishops, subject to the approbation of the House of Deputies in Gen-

---

* *Canon* X. sect. 3, 1853; also *Articles of Religion* in C. P. Book, Art. 34, § 2.

eral Convention, and the consent of the House of Bishops; they determine upon the mode of trying clergymen in the diocese, under certain restrictions; they appoint a standing committee, to be a council to the bishop, if there be one, and to act in the place of a bishop in certain cases, if there be none; they choose deputies, clerical and lay, from one to four of each order, to represent the diocese in General Convention; and attend to such other local matters as are not otherwise provided for.*

The General Convention meets once in three years; and is composed of all the bishops of the church, who constitute the upper house, or "House of Bishops;" and of an equal number of clerical and lay representatives, or deputies, from each of the dioceses connected with the Convention, who constitute the lower house, or "House of Deputies." The House of Bishops has a negative upon the proceedings of the other house.† This Convention has the power of establishing for the Church "A Book of Common Prayer, Administration of the Sacraments, and other Rites and Ceremonies of the Church, Articles of Religion, and a Form and Manner of Making, Ordaining, and Consecrating Bishops, Priests, and Deacons." ‡ And the 45th Canon of 1832, provides, that "every minister shall, before all sermons and lectures, and on all other occasions of public worship, use the Book of Common Prayer, as the same is or

---

* *Constitution of P. E.* Chh. Arts. 2, 4, 6. Canons III., IV. of 1832.

† *Constitution*, Arts. 1, 2, 3. Also *Bishop White's Memoirs of the Protest. Epis. Chh.*

‡ *Const.* Art. 8.

may be established by the authority of the General Convention of this Church. And in performing said service, *no other prayers shall be used than those prescribed by said book.*" All Missionary Bishops, whether for our own country or for foreign lands, are to be elected by "the House of clerical and lay Deputies, on nomination by the House of Bishops." *

From this outline of the general polity of this national church, it appears, that the rights and privileges of individual churches are not regarded, in several very important particulars: — (a) They are governed, not by the concurring voice of their own members, democratically, as were the apostolic churches, but by the bishops, clergy, and representatives of the laity. The bishops exercise a general supervision and government over all the congregations in their respective dioceses, and the *exclusive right* to "confirm," or admit persons to the communion of the church, and to ordain to the ministry. For the manner in which they exercise their power, they hold themselves amenable neither to their clergy nor their churches, but only to their fellow-bishops, who alone can try them.†

(b) The Scriptural rights of particular churches in selecting, ordaining, dismissing, and disciplining their ministers, are also disregarded by this system.

When a minister has been elected into any church or parish, the bishop of the diocese must be notified

---

* *Canon* X. of 1853.

† Art. VI. of the Constitution of P. E. Chh. provides, that "the court appointed for the purpose of trying Bishops shall be composed of Bishops *only.*" — See also *Bishop Onderdonk's Address to the Epis. Conv.* in N. Y., 1843.

of the same; or where there is no bishop, the standing committee of the diocese, who take the place of the bishop; and the approbation of the ecclesiastical authority of the diocese obtained, before said minister can be inducted into office.* Neither does this system recognize the right of a particular church to dismiss its minister, or that of a minister to leave his people, without the concurrence of the ecclesiastical authority of the diocese.† In the "Office of Institution of Ministers," the bishop tells the instituted presbyter: "In case of any difference between you and your congregation, as to a separation, and dissolution of all sacerdotal connection between you and them, *we, your bishop, with the advice of our presbyters, are to be the ultimate arbiter and judge.*" ‡ In regard to the discipline of ministers, Canon V. of 1835 provides, that "Every minister shall be amenable for offences committed by him, to the Bishop, and if there be no bishop, to the Clerical Members of the Standing Committee of the Diocese in which he is Canonically resident at the time of the charge." The bishop and his presbyters may settle *authoritatively* all such controversies between ministers, holding the rectorship of parishes, and their vestries or congregations, as cannot be settled by themselves.— *Canon* XXXIV. of 1832.

This system of church government does not recognize — so far as appears in its Canons and Prayer Book — the right of the brethren of particular

---

* *Canon* XIV. of 1853.

† *Canon* XXXIII. of 1832.

‡ *Office of Institution, in Book of Common Prayer.*

churches to say who shall be admitted to their fellowship, or who shall be excluded from their communion. It is made "the duty of ministers to prepare young persons and others for the Holy Ordinance of Confirmation:" . . . and "to present, for Confirmation, such persons as [*they*] *shall think properly qualified:*" * and these persons are confirmed, or admitted to the communion of the Church, by the Bishop.

Canon XLII. of 1832 provides, that, "If any persons within this Church offend their brethren by any wickedness of life, such persons shall be repelled from the Holy Communion, agreeably to the Rubric"—i. e. by the minister of the parish.† On complaint being made to the bishop, in writing, by the person thus expelled, the bishop may restore him if he think proper, or may institute an inquiry into the case: but unless such complaint is made to the bishop, it is not his duty to institute any inquiry.‡

Thus, so far as appears, the whole business of receiving to the communion of the church and rejecting from it, is in the hands of the minister of the parish and the bishop of the diocese. But for this we find no authority in the Scriptures.

And to the claims of Episcopacy, that her Bishops only have the right to ordain and confirm, to exercise a general supervision over the churches, and to be

---

* *Canon* XXVI. of 1832, and "The Order of Confirmation," in the Book of C. P. and the directions preceding.

† See the *Rubric*, or directions for the administration of the Lord's Supper, in C. P. Book.

‡ See *Canon*, Canon XLII. of 1832, and "The Order for the Administration of the Lord's Supper," in C. P. Book.

the chief administrators of spiritual discipline*— we are constrained to object as unscriptural assumptions.

(3) The 1st Canon of this church, enacts that "In this church there shall always be *three* orders in the Ministry, namely: Bishops, Priests, and Deacons." For this canon we can find no authority in the New Testament. Neither can we for those canons etc. which give to bishops the superintendence of several parishes, and the charge and government of their ministers.

(4) We object to the claim which this church sets up, of "power to decree rites or ceremonies," and authority to establish a Book of Service, and to require *entire conformity* to decreed rites, and to prescribed forms of prayer and religious service.† We find no warrant for these things in Scripture, and no example justifying them in the apostolic churches.

(5) We object not merely to the general claim of the Protestant Episcopal Church—of power to establish a Common Prayer Book, and to decree rites or ceremonies, etc.—as unscriptural, but we also object to many things in this C. P. Book and these decreed rites, ceremonies, and requisitions—as unauthorized by the Scriptures, and of dangerous tendency.

In "The Ministration of Public Baptism of Infants," for example, the Prayer Book teaches the doctrine of Baptismal Regeneration; or, in other words,

---

* *Bishop Onderdonk, Epis. Tested* by *Scripture*, p. 11.

† *Articles of Religion* in C. P. Book—Art. 20; *Canons* XLV. and XLVII. of 1832; *Constitution*, Art. 8.

that children baptized by the ministers of this Church, and in the form and manner prescribed in the C. P. Book, are "regenerate and grafted into the body of Christ's Church." And the officiating minister, after praying God to "sanctify this water to the mystical washing away of sin," and the application of the water to the child,—is required to say: "We yield thee hearty thanks, most merciful Father, that it hath pleased thee *to regenerate this infant with thy Holy Spirit, to receive him for thine own child by adoption, and to incorporate him into thy holy church*," etc. Thus we are taught, that the Episcopal baptism of infants is "*a saving ordinance*." * But where is the chapter and verse for this? And where shall we find scriptural authority for "god-fathers and god-mothers"—not the parents of the child—taking the part which they do in the baptism of infants? and where, for signing the child with the sign of the cross?

In "The Order of Confirmation" the officiating bishop utters language scarcely less objectionable than that employed in the Baptismal Service. Having laid his hands on the heads of the persons to be confirmed, he declares, that he does this, "*to certify them, by this sign, of* [*God's*] *favor and gracious goodness towards them*." And this declaration is made, not in respect to intelligent, and hopefully pious adult persons, only, but includes all such "children as are come to competent age, and can say the Creed, the Lord's Prayer, and the Ten Com-

---

* This has been distinctly and fully avowed by "The Churchman," while the official organ of the Bishop of New York.

mandments, and can answer to the other questions of [the] Short Catechism" in the Prayer Book, and are presented to the Bishop by the minister of the parish, for Confirmation.* Is such language authorized by the Scriptures? Is it safe — is it scriptural, for one erring mortal, to *certify* another of the favor of God, after this manner?

(6) We consider it a very serious objection to this church, that evidence of personal piety is not required, according to the C. P. Book, of those who are admitted to her communion. The rite of Confirmation admits one to full communion: but to enjoy this rite, the profession of an orthodox creed and a moral life, alone, are indispensable. Thus read the directions to the Order of Confirmation: "So soon as children are come to a competent age, and can say the Creed, the Lord's Prayer, and the Ten Commandments, and can answer to the other questions of this short Catechism, *they shall be brought to the Bishop*" — to be confirmed. "And there shall none be admitted to the holy Communion, until such time as he be confirmed, or be ready and desirous to be confirmed." — See also the last exhortation to the god-parents, at the baptism of a child.

Does not apostolic example require that all who are admitted to the holy communion of christian churches should intelligently believe, and publicly profess their belief, that they have been born of God, and become new creatures in Christ Jesus? But, it will hardly be maintained that all children who can say the Creed, the Lord's Prayer, and the Ten Command-

---

* See in *Book of C. P.*, Catechism and Order of Confirmation.

ments, and can recite the Catechism, give evidence of Regeneration.

(7) To this enumeration of unscriptural features in Protestant Episcopacy, we feel constrained to add another, touching various rites, and ceremonies, and outward observances, established by this Church and enjoined upon its members;—namely, that in many things, this Church symbolizes with Popery.

The Service-Book of the American Episcopal Church is the same, with slight alterations, as that used by the Church of England: and the English Book is chiefly compiled from Popish Service-Books.* Hence the Jesuit, Dr. Carrier, declared: "The Common Prayer and Catechism [of the Church of England] contains nothing contrary to the Romish Service."† Bishop Montague asserted: "that our [the English] Service is the same in most things with the Church of Rome; and that the differences are not so great that we should make any separation." ‡ The order of the Institution of Priests and Deacons is substantially the same in the Romish, English, and American Episcopal Churches. Their rites and ceremonies in public worship are strikingly alike; they stand, and sit, and kneel together; their confessions and absolutions, their Pater Nosters, Gloria Patri, Litanies, and Responses substantially agree together. Their method of rehearsing the Ten Commandments, and of reading the Psalms by alternat-

---

* See *Neal's Puritans*, Vol. I. p. 95, 96; *De Laune's Plea*, p. 47, 52; *Hist. Congregationalism*, p. 205, 206.

† *De Laune's Plea for the Non-Conformists*, p. 48.

‡ Ib., and *Neal's Puritans*, Vol. II. p. 164–342.

ing, is similar. Many of the Collects, Lessons, etc. of the English and American Episcopal Churches, are either word for word from the Romish Service-Books, or agree for substance. Their Saint's Days and Holy Days, their fasts and feasts — fixed and movable, are taken from the Calendar of Rome.

This conformity of the English service to the Roman ritual seems not to have arisen, originally, from any love for Popery, but from a fear, on the part of the early English Reformers, of doing violence to public prejudices, by a sudden and entire overturn of all the consecrated religious associations of the people; and a hope and expectation of drawing in the Papists, to a conformity with the Reformed Church of England.* And for some time their anticipations seemed likely to be realized. The Papists continued to attend the English service, until his Holiness, despairing of the recovery of his supremacy by fair means, interdicted the practice, and excommunicated Elizabeth. But, so imposing were the services of the English cathedrals in the days of Elizabeth, that the very messengers of the Pope declared, "that they wondered the Pope should be so ill informed and advised [as] to interdict a Prince, whose service and ceremonies *so symbolize* with his own." † And it is, I believe, a well-supported asser-

---

* *Stillingfleet*, in his "Irenicum," asserts this unequivocally; and commends the Reformers for their policy. He calls the English Liturgy "*a bait*" for the Papists. See p. 122, 123, 2d Ed. 1662.

† *Hume's England*, Vol. II. ch. 38, p. 572, Alb. ed., and Vol. III. ch. 40, p. 69; *Neal's Pur.* Vol. I. p. 273; *De Laune*, p. 49.

tion, that Pope Pius V. and Gregory XIII. both, offered to confirm the English Liturgy, on condition that Elizabeth would acknowledge the supremacy of Rome.* Thus stood church matters in the days of Elizabeth.

Some alterations were made in the Prayer Book by James I. and some by Charles II.; "yet, so as the main body and essentials of it (as well in the chiefest materials, as in the frame and order thereof) have still continued the same unto this day." This was said in the Preface to the Prayer Book, in the days of Charles II. (1661), and is equally true now; for no alterations have since been made in the English Book of Common Prayer. And the objections to the "main body and essentials" of the English Common Prayer Book — that they are borrowed from Popery, and cause the English Church to symbolize with Popery — lie with full weight against the "chiefest materials" of the Common Prayer Book of the Protestant Episcopal Church in the U. S. of America; for in most essential points and particulars the two books are alike.†

---

* *De Laune*, p. 48; *Neal*, Vol. I. p. 202, also p. 191, 192.

Neal says, Pius IV.; but this must be a mistake or misprint; for he says the offer was made in 1570; but Pius IV. died 1566. — See *Hume*, ut sup. and *Mosheim*, *Ecc. Hist.* Vol. III. p. 91, 92, Harper's ed.

† According to the Rev. M. Boyle, of Boston, a clergyman of the Protestant Episcopal Church, the service-book of the American Episcopal Church differs from the English in the following particulars: (1) "A shorter form of absolution is *allowed*," though "the English one is most generally recited in Divine service." (2) "The Athanasian creed is omitted." . . . (3) "In the office of Baptism, the sign of the cross may be dispensed with if re-

Regarding Popery as the "Mystery of Iniquity" — the grand device of Satan to overthrow the Church of God — we cannot but consider all symbolizing with this system of abominations as alike unscriptural and dangerous.

That this complicated and peculiar ritual of the Episcopal Church is not required by the New Testament, our only infallible guide, will sufficiently appear on the most cursory examination and comparison. That these things in the Episcopal Church are of dangerous tendency, is sufficiently evident to our minds from the history of English Episcopacy. Repeatedly has the Church of England been brought to the very verge of Popery. And for some years past her Protestantism has been most seriously threatened by this symbolizing with Popery, which her own Prayer Book sanctions — yea, *requires* in her members.

The reasons why Protestant Episcopacy in America has not developed more fully this same Popish tendency, are sufficiently obvious to such as consider that this Church, as an independent body, has existed but little more than half a century, and has been constantly surrounded by influences most decidedly hostile to Romanism, in the institutions of this country and in the vast predominance of dissenters "from

---

quested." . . . (4) "The marriage service has been considerably abridged." (5) "In the general service, some expressions in the English Prayer Book . . . are altered or omitted." (6) "A change was, of course, made in the prayers for Rulers." . . . (7) "And there may be a few other verbal differences of minor importance." — *Abridged from an article in Enc. Relig. Knowl. on P. E. Chh. in U. S. A.*

the bishop of Rome and all his detestable enormities." But the time is coming, yea, and now is, when the tendency of Episcopacy to countenance Popery, as a system of religious order and worship, will be more apparent.*

---

* Since the above was written, the public press has furnished a most remarkable confirmation of our apprehensions. On the 2d July, 1843, a young man was ordained by Bishop Onderdonk of New York, who openly avowed his agreement essentially with the Church of Rome: (1) "He did not see any thing to prevent or forbid" his having recourse to the ministry of Rome, if denied admission to the ministry of the Protestant Episcopal Church in this country. (2) "He did not deem the differences between [the P. E. Chh.] and the Church of Rome to be such as embraced any points of faith." (3) "He was not prepared to pronounce the doctrine of transubstantiation an absurd or impossible doctrine." (4) "He does not object to the Romish doctrine of Purgatory as defined by the Council of Trent." . . . (5) "He was not prepared to say whether she [the Romish Church] or the Anglican Church were the more pure." (6) "He regarded the denial of the cup to the laity [in the administration of the sacrament of the Lord's supper] as a mere matter of discipline." . . . (7) "He believes that the Reformation from the Church of Rome was an unjustifiable act, and followed by many grievous and lamentable results." (8) He was not disposed to fault the Church of Rome for using Apocryphal Books; "nor was he prepared to say that the Holy Spirit did not speak by these Books Apocryphal." (9) "He considered the promise of conformity to the doctrine, discipline, and worship of the P. E. Chh. as not embracing the 39 Articles in any *close* and *rigid construction* of them, but regarded them only as affording a sort of general basis of concord — as those which none subscribed except with certain mental reservations and private exceptions; and that this was what he regarded as Bishop White's view." — He further declared his conviction of the lawfulness of the invocation of saints — thought the souls in purgatory might be benefited by our prayers — received the creed of Pope Pius IV. so far as it was a repetition of the de-

I have now frankly expressed some of our reasons for regarding Episcopacy as less scriptural in its order and worship than Congregationalism. I have spoken of the *system*, not of the men who embrace it. Towards Episcopalians — so far as they exhibit the spirit of Christ — we cherish the kindest and most fraternal feelings. Their ecclesiastical polity we believe to be unscriptural in many particulars, and of dangerous tendency; and as honest, conscientious men, we hesitate not to say what we think.

THE METHODIST EPISCOPAL CHURCH.

The grounds of our preference for Congregationalism over the Protestant Episcopal Church having been briefly stated, we will turn next to the Meth-

---

crees of the Council of Trent, which decrees he could receive, the damnatory clauses only excepted, etc. etc.

Notwithstanding the avowal of these Popish sentiments, and the solemn protest of two of his most respectable clergy, the Episcopal Bishop of New York, with the concurrence of six of his presbyters, and of Bishop Ives of North Carolina, (who has himself since gone over to Romanism,) proceeded to ordain this Romanist as a minister of the *Protestant* Episcopal Church in the U. S. A. — See "*A Statement of Facts in Relation to the Recent Ordination in St. Stephen's Church, New York*, by Drs. Smith and Anthon, 1843."

The controversy which has grown out of this matter, has developed the arbitrary nature of the power claimed by high churchmen — Puseyites. It seems, that a bishop claims the right to say what motions may be made in Convention, and to refuse to put such as are offensive to him; and even to silence and put down the mover of any such motion. — See an account of the doings of the Episcopal Convention in New York, in September, 1843.

odist Episcopal Church, and cursorily examine its constitution and discipline.

(1) "The government of this church is strictly Episcopal." So says one of its leading members. Another says, "It is a moderate Episcopacy."

Like the P. E. Church, it asserts that there should be *three orders in the ministry* — Bishops, Elders, and Deacons; and its Book of Discipline contains the substance of the form and manner of making and ordaining these officers, which is found in the Book of Common Prayer of the Protestant Episcopal Church.* Their bishops, however, claim not the exclusive right to ordain, and may themselves be ordained by presbyters.† They are regarded as superior to elders in *office* rather than *grade*.‡ Still they appear to sympathize with Episcopacy. Soon after the establishment of an 'Episcopate' in the P. E. Church of U. S., Dr. Coke, the presiding Methodist bishop, expressed his entire accordance with the P. E. Church, in their order and discipline, and his earnest desire for a union between the two denominations.§ And though there is now, perhaps, less sympathy between these hierarchies than ever before, yet, as late as 1840, this proposal was renewed by a Protestant Episcopal Bishop.|| So far, then, as this Church approves of

---

* See *The Doctrines and Discipline of the Methodist Episcopal Church*, for 1856, p. 122–149.

† *Discipline*, p. 40.

‡ *Zion's Herald*, Oct. 6th, 1841.

§ See his letters to Bishop White, in Memoirs of P. E. Chh. p. 425–431.

|| In 1840, Bishop Smith, of the P. E. Church in Kentucky, addressed, through the "Protestant and Herald," a letter to the

the Constitution and Discipline of the P. E. Church, so far must we disapprove of Episcopal Methodism.

M. E. Church in Kentucky, proposing and urging a union of the two churches. We copy a few paragraphs from the letter, to show its spirit. The Bishop says:—

"Between the members of the Protestant and Methodist Episcopal Churches in these United States the sympathy is almost universal, that they approach each other much nearer in doctrine and practice than any two other denominations. Why are they not one and the same?

"The causes out of which the Wesleyan interest first arose, and which resulted in its becoming a great separate branch of the Church of Christ in Great Britain and America, no longer exist; or if they do exist, are not in the slightest degree applicable to the relative positions of Episcopalians and Methodists in this country; and if the CAUSES of separation have ceased, how unwise or even criminal must it not be, for the separation to continue.

* * * * * * * *

"Can a reunion take place? The answer depends, first, perhaps, on the question, how far each side is wedded to its own peculiarities, inconsiderable as they are; then, on the measure of real christian love and sympathy pervading both sides; and then, on the willingness to make mutual concessions.

"The writer speaks solely in his own individual capacity, when he says, that there is no measure of concession, reasonable or unreasonable, not *absolutely involving principle*, which he would not be willing to make, in view of an end so unspeakably auspicious and desirable. He would be cheerfully willing to adopt a modified itineracy, love feasts, and class meetings, and to take such gradual, but prospective measures for reunion as should shock no man's prejudices, and take, if necessary, a generation to bring about a perfect union.

"On the part of the Methodists, all that would be necessary would be a gradual return to the use of some Form of Common Prayer; and a slight concession to the Episcopalians upon the question of a succession in the Episcopacy."—*N. Y. Observer*, Nov. 21, 1840.

Quite recently movements have been made in England to bring about an ecclesiastical union between the Wesleyan Methodist

(2) Another objection to this church organization is, that it is National, or Provincial, in its character. All the M. E. societies (or churches, we should call them,) in the U. S. were once recognized as parts of one great, National Church; but since the great schism on the slavery question, the U. S. have been divided into two ecclesiastical provinces, and the M. E. Church has become provincial in its character. But, for neither provincial nor national churches can we find any authority in the New Testament.

In order to understand, and more fully to appreciate the character and workings of the Methodist Episcopal system of church order and government in the United States, let us, first, take a general view of this compact and symmetrical organism, as presented in the "Discipline of the Methodist Episcopal Church," 1856. Beginning with the individual societies, we find that these are organized into "classes" of about twelve persons each, over each of which is placed a "Leader," who has the general supervision and care of the members, and is required to report to the minister of the Society the state of the class every week. Every Methodist society is placed in what is called a "Circuit, or Station," in which there may be several societies and preachers. These, with the class leaders and stewards (who are the treasurers of the societies) are placed under the general supervision of an elder, deacon, or preacher, who has the special charge of the circuit. Each "circuit" goes to form a

---

Establishment and the Church of England. The subject has been introduced into Parliament, as we learn from the newspapers, and into the Convocation of Canterbury; but without success.

part of a "District," over which is placed what is called a "Presiding Elder;" who holds to the several circuits in his district very much the same relation which the elder in special charge of a circuit holds to all in that circuit. The several districts, in their turn, are united together in what is termed an "Annual Conference;" which may embrace within its bounds all the districts, circuits, and societies of an entire State, or the adjacent parts of several States. Finally, all the Annual Conferences are bound together by what is called a "General Conference;" which is the ultimate appeal, and the supreme power of the Methodist Episcopal Church.

Thus it appears, that the organization of this church is as complete and compact as human ingenuity can well conceive. From the class of twelve persons, with its appointed leader, up to the controlling power of this whole organism, the system is perfect,—a wheel within a wheel, all working as moved by the supreme power, the General Conference.

(3) Our objection to this organization is, that it is not scriptural. Who hath required such a cunningly devised system of church government at your hands?

And we particularly object, that this organization places the government of the M. E. Church absolutely in the hands of its ministers and office-bearers, to the exclusion of the body of the church, where Christ and his apostles originally placed all church power.

The general government of this church is in the hands of convocations of the clergy and official persons of the M. E. Church, called "*Conferences.*" Of these, there are three sorts—General, Annual, and

Quarterly Conferences. The "General Conference" is composed of one member for every twenty-one members of each Annual Conference,—all ministers; meets once in four years; and has "full powers to make rules and regulations for [the] church," under certain limitations and restrictions.* The M. E. Church North contains thirty-nine ecclesiastical divisions, called "Annual Conferences," including Oregon, California, and Liberia, each of which divisions holds a yearly convocation of the clergy, called the Annual Conference. These are made up of "all the travelling preachers—both those who are in full connection and those who are on trial." The Bishops appoint the times of holding these Conferences, and a Bishop, or a presiding Elder appointed by him, presides in them; or, in case of failure of these, a presiding officer may be chosen by the Conference. These Annual Conferences have the care of the church within their respective bounds. The general condition of the ministers and societies is inquired into; also "what amounts are necessary for the superannuated preachers, and the widows and orphans of preachers, and to make up the deficiencies of those who have not obtained their regular allowance on the circuits; and, what has been collected for Mission, Sunday School, Tract, and Bible Society purposes. This Conference likewise attends to the electing and ordaining of deacons and elders, and inquires where the preachers of the Conference are to be stationed during the year; their appointments,

* *Discipline*, p. 32–40.

and those of the presiding elders being fixed and changed by the Bishops.*

The "Quarterly Conferences" are composed of "all the travelling and local preachers, exhorters, stewards, and class leaders of the circuit or station, and none else;" though the male superintendents of Sunday Schools and the Missionary Committee have a right to sit and act with the Conference while questions relative to these objects are before the Conference; but at no other time.† The Presiding Elder of the District, or "the preacher in charge" presides over this Conference; the regular business of which is, to hear complaints, and to receive and try appeals; to get an estimate of the amount necessary for fuel, and table expenses for the family or families of the preacher or preachers of the circuit or station; to take cognizance of all the local preachers in the circuit or station; to license proper persons to preach, and renew their license annually; to recommend to the Annual Conference suitable candidates in the local connection for deacon's or elder's orders and for admission on trial in the travelling connection; and to try, suspend, expel, or acquit any local preacher in the circuit or station against whom charges may be brought; to appoint stewards (the preacher in charge having the right to nominate); and generally, to look after the local affairs of the circuit or station.‡

The General Conference, composed entirely of

---

* *Discipline*, p. 34–37, 40, 43, 45, 47.

† *Discipline*, p. 37, 38, Chap. III. § 4.

‡ *Discipline*, p. 37–40.

travelling preachers, elects and ordains the bishops; the bishops preside in the Conferences, form the Districts according to their judgment, fix the appointments of preachers; in the intervals of the Conferences, change, receive, and suspend preachers, "as necessity may require and as the discipline directs;" travel through the connections at large; oversee the spiritual and temporal business of the church; ordain bishops, elders, and deacons; and decide all questions of law in an Annual Conference, subject to an appeal to the General Conference.* In addition to these important, responsible duties, the bishops choose, station, and change the Presiding Elders; whose business it is to travel through their appointed districts, and, in the absence of the bishop, take charge of all the elders and deacons, travelling and local preachers, and exhorters in his district; to change, receive, and suspend preachers and fill vacancies in his district, during the intervals of the conferences and in the absence of the bishop; and in general, "to oversee the spiritual and temporal business of the church in his district." † Next to the Presiding Elder, in this hierarchal system, is the Elder, Deacon, or Preacher, who has "the special charge of a circuit." It is his duty to see that the other preachers in his circuit "behave well, and want nothing;" to renew the tickets for the admission of members into love feasts, quarterly; to regulate the bands (little associations of three or four believers for personal, religious improvement); and to meet

---

* *Discipline*, p. 40–43.

† *Discipline*, p. 43–45.

the steward and leaders as often as possible; to examine the accounts of the stewards; to appoint all the Class Leaders, and "to change them when he sees it necessary;" to receive, try, and expel members, according to the form of the Discipline; and generally, to look after the temporal and spiritual interests of his circuit.*

The discipline provides (Part I. ch. 9, § 4), that an accused member shall be brought to trial before the society of which he is a member, or a select number of them, in the presence of a bishop, elder, or deacon, or preacher; and if found guilty, expelled. But if the minister or preacher differ in judgment from the majority of the society, or the select number, concerning the innocence or guilt of the accused person, the trial, in such case, may be referred by the minister or preacher to the ensuing Quarterly Conference, which shall finally determine the case. Excluded members, also, have the right of appeal to this Conference.

In relation to the admission of members to the church, it does not appear from the Discipline that the churches, or local societies of believers, are called to vote. Part I. ch. 2, § 2, p. 30, directs that "none be received into the church until they are recommended by a leader with whom they have met at least six months on trial, and have been baptized; and shall on examination by the minister in charge, before the church, give satisfactory assurances, both of the correctness of their faith and their willingness to observe and keep the rules of the church." And in order

---

* *Discipline*, p. 58–63.

to be more exact in receiving and excluding members, the official minister or preacher is directed, at every quarterly meeting, to read the names of those that are received into the church, and also those that are excluded therefrom. But from all this, it does not appear that a vote of the church is essential to the reception or the rejection of a member.

Now, from this brief and summary survey of the order and discipline of the Methodist Episcopal Church (North) of the U. S. it must be apparent, that the government of this church is not in the hands of the *brethren of the church*, where Christ and his apostles placed it, and where it long remained; but has been engrossed, almost completely, by the ministers of the church.

John Wesley was certainly right, when he said of himself and his Methodist friends, — WE ARE NO REPUBLICANS.* And Richard Watson, a standard writer among the Methodists, but echoed Mr. Wesley's sentiments, when he said: "A popular form of church government . . . could only be tolerable, in very small, isolated societies, and that in times of their greatest simplicity and love." † Mr. Wesley's notions of church government were highly monarchical, if not despotic. Bishop Coke and Asbury tell us, that "Mr. Wesley, as the venerable founder (under God) of the whole Methodist Society, *gov-*

---

* See *Letter to John Mason.* — "As long as I live," said Mr. Wesley, "*the people* shall have no share in choosing either stewards or leaders among the Methodists."

† *Theol. Institutes*, Part IV. ch. 1, republished in New York by M. E. Book Concern.

erned without any responsibility whatever. . . . He was the patron of all the Methodist pulpits in Great Britain and Ireland for life; the sole right of nomination being invested in him by all the deeds of settlement; which gave him exceeding great power." *

The present Methodist Episcopal Church in the United States, received its first bishops from the hands of Mr. Wesley; and if not actually organized by him, was shaped, and for some time controlled, by men imbued with his spirit. The first preachers of the denomination in this country, came from Ireland and England, in 1766–1771; and in 1784 Mr. Wesley sent over three regularly ordained clergy; but "preferring the episcopal mode of church government to any other, he solemnly set apart, by the imposition of his hands and prayer, one of them, namely, Thomas Coke, doctor of civil law, late of Jesus College, in the University of Oxford, and a presbyter of the Church of England, for the episcopal office, and having delivered to him letters of episcopal orders, commissioned and directed him to set apart Francis Asbury, then General Assistant of the Methodist Society in America, for the same episcopal office," &c. And Mr. Asbury having been set apart accordingly, was, with Mr. Coke, then received by the General Conference, held at Baltimore, as their bishops, "being fully satisfied of the validity of their episcopal ordination." †

It is for the reader to judge between Episcopal

---

* See *Bishop Hedding on Meth. Discip.*, Zion's Herald, Dec. 1, 1841.

† *Discipline*, p. 13 and 14.

Methodism and Congregationalism, "whether of the twain" is the more scriptural in its character.

PRESBYTERIANISM.

Let us next look at Presbyterianism. I denominate this *aristocratical*, because it recognizes no presiding and controlling head, under the title of a bishop, but commits the government of the church to the ministers and a few select persons from the churches. Its clergy are all on a footing of equality. Each congregation has the right of electing its own officers.* These consist of a pastor, ruling elders, and

---

* They cannot, however, *call* a pastor except it be *through* the Presbytery to which the church belongs. Neither can they have a pastor ordained or installed over them, except it be by the consent and concurrence of their own presbytery, and that with which the candidate is connected. — See "*Form of Gov.*" ch. 15 and 16. I am now speaking of American Presbyterianism. In Scotland, Presbyterianism is the Established and endowed religion of the State. This took place in 1592, after a struggle of about fifty years with Popery and Prelacy; and, after several changes, was confirmed soon after the Revolution in 1688; and thus has continued to the present time. This connection of Church and State has given the State a right to legislate for the Church, and has introduced the law of Lay Patronage. This law takes from the several parishes the right to elect their pastors. The patron of the living has the right to present any duly qualified minister to a vacant parish; and the presbytery, within whose bounds the vacant parish lies, is obliged to receive such presented minister. Great opposition to this law has of late appeared; and the Presbyterian Church is now in a ferment upon this subject.

In other respects, the order and government of the Scottish Kirk is substantially the same with the Presbyterian Church of

deacons, in number according to the wants of the congregation. Thus far the difference between Congregationalism and Presbyterianism is not so essential: but, from this point the two denominations rapidly diverge.

(1) A radical difference between us is found in our definitions of *a church.* One of the "radical principles of Presbyterian church government is, that the several different congregations of believers, *taken collectively* constitute *one church* of Christ, called emphatically — *The Church.*"* This principle is the groundwork of all our differences in respect to church government and discipline.

(2) Acting upon this principle each Presbyterian congregation is governed, not by the united brethren thereof, but by "*The Church Session;*" that is, by the pastor and ruling elders of the congregation, who are "charged with maintaining the spiritual government of the congregation: for which purpose, they have power to inquire into the knowledge and Christian conduct of the members of the Church; to call before them offenders and witnesses, being mem-

---

the United States — *McCulloch*, vol. ii. ch. 7, § 3. — *Blackwood's Mag.* for Dec. 1840 and Aug. 1841.

Since the above was written, this ferment has burst forth into a secession of nearly five hundred ministers of the Church of Scotland, embracing a large proportion of the piety and talent of the Establishment. These men have separated from the National Kirk, surrendered their livings, organized themselves into a new body, under the title of *The Free Church of Scotland*, and thrown themselves on the voluntary contributions of the people for a support.

* See "*Form of Government of Presbyterian Chh. in U. S.*" p. 397. 18mo. 1821.

bers of their own congregation, and to introduce other witnesses, where it may be necessary to bring the process to issue, and when they can be procured to attend; to receive members into the church; to admonish and rebuke, to suspend, or exclude from the sacraments those who are found to deserve censure; to concert the best measures for promoting the spiritual interests of the congregation; and to appoint delegates to the higher judicatories of the church." *

Thus it appears, that "The Church Session" is, virtually, *the church.* A few leading men are invested with authority to control and manage all the affairs of the congregation. And these men are *permanent* officers, independent of the congregation, and, after their election, not subject at all to the controlling voice of the brethren. They can be removed from office only by death, or regular trial for misdemeanors. I speak particularly of the ruling elders, who are considered as the representatives of the congregation. The pastor, if obnoxious, may undoubtedly be induced to remove by other means; but not without the concurrence of the Presbytery. The government of each congregation is, then, to all intents and purposes, *aristocratical.*

(3) From the decisions of this court, *The Session,* an appeal may be made to a higher, called "*The Presbytery.*" This is composed "of all the ministers, and one ruling elder from each congregation within a certain district," larger or smaller, according to circumstances. The Presbytery has, substan-

---

* *Plan of Gov.* ch. 10, § 6.

tially, the same power over *all* the congregations within its limits, that the Church Session has over a single congregation.

(4) From the decisions of this second judicatory, an appeal may be made to a third, called "*The Synod.*" This is composed of the ministers and elders of at least three presbyteries. This court exercises a controlling influence and authority over all the presbyteries, church sessions, and congregations within its bounds.

(5) From this body an appeal may be carried up to the "General Assembly;" which is the highest judicatory of the Presbyterian church. This is the end of controversy; or, perhaps I should say — the reservoir into which all obstinate controversy finally runs, there to be disposed of as it best can be.* This body is thus constituted: Every presbytery is entitled to send one minister and one ruling elder; and, if the presbytery embraces more than nine ministers, it may send two ministers, and an equal number of ruling elders; and so on, one minister and one elder for every nine ministers in any presbytery. The

---

* The Secession Church of Scotland, a large and increasing body of Presbyterians, differs from the Established Church (1) in having no General Assembly; the Synod, which meets twice a year, being their highest Ecclesiastical court; (2) in abjuring patronage; (3) in giving the right to choose its own pastor, to the communicants of each congregation. — *McCulloch*, ut sup. Sect. 4.

The "New-School" Presbyterians (as they are often called) of this country, agree with the Secession, in making their Synods the highest judicatory body. Their General Assembly, which meets but once in three years, has no appellate jurisdiction.

General Assembly has the same authority over the whole Church that each of the inferior judicatories has over the particular portion assigned to its care. It is the bond of union among all the congregations. It is the General Assembly of the Presbyterian Church in the United States — *The Presbyterian Church itself.*

No one will deny that this system of church government is orderly and methodical; that its movements are systematic and regular: but the question at issue is — Where is the Scriptural model and authority for all this? I go not into the specification of objections to this system — I will not dwell upon the recent developments of the workings of this consolidated system; but, with the Scriptures in his hands, I put it to any unbiassed mind to decide, which is the more Scriptural form of church government, the Presbyterian or the Congregational.

OTHER DENOMINATIONS.

The Lutheran Church on the Continent of Europe, holds an intermediate position between Episcopacy and Presbyterianism, except in Denmark and Sweden, where the Episcopal form prevails — or rather, Romanism "with its offensive parts lopped off."

The sovereigns of the respective countries in which Lutheranism is established, "possess the supreme power in Ecclesiastical affairs." The highest Ecclesiastical tribunal is the *Consistory,* which is composed of civil and ecclesiastical jurists, who manage the affairs of the Church in the name of their respective sovereigns. Where the Episcopal form prevails, it is rather on the ground of expediency, than from any belief in its Divine origin: "for the Lutherans are persuaded, that, by Divine right, there is no difference of rank and prerogatives among the ministers of the Gospel." * They admit of Superintendents — sometimes called inspectors, seniors, or presidents — who have the oversight of ministers and ecclesiastical affairs, but are superior to other ministers only in office. The churches use liturgies, practise confirmation, confession, and absolution. Their liturgies, though essentially the same in the articles of religion, differ widely in different countries; and are much more simple than those of strictly Episcopal Churches, and admit of more liberty in using them.

It is deemed unnecessary to go into any further comparison of different forms of church order and discipline. All other denominations are believed to recognize more or less of the general principles of government which have been already considered; and may be classed under one or other of these great denominations, as the peculiarities of one or the other predominate. *The Calvinist Baptists* are Congregationalists in their government. Indeed, they are one with us, so far as the principles of church polity are concerned. *The Freewill Baptists* recognize a form of government, and order, substantially Congregational. "Government is vested primarily in the churches, which are usually composed of such

---

* *Mosheim*, B. IV. Cent. XVI. Part II. ch. 1, § 3, 4.

believers as can meet together for worship."* *The Protestant Methodists*, or Reformed Methodists have introduced into their government the *representative* principle — allowing the laity an equal voice with the clergy in their church judicatories. They do not recognize the order of bishops, as distinct from that of elders; but, in most other particulars, symbolize with the Protestant Episcopal Church, in their government. "*The Christian Connection*" maintain the strict independence of the churches. So do the *Unitarians*.

Believing Congregationalism to be entirely Scriptural, we are constrained to regard this form of church order and discipline as *more* correct and Scriptural than any other, in just that proportion in which any other varies, in essential particulars, from this. And in the maintenance of this opinion of our favorite model, we do not regard ourselves as guilty of any arrogance in relation to other systems; for, consistently with our principles, we can do no less than to esteem our own above all others. We maintain that the Scriptures are a sufficient guide to all that is essential to the good order and correct discipline of a church of Christ. We have carefully examined the Scriptures to ascertain what this order and discipline should be; and have arrived at conclusions, which these pages partially, at least, detail. We have compared this system with others, and have briefly detailed the result: and if, in our investigations and

---

* *Elder Beede*, in Relig. Encyclopedia. See also the Appendix to their "Treatise on the Faith of the F. W. B."

our deductions we have not erred, then, in our conclusion we are correct, that—*of all the systems of church government known to us, Congregationalism is the most Scriptural.* And this we conceive to be one of the advantages—and not a trifling one, either—which this system possesses over every other.

II. Another advantage of Congregationalism is, that *it encourages self-government beyond that of any other system.*

In proportion as you abridge men of the privilege of governing themselves, and deprive them of the inducements to attempt it, in just that degree you encourage the doctrine that they are *incapable* of self-government, and discourage all attempts to exercise this inalienable and all-important right. Now, the Congregational system of church government, beyond all others, encourages every man to exercise this important birthright. It teaches him that Christ has intrusted the management of his kingdom upon arth to the hands of his people, with certain general rules for their guidance. And he who has learned from the Scriptures that Christ has committed such interests to his people, will not be slow to perceive, that if men are judged competent to manage affairs which pertain to their eternal interests, there is a gross inconsistency in denying their ability to manage affairs which pertain only to the present life. The direct tendency of this system of church government, then, is to a democratical form of State government.

The early English Congregationalists seem to have had no design upon the State when they asserted their rights as Christians; indeed, they expressly avowed their cordial attachment to the monarchical, and all but despotic government under which they lived. And this was true of the Brownists even, the pioneers of our denomination, who were rigid separatists from the Episcopal Church, and often violent in their denunciations against those who upheld it; and who denied the right of State governments to interfere at all with the affairs of the churches.

Penry, one of the last of the Brownists who suffered death for his religious sentiments during the reign of Elizabeth, when accused of disloyalty, protested against the accusation; declaring that the queen had a daily remembrance in his prayers; and with his dying breath, sent to her majesty the assurance of his loyalty.* Nevertheless, the politicians of those times were not slow to perceive the natural tendency of these principles of church government; and could not be persuaded that the men who claimed independence in church matters, did not aim at the same independence in civil affairs. Hence it was, that the persecution of the Brownists during Elizabeth's arbitrary reign, was even more violent than that of the Protestants under the bloody Mary, Elizabeth's Popish predecessor.

However it may have been with the English Independents while they remained in their native land, it is very obvious that the Leyden church early entertained democratical prepossessions in respect to civil

---

* See an account of Penry's martyrdom in *Waddington's Life of John Penry*, or in the *History of Congregationalism*. See note, *ante*, p. 14.

government. How much influence their residence in Holland may have had in modifying their views, it is difficult to say; but it is certain that the very first act of the emigrating Pilgrims, in a civil capacity, was one which savored strongly of democracy. Before landing upon the rock of Plymouth, they drew up and subscribed an instrument, by which they covenanted and combined together "*into a civil body politic*; to enact, constitute, and frame such just and equal laws and ordinances, acts, constitutions, and officers, from time to time, as should be thought most meet and convenient for the general good of the colony." "This brief, but comprehensive constitution of civil government," says Pitkin, "contained the elements of those forms of government peculiar to the new world."

From the outset, the English government was jealous of the spirit of independence manifested by the Pilgrims; and, to counteract this, the project of introducing *Episcopacy* and a Governor-general into the colonies of New England, was early entertained by the Court. The commissioners appointed by Charles II., in 1664, to visit New England, with "full power and authority to heare and receive, and to examine and determine all complaints and appeales, in all cases and matters;" or in other words, to overturn the government of the colonies if not found sufficiently loyal — reported of Massachusetts: "Their way of government is *Commonwealth-like;* their way of worship is rude, and called *Congregational*." * The last

* *Hutchinson*, Vol. I. App. No. 15, and *Am. Encyc.*, Art. New England.

word in this sentence, whether by design or not, explains the first clause. That the English government was prepared to believe this report, is evident from the fact, that Lord Clarendon, in his draft of the plan for sending over commissioners, declared that the colonies "*were already hardened into republics.*" And when the struggle for civil independence actually began in this country, it was found that New England, the hotbed of Congregationalism — in which, in 1760, there were 440,000 Congregationalists, out of 500,000 inhabitants — was also "the hotbed" of revolutionary principles. And to this form of *Church* government, we unquestionably owe our peculiarly free and excellent forms of *State* government.*

To those who regard a democratical form of government as the inalienable gift of God and birthright of man, it will be no slight recommendation of Congregationalism, that it favors, if it does not unavoidably lead to, this form of civil government.†

---

* "Several years before the American Revolution, there was, near the house of Mr. Jefferson, in Virginia, a church which was governed on Congregational principles, and whose monthly meeting he often attended. Being asked, how he was pleased with the church government, he replied, that it had struck him with great force, and interested him very much; that he considered it the *only form of pure democracy that then existed in the world*, and had concluded that it would be the best plan of government for the American colonies." — See an able article on Congregationalism in *Encyclopedia of Religious Knowledge.*

† A writer in the *London Quarterly Review* (Vol. XVI. p. 517, 518), says: "It soon became apparent (in the reign of Elizabeth in England) that they (the Puritans) *tended naturally towards republicanism;* for certain it is, that *monarchy* and *Episcopacy*,

III. Another important advantage of this popular form of church government is, that *it promotes general intelligence beyond any other.*

As no people are fit to manage their civil affairs unless intelligent and virtuous, so no body of men are qualified to conduct ecclesiastical affairs who are destitute of intelligence and piety. The motive in either case to be qualified for self-government is wellnigh irresistible. Every Congregationalist is ex-

---

the throne and the altar, are much more nearly connected than writers of bad faith, or little reflection have sought to persuade mankind. Besides *this insensible, but natural inclination towards democracy, which arises from the principles of* a *popular church government*, there was another cause why the current should set in that direction; it was only under Commonwealths that the Puritans saw their beloved discipline flourish."

So, Bishop Laud told Charles I. and his second parliament: "They, whoever they be, that would overthrow '*sedes ecclesiæ*,' the seats of ecclesiastical government, [alias, the bishops' thrones], will not spare — if ever they get power — to have a pluck at the 'throne of David,' [i. e. the monarchy of the kingdom.] And, there is not a man that is for *parity*, — all fellows, in the Church, — but he is not for monarchy in the State. And certainly, either he is but half-headed to his own principles, or he can be but half-hearted to the house of David." Or, in plain English — no man can be an enemy to Episcopacy, and yet a friend to monarchy. — See *Hanbury's Historical Memorials*, Vol. I. p. 476.

Thus, too, that organ of Toryism in Church and State, Blackwood, tells us, that "the anomaly of a popularly elected church [he is protesting against the right of the people to elect their own spiritual guides] and a hereditary monarchy cannot co-exist in the same country." And again he asks: "If the cause of universal suffrage is triumphant in the *Church*, how is it to be resisted in the *State?*" — *Magazine*, Vol. XI. No. 6, Art. "Non-Intrusion Question."

pected to take part in the most important business that is done on earth — the business of the Church of Christ. He recognizes his accountability to Christ for the manner in which he does the work assigned him. He feels — if he feels as he ought — that there is deep responsibility incurred by him. Acting under this conviction, he is constrained to seek that preparation of heart and mind which will fit him to act well his part as a Congregational professor.

I do not say, that such are actually the feelings and practice of all who embrace this form of church government; for many, we have reason to fear, are merely *nominal* Congregationalists, have little acquaintance with the nature and operation of the principles which they profess, and no suitable sense of the responsibilities which they incur in transacting the momentous business of a christian church. I speak not of all who profess this system, but of the *tendency* of the system itself, and of its *actual results* in multitudes of instances.*

In saying what I have of the tendencies of Congregationalism, I would not be understood to intimate, that other Protestant denominations do not encourage intelligence and piety among their members; but this I do say, — that the more free any

---

* I have somewhere met with the remark, that the French nation were much less frivolous immediately after their late revolution than before. The responsibility of sustaining the government for which they had fought, made them comparatively grave. A sense of responsibility always makes men thoughtful and sober-minded.

system of government is, and the greater the responsibility laid upon men, the stronger will be the motive to be intelligent, in order to manage that government and to meet that responsibility. Now, as in no denomination so much is expected of the members of a church as in ours, so, in none are intelligence and other suitable qualifications for church membership so urgently demanded. Other forms of church government favor these things just in proportion as they approach towards, or recede from, the standard of pure Congregationalism.*

---

* In reply to a letter of inquiry, whether there were any Congregational churches in a particular section of our country; an intelligent correspondent says—"No." And assigns as a reason, the want of general intelligence among the people of that section of country. "I do sincerely think," says my correspondent, "that out of New England, it is exceedingly difficult to make Congregational churches live; and why? Because, out of New England, there is (comparatively speaking) only here and there an enlightened man. He must be an elder and take care of the rest."

I give this extract, in illustration of what is said in the text; not because I accord entirely with my correspondent. Another correspondent, equally intelligent, and with far more extensive observation and experience, writing from a city full of Presbyterianism and Episcopacy, tells me, that Congregationalism *can* live and flourish at the South or the West, if good men will but try it, and boldly and faithfully maintain its precious principles and usages. This I most fully believe. Facts, as well as reason, testify to this truth. What surer method to keep men ignorant and unfit to govern themselves can be pursued, than to persuade them that they are so? and to adopt a system of church government (or civil, if you please) which makes no demand on them for intelligence?

Richard Watson, a standard author among the Methodists, grounds an objection to "a popular form of church government"

Some of the legitimate effects of this system are seen in the early efforts of the Pilgrims to establish schools and seminaries of learning, as well as to plant churches and to propagate the gospel, in this land of their exile; for these schools were established, mainly, as auxiliaries to the churches. Scarcely had these venerable men felled the forest of New England, when they began to provide means to insure the continuance of their churches and the stability of their civil government. "Learning and Religion," they wisely judged to be "the firmest pillars of the church and the commonwealth." Harvard College, which had previously existed as a high school,* was established at Cambridge as early as

---

on the supposed ignorance and youth and inexperience of the mass of every religious community. He speaks with a sort of holy horror, of "referring every decision to numbers and suffrages, and placing all that is good, and venerable, and influential among the members themselves, at the feet of *a democracy*." — *Theological Institutes*, Part IV. Chap. I.

Congregationalism unquestionably demands a greater measure of religious intelligence in the mass of the church, than any other system of church government. And it is too obvious to require argument, that the very necessity for intelligence, will, with good men, be a strong inducement to become intelligent. And, it seems to me altogether reasonable to believe, that in those very communities where it is now supposed that the want of intelligence forbids the existence of Congregational churches, there would have been a vastly greater amount of religious knowledge and general intelligence, if such churches had long ago been there established. If the intelligence of New England originally established Congregationalism, it is equally true, that Congregationalism has preserved for New England that intelligence.

* "In 1636 the general court gave £400 towards a public school at Newton." — *Hutchinson*.

1638; *eighteen years*, only, after the landing of the Plymouth pilgrims, and only eight or ten years after the commencement of the Massachusetts colony.

To Congregational principles we are indebted for most of the colleges of New England. From the same source has flowed down to us that system of common schools which, notwithstanding its defects, has so long and so richly blessed our land and the world. The same spirit has founded and endowed the Theological Seminaries of New England. The influence of Congregationalism in establishing theological and literary Institutions at the South and West, is well known.

Can any man consider the facts now alluded to, without perceiving that this system of church order and discipline is preëminently favorable to general intelligence? *

---

* Pitkin, in his *Civil and Political History of the United States*, says: — "Primary Schools first commenced in New England. Aware of the importance and necessity of information among the people, in order to secure and perpetuate their liberties, the legislators of New England, at an early period, made provision for instructing all in the first rudiments of learning. In this, the *clergy*, who were not less distinguished for their literature than their piety, cordially coöperated. In making this provision for the general and early education of their children, their views were not limited to the single object, though an important one, of making them better men and better citizens, but, what was justly deemed by them of infinitely more importance — better Christians. . . . .

"Schools for general education were established in Boston, in 1635, by the inhabitants of that town; and in 1647, the legislature of Massachusetts declared, by a general law, 'that every township with fifty families, should provide a school, where chil-

IV. Another advantage of this system of church government and discipline is, that *it presents the most*

---

dren may be taught to read and write; and that every township of one hundred families, should provide a grammar school, where youth could be fitted for the University.' This law was substantially adopted in the code of laws established by the colony of Connecticut, in 1650, with a preamble, declaring, in the quaint language of the day, that, 'It being one chief object of that old deceiver, Satan, to keep men from the knowledge of the Scriptures, as in former times, keeping them in an unknown tongue, so in these latter times, by persuading them from the use of tongues, so that at least, the true sense of the *original* might be clouded by false glosses of saints-seeming deceivers; and that learning may not be buried in the graves of our forefathers in church and commonwealth,' etc.

"In the system of New Haven colonial laws, published in 1656, it is ordered, 'that the deputy for the particular court, in each plantation in this jurisdiction, for the time being, or where there are no such deputies, the constables and other officers in public trust, shall, from time to time, have a vigilant eye on their brethren and neighbors, within the limits of said plantations, that all parents and masters do duly endeavor, either by their own ability or labor, or by improving such schoolmasters or other helps and means as the plantation doth afford, or the family may conveniently provide, that all their children and apprentices, as they are capable, may, through God's blessing, obtain, at least, so much as to be able to read the Scriptures and other good and profitable books in the English tongue, being their native language, etc.'

"In 1663, it was proposed by the court of Plymouth colony, to the several towns within that jurisdiction, as a thing that they ought to take into their serious consideration, that some course may be taken, that in *every town* there may be a schoolmaster set up, to train up children to reading and writing.

"These laws laid the foundation of the system of free schools in New England." — Vol. I. p. 151, 152.

In estimating the influence of Congregationalism in promoting

efficient barrier to the inroads of heresy, and false doctrine, and general corruption.

I am not ignorant, that some persons regard Congregationalism as the very parent and nurse of all heresy, and the fruitful cause of all errors in doctrine and religious practice with which the country is now, or ever has been, afflicted. The freedom of our government — the right which our churches claim, to choose whom they will for pastors, and to adopt what articles of faith, and to pursue what particular practices they please, are regarded by many as exceedingly objectionable — not to say abominable peculiarities. But these features of our system are, after all, the best rampart against general defection and corruption. The very liberties of our churches — so terrific in the eyes of those who plead for a "strong government" — are, under God, our surest defence against universal defection. That this liberty may not be abused, I shall not contend. That any other than a virtuous people are capable of self-government, I do not believe. That the Congregational system of church government is unsuited to any but truly pious persons, I have already asserted: for none others was it designed. But for these, it is admirably adapted. An unconverted, proud, ambitious, worldly minded church member may, perhaps, do more injury in a Congregational church, than in

---

general intelligence, let it be borne in mind, that these laws were emphatically *Congregational* — that nearly every man concerned in the formation and execution of them, was a decided Congregationalist.

any other.* For men of this description our church government was never designed. Such men, however intelligent, have not the first qualification for church membership. But, let our churches be constituted as they ought to be, and kept pure by discipline, and there will be no danger of intrusting to them the power of electing their own officers, making their own by-laws, and regulating all their own affairs, under Christ.

It may perhaps be said: "It is impossible to keep out unworthy members; they are in the church now, and they will always be found there." It is true, this matter demands great watchfulness on the part of our churches; and after all, some unworthy members may creep in: if, however, the great mass of any particular church be sound and pious, there will be, under ordinary circumstances, comparatively little danger from the unsoundness of a few individuals. Certain it is, that there is much less danger that the majority of a church will become unsound and heretical, than that a few men, constituted governors of the church, will swerve from the faith. Every system of church government which takes the power out of the hands of the brethren — or the church itself — places it in the hands of individuals. Now, it appears to us that the danger to the church will be in proportion to the *fewness* of those who take part in her government and are interested in the maintenance of her orthodoxy: that is to say, there will be more danger that *one* man will become unsound and heretical,

* Unless he should chance to be a "vestry-man" or a "ruling elder."

than that *five* will; and more danger that *five* will swerve from the truth, than that *one hundred* will. Samuel Mather well says: "When a bishop or a small number of ministers [and he might have said — or laymen] have the supervision, or oversight and management of affairs, it is next to impossible but that pride and ambition, faction and envy, political regards and secular interests, should govern; and indeed, this is no more than what is observed by the historians, Socrates and Sozomen, as well as by several other Fathers." *

Upon this subject, Ecclesiastical History lifts an admonitory voice. It is notorious, that when the control of the churches fell into the hands of synods, then the purity of the churches began visibly and rapidly to decline. This declension became more serious, as the influence of *many* in the government of the churches diminished to a *few;* and it became *total,* when "THE MAN OF SIN" mounted the Papal throne and claimed to be the Head of the Church — the Vicegerent of Christ — the Infallible Interpreter of the mind of the Spirit — and the Unerring Guide of the Faithful.

Now, inasmuch as our Congregational polity places all church power in the hands of the brethren of the church, it provides a very important safeguard against the inroads of heresy.

I anticipate an objection to these remarks, founded on the fact that Arminianism and Unitarianism have corrupted so many of the Congregational churches of New England. With persons not well acquainted

---

* *Apology,* p. 104.

with our history, this is considered a sufficient and conclusive argument against our System. But I must take the liberty to say to such persons — You understand not whereof you affirm. It was not *Congregationalism* which introduced Unitarianism into New England; but it was the disregard of Congregational principles, even by some of the Fathers of our churches, which opened the way for Unitarianism.

The half-way covenant, and afterwards, the admission of baptized, but unregenerate persons to the Lord's Supper as "a converting ordinance" — were the things which broke down our defences, and introduced unconverted men into the churches and the ministry, and prepared the way for the prevalence of Arminianism, and after that, of Unitarianism. I will only add, that this objection to our system comes with a peculiarly ill grace from our Presbyterian brethren; because Stoddard, the leader in these innovations upon our church polity, was himself, "in principle, a Presbyterian, and hoped to introduce substantially that mode of government" into New England.*

Again, the *independency* † of our churches, furnishes a further barrier against general defection from the faith. The more closely you connect the different communities of Christian professors, for purposes of government, the more readily are they affected by each other. Bring these associated com-

---

* *Dwight's Life of Edwards*, p. 381 — quoted in "The Great Awakening," p. 5. See also *Allen's Biog. Dictionary*, Art. Stoddard.

† I mean not absolute independency — but, *completeness — all-sufficiency* for their own government, etc., as before explained.

munities under the government of one man, or of a few men, and you increase the danger of corruption in the whole mass in proportion to the intimacy of the association and the influence and power of its governors. But, should a Congregational church become heretical in its faith and erroneous in its practice, it will not necessarily affect sister churches. It cannot injure them except by the force of bad example. Each church, standing independently of every other so far as its internal management is concerned, has the means of defence in its own hands. It can shut the door, and no man can open it.

Then, in respect to its *teachers*, this system furnishes as complete a barrier against false and dangerous doctrine as it is possible to raise. It recognizes no man's right to send to a church a preacher, or to place over it a pastor. We know no Metropolitan — no General or Yearly Conference, having authority to say to this man, go, and he goeth; and to another come, and he cometh; — no Presbytery to tells us whether we may, or may not, call a pastor. Each church judges and chooses for itself. Every brother in the church has a perfect right to object to the call of a pastor; and every man's vote counts equally in an election. The whole church being constituted judges, and being qualified by intelligence and piety to act their parts, the danger of being imposed upon by an unsuitable man is comparatively small; especially, if the scrupulous care of our fathers in trying their candidates for settlement, be imitated by their sons.*

* It was not uncommon for candidates for settlement, to be on trial for several months before they received a call. Our

But, should a pastor prove an unsound and dangerous man, his influence does not necessarily affect any church but his own: and this has the power to discipline the offender, and thus to bring him to repentance; or, at least, to purge out the leaven from their own body, and to make known his true character to others, and thus to impair his ability to injure them.

Thus does Congregationalism protect the churches from heresy and error. Thus does it provide a simple but effectual remedy, in case all previous caution should fail, for the extirpation of every thing false and dangerous.

It is not denied, that notwithstanding all, errors in doctrine and practice have crept into our churches. And into what denomination of professing Christians have they not gone? Who — what — can guard effectually against the depravity and deceitfulness of human nature? A Judas was among "the twelve." A Simon Magus, and "damnable heresies" corrupted the apostolic churches. Congregationalists claim not entire exemption from error. But, who shall cast the first stone at us? Shall the Church of Rome? We point her to "the mark of the beast"

---

fathers had no fellowship with the *touch-and-take* system of modern days.

John Milton's answer to such as object, that the brethren of a church are not competent to judge of the qualifications of a pastor, deserves repeating: "Many," says he, "may be able to judge who is fit to be made a minister, that would not be found fit to be made ministers themselves; as it will not be denied that he may be the competent judge of a neat picture, or elegant poem, that cannot limn the like." — *Hanbury*, Vol. I. p. 192, note.

upon her forehead. Shall the high-church Episcopacy of England? We beg her to stop long enough to reflect on the Arminianism of Laud's administration, and the rapid strides which she made towards Popery itself during his reign. Or, if she prefer something of later date, we point to the admitted diversity of religious sentiment which now exists among her clergy; and this, too, upon fundamental points, in spite of her liturgy, and creed, and subscriptions, and test-oaths.* Shall the Protestant

---

* A clergyman of the Church of England, Rev. John Acaster, vicar of St. Helen's, York, in a work entitled, "The Church of England in Danger from Itself," fully admits the truth of the assertion in the text. He says: "To this (the neglect of a proper examination of the candidates for the ministry), more than to any other thing must be ascribed *that great difference of opinion which exists among her ministers*, ON SOME OF THE MOST IMPORTANT DOCTRINES OF RELIGION, *dangerous to the souls of men, and inimical to the peace and stability of the church*," p. 44; quoted by Rev. J. A. James, in his "*Defence of the Principles of Nonconformity*," p. 75.

In a note to the above, Mr. James adds: "No one can for a moment doubt, that the Church of England comprehends within her pale, persons holding *the widest possible variety of religious opinions:* Socinians, Arians, Arminians—from Pelagianism to the modified Arminianism of Tillotson; Baxterians, Calvinists of all grades, from the supralapsarianism of Dr. Hawker to the more moderate views of Davenant and South; Hutchinsonians, Baptismal Regeneration Advocates, and their opponents; Swedenborgians, the followers of Joanna Southgate, modern Millenarians, Believers in the unconsciousness of the soul from death till the resurrection, Followers of Mr. Irving on the subject of the peccability of Christ's human nature, etc. etc."—*Ib.* p. 75, 76, note. This catalogue was made out in 1830; whether it should now be enlarged or diminished, on the whole, I am unable to say; but doubtless the author, were he now revising it, would

Episcopal church of this country, claim greater purity? Will it be denied, that even in this country, the line is becoming more and more distinct between high-church and low-church?—that it is not uncommon, even now, to designate their clergy as Evangelical or Arminian?—that the Oxford controversy is already fermenting in the bosom of the P. E. church of the U. S.? and that her bishops, and ministers, and laymen, are openly taking ground on either side? The very extensive prevalence of Arianism and Unitarianism among the Presbyterians of England, and the diversity of sentiment which prevails in the Presbyterian Church of the United States, prove the entire possibility of "grievous wolves" entering the Presbyterian fold, high as are its walls, guarded as are its entrances.

While, therefore, we claim not for our system of church order and discipline, that it is a complete defence from error—to which all denominations are more or less exposed—we confidently believe, that the Congregational churches of Great Britain and America, will bear a favorable comparison, in point of purity, with any denomination in either country.

---

add—Travellers towards Rome, under the title of PUSEYITES.

See Prof. Newman's admission, *Oxford Tracts*, Vol. I. p. 238, quoted in Smyth's "Apostolical Succession," p. 17. Among other things, Prof. Newman says: "In the English Church may be found differences as great as those which separate it from Greece or Rome—Calvinism and Arminianism, Latitudinarianism and Orthodoxy—all these, sometimes simply such, and sometimes compounded together into numberless varieties of school, . . . each denouncing all the rest as perilous, if not fatal errors."

It would be easy to swell this list of advantages of Congregationalism. But, if any thing like a just estimate of the system advocated in these pages has been expressed, there can be no occasion to say more, to commend to the consideration, to the confidence, and to the love of the descendants of the Pilgrims, a system which their fathers considered as essential to the highest welfare of their posterity, to the promotion of holiness in the land, and to the advancement of the Divine glory in the world.

CONCLUSION.

In conclusion, I commend to the friends of Congregationalism, the warning words of one of the fathers of New England, and the concluding address of one of the ablest defenders of our system: "Consider what will be the end of receding or making a defection from the way of church government established among us. I profess, I look upon the discovery and settlement of the Congregational way, as the boon, the gratuity, the largess of Divine bounty, which the Lord graciously bestowed on his people that followed Him into this wilderness; and a great part of the blessing on the head of Joseph, and of them who were separate from their brethren. These good people that came over, showed more love, zeal, and affectionate desire of communion with God in pure worship and ordinances, and did more in order to it than others; and the Lord did more for them, than for any people in the world, in showing them the pattern of His house, and the true scriptural way of church government and administrations. God was certainly in a more than ordinary way of favor present with his servants in laying of our foundations, and in settling the way of church order according to the will and appointment of Christ. Consider what will be the sad issue of revolting from the way fixed upon, to one extreme or to another, whether it be to Presbyterianism or Brownism; as for the Presbyterians, it must be acknowledged that there are among them, as pious, learned, sober, orthodox men, as the world affords; and that there is as much of the power of godliness among that party, and of the spirit of the good old Puritans, as among any people in the world. And for their way of church government, it must be confessed, that in the day of it, it was a very considerable step to reformation. The reformation in king Edward's days was then a blessed work. And the reformation of Geneva and Scotland was then a large step, and in many respects purer than the other. And for my part, I fully believe that the Congregational way far exceeds both, and is the highest step which has been taken towards reformation, and for the substance of it, it is the very same way that was established and practised in the primitive times, according to the institution of Jesus Christ." *

"Thus I have endeavored to state and vindicate the more distinguishing liberties of the churches in New England. As these privileges have been purchased by the blood of the Lord Jesus, they ought to

---

* Election Sermon of President Oaks of Harvard College, 1675–1681.—*Magnalia*, Vol. II. p. 64, 65.

be very precious in our esteem, nor, upon any pretence whatever, to be slighted and undervalued by the happy people who enjoy them.

"It is worthy to be always remembered by these churches, that it was not on account of any peculiar sentiments in doctrinal matters, that our wise and good fathers left their native country and came into this then howling wilderness; for they agreed to the doctrinal articles of the Church of England, as much as the Conformists to that Parliamentary Church, and indeed, much more so than most of them; but it was from a pure respect to ecclesiastical discipline and order, and to a more refined worship, that these excellent men, our ancestors, transported themselves, with their families, into this land.

"The Church of Rome, as far as in them lies, have divested our great Saviour of his prophetical, sacerdotal, and kingly offices; other churches have been so far overcome by the light of reason and revelation, that they have restored, as one may say, his sacerdotal office to him, and his prophetical office also: but our gracious predecessors, observing that their brethren in England were not willing to allow our Lord Jesus Christ to be the king and ruler of his church, nobly resolved, as the children of Zion, to acknowledge and rejoice in their king: and hence they quitted their ungrateful country, that so they might observe that refined worship and order, which their Lord and Sovereign had in his word appointed to be observed. It follows, therefore, that any degeneracies from the pure worship and scriptural order in these churches, would be a direct rejection of the kingly authority of Christ Jesus, and a means of setting up another king or captain to lead us backward, in the steps we have taken from Babylon, towards it again. May God of his rich grace, therefore, preserve these churches from any such degeneracies!

"It is evident, indeed, that great pains are taken to draw our people, especially our inconsiderate young people, who are too unmindful of the King and God of their fathers, from their love and attachment to those first principles of these churches, which I have been explaining and enforcing: but, as Naboth said to Ahab concerning his vineyard, in 1 Kings 21: 3,—'The Lord forbid it me, that I should give the inheritance of my fathers unto thee;' even so it is fit, that we should say to such as would entice us to part with the pure order of these churches, this was our father's inheritance; and God forbid, that any should persuade us to give up our inestimable rights; for the very thought of parting with them is shocking.

"Dear people, the liberties which have been challenged for you, are the same as the brethren in the times of primitive Christianity enjoyed for hundreds of years together: and, whatever specious pretences some may make to the contrary, the dispossessing of the brethren of these their valuable liberties, was a considerable instance of the Romish apostasy. And, indeed, they have but a slender acquaintance with ecclesiastical history, who do not know, that the rise of Popery was owing to the people's tamely giving up their rights and privileges, either through ignorance or imprudence, to the clergy; who unreasonably engrossed to themselves, and grasped in their own clutches, all things in the churches that were of any worth and importance.

" There can be no doubt, that there are many who are sworn and inveterate enemies to the pure order in these churches: and, besides these, we have reason to think that there are many false friends to it; by which sort, I mean those that pretend some regard to the order of the gospel in these churches, but yet, at the same time, would gladly subvert it. And it is well, if there are not sundry ministers in these churches, who are disaffected to it: for, as Luther has somewhere remarked concerning religion: *Nunquam magis periclitur quam inter reverendissimos;* so it may be said in respect to the order in these churches; probably it may be in most danger from some of the reverend body. But, surely, all such in these churches are very unadvised and blameworthy; and, if they are not duly sensible of the tendency of their disaffection and undertakings, it is a pity but their brethren should be, and carefully guard against them.

" And, in fine, much honored and entirely beloved churches; be pleased to accept of this attempt of one, the most unworthy of your sons; who, being set for the defence of the order of the gospel among you, has endeavored to illustrate and confirm that order in its primitive purity for your advantage. And wherein he has failed of giving the true sense of his and your fathers — though from a diligent search of their meaning he has endeavored it — be pleased to impute it to human frailty and undesigned mistaking; for into these alone his failing must be resolved.

"Ut desint vires, tamen est laudanda voluntas." *

* *Samuel Mather's Apology for the Liberties of the Churches in N. E.* p. 142–146. Published 1738.

APPENDIX.

[In the forms of letters, votes, etc. given in the following pages, I shall not of course be understood as settling the precise form in any given case; or, as intimating that a hundred other modes of expression may not be equally proper. But, having had occasion to know that intelligent church members, and even young ministers, are often at a loss how to express themselves suitably in communications of this description, I have thought that some brief forms would be acceptable, as guides to the general style, etc. of these documents. I have studied brevity, for obvious reasons: should any judge these forms too skeleton-like, they can clothe them to their taste.]

No. 1.

LETTER MISSIVE FROM PERSONS WISHING TO BE ORGANIZED INTO A CONGREGATIONAL CHURCH.

———, ——, 18.

To the Congregational Church of Christ in ——,

Reverend and Beloved,

Whereas the Great Head of the Church has disposed a number of persons in the town of ——, to unite together, for public worship and the celebration of religious ordinances, under a Congregational form of church government, the undersigned, in behalf of their brethren, respectfully solicit your attendance, by your Rev. pastor and delegate, at

——, on the —— of ——, at —— o'clock, to take into consideration the propriety of organizing us into a Congregational Church of Christ; and, should it be deemed expedient, to assist in the appropriate services of such an occasion.

Wishing you grace, mercy, and peace, from God the Father and our Lord Jesus Christ, we subscribe ourselves,

Yours in the gospel,

——, ——, ——, } *Committee of Arrangements.*

No. 2.

CALL FROM A CHURCH TO A PASTOR-ELECT.

*To Mr.** —— [*or, the Rev. Mr.* ——,]

The undersigned, a committee of the Congregational church of Christ in ——, would respectfully submit to your consideration the following votes of the church:—

"At a regular meeting of the Congregational church in ——, on the —— day of ——,

Voted, That the members of this church are entirely satisfied with the piety, orthodoxy, and ministerial qualifications of Mr. —— [or Rev. Mr. ——, as the case may be].

[The state of the votes should be given, whether unanimous, or by what majority.]

Voted, That Mr. —— be invited to become the pastor and teacher of this church.

Voted, That brethren A, B, and C, be a committee to communicate these votes to Mr. ——, and to make other

---

* If the pastor-elect has not been ordained, it is proper to address him as *Mr.* and not Rev.

arrangements which may be necessary to carry out the wishes of the church in relation to the premises.*

———, *Moderator.*
———, *Clerk.*"

The committee are happy to say, that an entire unanimity of feeling [or as the case may be] prevails in the parish, in reference to your settlement among us. The doings of the society will accompany this communication.

And now, dear sir, permit us personally, and in behalf of the church which we represent, to express our earnest desire that you will accept of our invitation to the pastoral office among us, and name an early day for the ordination [or installation] services.

Praying that God would guide you to a favorable decision, we subscribe ourselves, in behalf of the church,

Your brethren in Christ,

———,
———, } *Committee of the Church.*
———,

———, ———, 18—.

No. 3.

LETTER MISSIVE FOR AN ORDAINING COUNCIL.

The Church of Christ in ——, to the Church of Christ in ——, Sendeth Greeting.

The Great Head of the Church having kindly united the hearts of this church, and the congregation statedly wor-

---

* The other things referred to here, are the calling of a parish, or society meeting, for the purpose of concurring with the church and fixing the salary, etc.

It would be equally proper to have the church vote "*a call*" to the candidate, embodying the substance of the votes and the statements of the committee.

shipping with us, in the choice of Mr. —— [or Rev. as the case may be] for our pastor and teacher, and he having accepted our invitation to settle with us in the gospel ministry, and suitable provision having been made for his temporal support — we affectionately solicit your attendance, by pastor and delegate, at ——, on the —— day of —— next, at —— o'clock in the ——, to assist in the examination of the candidate; and, if judged proper, in the ordination services.

May grace, mercy, and peace be multiplied unto you all.

Your brethren in Christ,

——, } *Committee of*
——, } *the Church.*
——, }

The other churches invited to sit in council, are —— [here name them.]

Rev. Mr. —— and delegate will please call upon Mr. —— for entertainment.

No. 4.

LETTER OF INTRODUCTION.

To whom it may concern.

This may certify, that the bearer, Mr. —— ——, is a member in regular standing of the Congregational church in ——. Expecting to be absent from us for some months, and desiring christian intercourse during his absence, he has requested a letter of introduction to any church of Christ with which he may wish to commune; he is, therefore, hereby affectionately recommended to the occasional communion and fellowship of any who love our Lord Jesus Christ.

——, *Pastor of the Cong. Chh.*
[*or, Clerk, as the case may be.*]

——, ——, 18—.

[This sort of letter does not require a vote of the church. The pastor, or if the church has no pastor, the moderator or stated clerk may give such a letter as this. No member should leave the place of his residence for any considerable number of weeks without taking such a letter.]

No. 5.

LETTER OF DISMISSION AND RECOMMENDATION.

The Congregational Church in ———, *to the Congregational Church in* ———.

Reverend and Beloved,

The bearer, —— ——, a member of this church in regular standing, having requested a letter of dismission and recommendation to you, the church have voted the same. When received by you, his particular relation to us will be considered at an end.

Wishing you grace, mercy, and peace,

We are yours in the Lord, in behalf of the church,

———, *Pastor.*
——— *Church Clerk.*

———, ——, 18—.

No. 6.

LETTER MISSIVE FOR A DISMISSING COUNCIL.

The Congregational Church in ———, *to the Congregational Church in* ———, *Sendeth Greeting.*

Whereas difficulties have arisen among us, which seem to render the dissolution of the pastoral connection between the Rev. Mr. —— and this church desirable, [or this church having become impoverished by deaths and removals, so as to be unable any longer to sustain the ministry among us; — or, whatever the case may be] we respectfully request the advice of your Rev. pastor and a delegate, in relation to the question, — Whether, under existing circumstances, this connection ought not to be sundered?

[Time and place of the meeting.]

In the bonds of the Gospel, we are yours,

——, *Pastor.*

——, *Clerk, or Comm. of the Chh.*

[Date.]

P. S. [Place of entertainment. — Other churches invited.]

No. 7.

LETTER MISSIVE FROM A CHURCH AND AN AGGRIEVED BROTHER OR BRETHREN, FOR A MUTUAL COUNCIL.

The Congregational Church in ——, to the Congregational Church in ——.

Rev. and Beloved,

This church have recently felt it their painful duty to exclude from their fellowship Mr. ——, for [heretical sentiments, disorderly walk, or unchristian conduct — or all, or either, as the case may be]; and, though a majority [or a large majority] are persuaded of the propriety and scriptural correctness of the course pursued, yet, as Mr. —— feels himself aggrieved and injured by our act, and some of our brethren are not altogether satisfied — we have thought proper to yield to his and their earnest request, that the advice of a mutual council might be taken. To the end, then, that all things may be done to the edification of the body of Christ, we respectfully invite you, by your Rev. pastor and delegate, to meet in council, on ——, at —— o'clock, at ——, to review the doings of this church, and to give us such advice as your christian wisdom may suggest.

May the blessing of the great Head of the Church be with you all.

Yours, in the Gospel,

———, *Pastor.*

———, *Clerk, or Committee.*

The subscriber [or subscribers] unites in the above request. ———, *The Aggrieved.*

——, ——, 18—.

P. S. The other churches invited are ——.

Rev. Mr. —— and delegate will find accommodations at the house of Mr. ——.

No. 8.

LETTER MISSIVE FROM AN EXCOMMUNICATED INDIVIDUAL, ASKING FOR AN EX PARTE COUNCIL.

To the Congregational Church in ——,

The undersigned feeling himself aggrieved by the recent action of the Congregational Church in ——, and having solemnly protested against their proceedings, and earnestly solicited them to unite with him in asking advice of a mutual council, but without success, begs leave to lay before an ex parte council the following brief outline of the charges made against him, and of the proceedings of the church in reference to them. [Here may follow the charges, an account of the doings of the church, and a distinct annunciation of the several particulars in respect to which the church are believed to have erred.] In view of the whole case — which I have endeavored fairly to state — may I not confidently ask the aid of your Rev. pastor and a delegate, to sit in council with others, and investigate the case submitted, and advise in the premises?

With sentiments of Christian regard, I am

yours in affliction,

———.

P. S. The other churches sent to, are ——. The council are desired to meet at —— on —— ——, at —— o'clock.

[Date, &c. &c.]

No. 9.

LETTER MISSIVE FOR A MUTUAL COUNCIL.

The Congregational Church in ——, to the Congregational Church in ——,

Rev. and Beloved,

Difficulties having arisen between the pastor and sundry members of this church, in the adjustment of which we feel our need of your counsel, this is to invite your attendance, by pastor and delegate, at a mutual council, to be held at ——, on —— day of ——, at —— o'clock, to advise us respecting the following matters, namely: — [Here let every material point in the case be mentioned distinctly; as the church send their pastor and delegate to act upon these points, and none others, the letter missive being the warrant on which the assembled council proceed]; and such other incidental matters as may grow out of these main points of difficulty between us.

Wishing you grace, mercy, and peace,

We subscribe ourselves yours,

———, *Pastor.*

———, *Comm. of the Chh.*

——, ——, 18—.

P. S. The Rev. Mr. —— and delegate will be accommodated at the house of Mr. ——.

No. 10.

LETTER MISSIVE FOR AN EX PARTE COUNCIL.

[The same form may be used as for a mutual council, with this exception: — It must be distinctly stated, that a *mutual* council has been proposed by the inviting party, and been rejected by the other party. No church should send their pastor and delegate, to assist in an ex parte council, unless assured that a *mutual*, has been first proposed and refused.

The letter will be signed, of course, only by the sending party — the pastor of the church, or the aggrieved brother or brethren, as the case may be.

The names of the invited churches should always be given, that every church may know with whom it is expected to associate in council.]

No. 11.

MINUTES OF AN ECCLESIASTICAL COUNCIL.

[It is important that these be accurately and intelligibly made, as they should be placed among the records of the church which calls the council, and should also be preserved by the scribe of the council for future reference. Something like the following form may be adopted: —]

Minutes of an Ecclesiastical Council held at A——, ——, 18—, for the purpose of —— [here state the object.]

Pursuant to letters missive from the Congregational church in A——, the pastors and delegates of the following churches assembled at ——:

From the Congregational Church in B——, Rev. —— ——, Pastor, Brother, —— ——, Delegate.

[Giving each church in alphabetical order.]

The brethren were called to order by the Rev. ——, who read the letter missive.

The council was then organized by choosing Rev. —— ——, Moderator, and Rev. —— ——, Scribe.

After prayer by the moderator, the council proceeded to business.

[Here should follow a brief statement of the proceedings, with notices of adjournments, devotional services, etc. If the council are called to assist in adjusting difficulties in the church, these should be succinctly, but clearly stated; and the decision of the council upon each successive point given. In a word — the scribe should endeavor to give a distinct outline of the case submitted to the council, and their treatment of the same. This document, after being carefully read and corrected by the council, should, if necessary, be rewritten, and then subscribed by the moderator and scribe, in the name of the council.

RESULT OF COUNCIL.

Sometimes it is deemed expedient to appoint a committee to embody in what is called a *Result of Council*, the case submitted and the action of the council upon the same; and if so, the entries of the scribe may be of a more general nature. Sometimes the labor of making out a Result is assigned to the scribe; and an *assistant* is appointed to perform the ordinary work of keeping minutes, etc.]

No. 12.

The Congregational Church in ——, to the Council who may assemble to organize —— Congregational Church in ——,

Rev. and Beloved,

This may certify you, that the bearer, —— ——, [where there are several persons going from the same church, their names may be all put into one letter] has for some time been a member, in good standing, of the Congregational church in ——. Proposing to unite in forming a new church, to be called —— ——, he has asked a letter of dismission and recommendation for this purpose. We therefore heartily commend him to your christian confidence, as a brother beloved in the Lord; and if received and recognized by you as a member of the church —— —— his particular connection with us will be considered at an end.

Craving God's blessing on your proceedings, we subscribe ourselves, yours in the fellowship of the Gospel, in behalf of the church, ———, *Pastor.*

———, *Clerk.*

——, ——, 18—.

No. 13.

DISCIPLINE OF A PASTOR BY HIS CHURCH.

Note to pages 188, 209.

It may be proper to apprise the reader, who is not already familiar with the fact, that those churches and ministers who adopt the Consociational system, generally deny the right of a church to discipline its pastor.

The Rev. Mr. Mitchell, in his Guide to the Principles and Practices of the Congregational Churches of New England, (p. 236,) says: "A church would, in most cases, find it a most embarrassing business, to undertake the discipline of its minister. It is wisely relieved from such a duty." And, again, (p. 235, note,) "I do not see how a church in such circumstances, (i. e., in case a pastor becomes heretical or scandalous,) or at least, in certain *supposable* circumstances, can act in its *collective* capacity at all. Who is to *convene* the church? and who is to *preside?* The pastor may refuse to convene it; and if it do convene, may claim to act as its moderator by virtue of his office, (*Cambridge Platform*, ch. X. § 8,) and in that capacity, if he be a bad man, may effectually embarrass its proceedings."

It may be replied to these objections: that there is scarcely any end to the difficulties which "a bad man," whether he be a minister or a layman, may throw in the way of church discipline. It is in vain to think of guarding against all "*supposable*" difficulties. A minister *bad* enough, or *mad* enough, to insist upon embarrassing and interrupting the orderly proceedings of a church, under such circumstances, would expose himself to legal process, for disturbing a religious meeting; and a church would be justified in having him arrested and put under bonds for his good behavior, while they proceeded under the moderatorship of the senior deacon, or some one chosen for the occasion, to examine the charges against their pastor. And this would be no invasion of the pastor's rights; for, so soon as a regular charge against a pastor is laid before a church, and the church vote to examine that charge, their pastor is, *virtually*, suspended from the exercise of his pastoral office, and his right to moderate the church, for the time being, ceases.

CHURCH-MEMBERSHIP OF PASTORS.

Connected with this question, respecting the right and power of a Congregational church to discipline its pastor, is another, namely: *Ought a minister to be a member of the church of which he is pastor?* Those who deny the disciplinary authority of a church over a pastor, take of course, in order to be consistent, the *negative* of the question. Mr. Mitchell says (p. 237): "It is insisted on by some, that a minister shall be a member of the church of which he is the pastor; and subject, 'like any other member,' to its watch and discipline. But neither the reasons, nor the passages from Scripture, which are adduced in support of the position, are satisfactory; and by the great majority of the denomination it is not, I believe, admitted." Again (p. 238): "It seems inconsistent with the relations the pastor sustains to the church, as one whom the Holy Ghost hath made its overseer, and with the respect which is required to be paid to him for his office sake, that he should be subject to its watch and oversight, *in the same manner*, as any other member." And again (p. 241): "Leave a minister to the watch and discipline of his *peers*. This is the common privilege of the brotherhood, and ought to be his."

The unsettled state of every thing connected with the pastoral office for some years past, has undoubtedly introduced irregularities into the practice of our denomination upon this point, as well as upon many others. In many cases, the pastoral connection is now formed with the understanding that it will be short-lived. A stipulation is often made that the connection may be dissolved, by either party, the church or the pastor, giving the other three months' notice. In other cases, a settlement is made for a stipulated number of years,—*five* being a favorite number. The system of rotation has thus been pretty thoroughly introduced into the pastoral office. Our pastors have become *travelling* preachers. In the county where the writer was located, there were *thirty-one* Congregational churches. A settlement of thirteen years, gave him the painful opportunity of witnessing overturns in *thirty* of these *thirty-one* churches. There was but one church in the county, besides his own, which had not changed pastors during the time, and many of them *repeatedly*. Now, if this is a specimen of the state of things in our churches generally, can we wonder, that the *practice* of our denomination should be opposed to the admission of ministers as members of the churches of which they are pastors? In this unsettled state of things, it is natural that the churches should be inattentive to the church-membership of their pastors; and *as* natural for our pastors to wish to retain their connection with the churches with which they originally united by profession. But, it was not always so in New England;* and our principles, as well as the early practice of our churches, are diametrically opposed to this innovation.

And it is believed that even now the pastors of most of our best regulated and most stable Congregational churches, out of Connecticut, will be found to be members of their own churches. And what is there in this relation inconsistent with the "respect which is required to be paid to a pastor, for his office' sake?" Nothing more than in the accountability of a presiding officer of a legislative assembly to the rules of that body. As *church members*, ministers and laymen are on equal footing: they are alike accountable to the laws of Christ's kingdom. The administration of these laws is intrusted to *the church*, as such; and not to any other association of men, however wise or good. A

---

* See *Mather's Ratio,* p. 167–169.

church has no more right to delegate the duty of disciplining *any* of its members to other hands, than it has to delegate to others any other christian duty.

Prof. Upham, in his "Ratio Disciplinæ," (p. 167,) says: "It is settled, both in principle and practice, that the minister is accountable to his church; and in the first place, *in virtue of his church-membership*. According to Congregational usage, no person becomes and remains the minister [pastor?] of a church, without also transferring his relationship, and becoming a member of the same. The reasons of this are various; but one undoubtedly is, that he may feel himself subject to the needful restraint of its watch and discipline."

Mr. Mitchell intimates, that Prof. Upham has been "*misled* by some of the early writers whom he consulted." If so, the soundest and most learned writers of the denomination are unsafe guides. "The Cambridge Platform," "Cotton's Way of the Churches in New England," * "Cotton's Book of the Keys," † "Thomas Hooker," ‡ "Mather's Apology," and "Mather's Ratio Disciplinæ," all maintain this doctrine.

Cotton Mather's words are: "When a pastor has fallen into scandal, the brethren that are acquainted with it, proceed *as they would with another brother in such cases; only with more special terms of respect and repetition of addresses*, as the relation of a father may call for." ||

The Cambridge Platform, ch. 10, § 6, speaking of an incorrigibly offending elder, says: "as the church had power *to call him to office* so have they power, according to order, (the council of the churches, where it may be had, directing thereto,) *to remove him from his office:* and being

---

* See p. 99–102.

† "*Keys of the Kingdom of Heaven,*" p. 31, 41–43.

‡ See *Part I.* p. 51, 52, 155, 192; Part II. p. 68.

|| See *Mather's Ratio*, p. 162–165.

now but a member, in case he add contumacy to his sin, the church that had power to receive him *into their fellowship*, hath also the same power to *cast him out*, that they have concerning any other member."

It is an important principle of Congregationalism, that the call of the church, and the acceptance of the same by the pastor elect, constitute the pastoral relation to any particular church. The ordination is only the *induction into office* of the individual, who, by virtue of his *election*, is entitled to that office.

In ch. 9, § 2, of the Platform, we read: "This ordination we account nothing else but the solemn putting of a man into his place and office in the church, *whereunto he had right before by election;* being like the installing of a magistrate in the commonwealth. Ordination therefore is not to go before but to follow election. The essence and substance of the outward calling of an ordinary officer in the church, doth not consist in his ordination, but in his voluntary and free election by the church, and his accepting of that election; whereupon is founded that relation between pastor and flock, between such a minister and such a people. Ordination doth not constitute an officer, nor give him the essentials of his office. The apostles were elders without imposition of hands by men; Paul and Barnabas were officers before that imposition of hands. Acts 13: 3. The posterity of Levi were priests and Levites, before hands were laid on them by the children of Israel. Numbers 8: 10. Acts 6: 5, 6. 13: 2, 3. 14: 23. 1 Tim. 4: 14. 5: 22."

Cotton Mather, in speaking of the doctrines of the fathers of New England, says: "They reckoned not *ordination* to be essential unto the *vocation* of a minister, any more than *coronation* to the being of a king: but that it is only a consequent and convenient *adjunct* of his *vocation*, and a solemn acknowledgment of it, with an useful and proper benediction of *him* in it." *Magnalia*, Vol. II. p. 208. See also, *T. Hooker's Survey*, P. II. p. 60; *Calvin's Inst.* B. IV. c. 3, § 10; *Milton's "Animadversions upon the Remonstrant's Defence,"* etc. ut sup. p. 193, note.

The principle here recognized, puts the power of discipline into the hands of the church: and this is clearly the right of the church. No other body has been invested with power by Christ to open and shut the doors of the church — to discipline offenders against the laws of his kingdom. In ch. 8, § 7, of the Platform, it is said: "If the church have power *to choose* their officers and ministers, then, in case of manifest unworthiness and delinquency, they have power also to *depose them:* for to open and shut, to choose and refuse, to constitute in office and remove from office, are acts belonging to the same power." Speaking of the power and right of a church to discipline, and even depose its pastor, the learned and excellent Samuel Mather, in his Apology, etc., says: "It is entirely just and reasonable that particular churches should have this power: for they are ecclesiastical societies confederate, that is to say, they are churches, before they have officers, and even without them. And, although they may be in such a state as this, yet even then a subordinate ecclesiastical power is under our Lord Jesus Christ, and by Him delegated unto them: so that, having the nature and essence of a church, as they surely have, they may act as such: and, as it is natural to all societies and bodies whatsoever to preserve themselves, the churches of Christ also are doubtless furnished with sufficient power for their own preservation and comfortable subsistence. It follows, therefore, that, if the elder of a particular church should be found guilty of maladministration, and break in upon the known and fundamental privileges which every Christian society has in common with other societies, that particular church may and ought, from a sacred regard to the law of self-preservation, to depose such an arbitrary and tyrannical elder, if upon their admonitions he do not repent and give them satisfaction.

"Nor indeed can it well be disputed, that the churches in the days of primitive Christianity were possessed of this most valuable right and privilege, when there are such testimonies in the ancient approved writers, which fully demonstrate it. It is as clear as the light, from that deservedly prized remain of antiquity, CLEMENT's first Epistle to the *Corinthians*, which is worthy of frequent citations from it, that the church of Corinth at that time, had, and exercised this privilege. For, he says to them in that epistle, '*We perceive that ye have removed some, who have performed their office well, from the ministry which they were thought to deserve, as having no fault to be found with them: Ye are too contentious, brethren, and too hot about these things which appertain not to salvation.*' Now, is it not very plain from these passages, that the *Corinthians* had deposed and laid aside their ministers, merely because, in lesser or disputable points, their judgments did not please them? 'Tis true the good CLEMENT blames them, and it must be confessed that they deserved to be blamed, for casting off those persons *who had holily and unblamably performed the duties of their Episcopacy:* But, CLEMENT never twits or blames them at all for exercising a power which did not belong to them: no, far from it. All that he faults them for, and indeed all that can be objected against them is, that they exercised the power, of which they were possessed, in an irregular manner, when the occasion did not require it.

"And it is also certain, that the particular churches of our LORD JESUS CHRIST, enjoyed this privilege, at least until the two hundred and fifty-eighth year after CHRIST: For, in that year, a Synod convened, in which CYPRIAN presided: And that Synod approved and commended the proceedings of some churches who had deposed their bishops, upon the application of those churches to the synod in order to obtain their opinion concerning their conduct. As for CYPRIAN's own judgment in this matter, it may easily be seen by reading some of his epistles: For, in one of his epistles, he expressly acknowledges, that in his time the people had the power, as of choosing worthy ministers, so likewise of refusing and casting off those who were not so; and in another epistle, he affirms, that this power belongs to the church, and that it was given to the church by divine authority. And the learned ORIGEN, was of the same mind: For he freely declared to his people, 'If I seem to you to be a right hand, and am called a Presbyter and seem to preach the word of God; yet if I shall do any thing contrary to ecclesiastical discipline and the rule of the gospel, so that I give scandal or offence to the church, let the whole church conspire, and with one consent cut me off, although I am their right hand.' And this right and liberty of the brethren for which we plead, is so fully represented by CYPRIAN, and so strongly proved to belong to them, from passages which he urges out of the Old and New Testament, that I shall refer you unto him: In the mean time, I cannot but transcribe a few sentences from him. 'For this cause,' says he, 'the people obedient to the commands of the Lord, and fearing God, ought to separate themselves from a wicked bishop: For they principally have the power of choosing worthy priests and rejecting the unworthy, which comes from divine authority.' Nor, may I omit the testimony of the prodigiously learned GROTIUS, with reference to this right of the people in the early ages of Christianity: Now he testifies, that it was not only the right of the people to flee and avoid an unfaithful pastor, but that such a pastor, by virtue of the sentence against him, lost his pastoral right, and whatsoever of that kind was once ascribed unto him.

"To conclude; as JESUS CHRIST has made these churches free in this liberty, it is to be hoped, that they will stand fast in it, as occasion shall require, nor suffer their pastors under their maladministrations, to deprive them of it." *

If it be objected, that the authorities cited are *ancient*, and that modern Congregationalists have adopted different views and practice; I beg leave to refer to a sermon, published in 1826, by that close reasoner and consistent Congregationalist, Dr. Emmons; entitled "The Platform of Ecclesiastical Government, established by the Lord Jesus Christ." At page 16th he says: "If every church be formed by confederation, and has an independent right to exercise all ecclesiastical power, [as he had before shown] then *they have a right to dismiss their own minister, whenever they judge he has forfeited his ministerial character.* Those who have a right to put into office, have a right to put out of office. The church either puts their minister into office, or delegates power to a neighboring minister to do it for them, which is the same thing as doing it themselves. Therefore, as neighboring ministers could not place a pastor over them without their consent, so they [the neighboring ministers] cannot put away or dismiss their pastor without their consent. *The voice of the church must always be had in every act of discipline.* Now, if a council cannot dismiss a minister without the consent of the church, then it clearly appears, that the right of dismission belongs *solely to the church,* who may dismiss their minister without the advice, or contrary to the advice of a council, if they think he has forfeited his ministerial character; but not otherwise."

None who know the character of Dr. Emmons — and who is there that does not know it — will question his competency to give an opinion of what is essential to sound

* See *Mather's "Apology for the Liberties of the Churches of New England,"* p. 81–85. F. Johnson maintained the same doctrine. — *Hanbury,* Vol. I. p. 242. Also, *Hanbury,* p. 94; Ainsworth and others.

Congregationalism. Throughout his discourse, he insists, that all ecclesiastical power is vested in each duly constituted church, by Jesus Christ, the head of the church. The church is the ultimate appeal in all cases of discipline, and has an undoubted right to perform all necessary acts of discipline. "It is at the option and discretion of any particular church, whether they shall, or shall not ask counsel in any case of church discipline, and if they do ask counsel of others, their advice is only advisory, which they have a right to accept or reject." — *Discourse*, p. 15, 16.

The above extracts go to show, that the doctrine maintained in these pages, has the countenance of one of the most distinguished Congregational divines of modern days; as well as the support of ancient authorities.

If we may erect a distinct tribunal to try *ministers*, we need but one step more, and the power of disciplining *any member* is taken from the church. Every minister must be either a member of the church of which he is pastor, or of some other church. To *that* church of which he is a member, he is amenable; and to the discipline of that church he is subject, just as much as any other member; otherwise, we have the anomaly of a church, professing to believe itself empowered to discipline its members, having within its bosom one, at least, over whom it has no disciplinary power. As a church member every minister stands on precisely the same ground as every other member does; he is amenable to the same laws; and his official character cannot, — will not shield him. As a church member he has no rights or immunities which other members have not. His superiority over the church is *official* merely, — he is chief among equals.

It is objected, that every man should be tried by his "*peers*." If *pastors* are to be tried by *their* "peers," by whom are the *deacons* to be tried? have not they the same claim to exemption from church jurisdiction that the other officers of the church have?

If it be further objected, that the church is much more liable to be swayed by prejudice, than an association of clergymen: it may be answered, that a pastor may have the advice of a council, if he desire it; and has, therefore, as complete protection from injury as any of his lay brethren; and more than this he cannot reasonably ask.

Presbyterians and Episcopalians object to Congregationalism, that it does not give ministers sufficient power. Dr. Campbell says, we "have gone to an extreme, though" — as he honestly admits — "not the most common extreme, in bringing the pastoral authority too low." *Lecture* 6, p. 91. My own humble labors have been criticized, for not sufficiently guarding against the encroachments of the people on the rights of the ministry. In reference to this objection, we answer: That we give to ministers all the authority which the New Testament gives them. We acknowledge them to be bishops or *overseers* of their respective churches; to be *guides* (ἡγουμενοι) to their churches; and *governors* (προϊστάμενοι presidents) in them. And we maintain, that the churches are bound to "*remember* them which have the rule over them," or are their guides; "*to know*," i. e. respectfully and affectionately to regard, "them which are over [them] (προϊστάμενους) in the Lord, and to esteem them very highly in love *for their work's sake;*" to "*obey them* which have the rule over [them] and submit [themselves]."

Still, we cannot conceal from the churches, if we would, the fact that their submission and obedience to their pastors are to be based on the conformity of these overseers, guides, and presidents, to the requisitions of the gospel; or, in other words, that the churches are bound to obey and submit themselves to their ecclesiastical rulers, no further than these rulers conform to the Word of God. As officers, they preside over the churches — they are *presidents*, but not monarchs, nor tyrants; and while they act worthily of their office, they are respected and obeyed. They are guides to be followed, not blindfold, but in the light of truth; and when they cease to walk in that light, they have no further claim upon the obedience of the people. And what more can we give to the pastors, without intrenching upon the free spirit of the Gospel Institution?

Is it objected, that the churches are made judges of their pastor's conformity to the gospel standard? And pray who should be, if not the churches? Not the ministers themselves, surely! For this would make them the most absolute despots. Not neighboring ministers solely; for this would destroy the independence of the churches. The rights of private judgment in matters of *faith*, will not certainly be denied by any consistent Protestant: with what propriety then can individual churches be denied the right of deciding, from the Word of God, whether their pastors and spiritual guides and overseers conform in their disciplinary measures to this infallible standard? It is freely admitted, that the authority of a Congregational pastor in the government and general direction of the affairs of his church, very much depends upon his personal integrity, wisdom, piety, and careful conformity to the principles of church government laid down in the New Testament. And these are the best foundations for all authority: they most effectually insure the integrity, and piety, and humility of the ministry, while they guard the individual rights of the churches. Indeed, we see not how we can give to the pastors of churches founded on such principles as ours are, greater power over the churches. We must either govern by brute force, by hierarchal machinery, or by moral power. We reject the two first, as inconsistent with the spirit of Christianity: we have only the last remaining. Dr. Campbell is honest enough to admit this;

and by his admission answer his own objection to Congregationalism, "of bringing the pastoral authority too low." For he adds: "it is however certain, that when authority of any kind is unattended with what are commonly called coercive measures, or the power of the sword, and unsupported by temporal splendor, or worldly sanctions, it is impossible to preserve it otherwise amongst an enlightened people, than by purity of character in those vested with it, and by diligence in the discharge of the duties of their station." — *Lec.* vi. p. 91.

Sound Congregational principles and practice, then, are decidedly opposed to the doctrine, that a pastor should not be a member of the church over which he presides, and should be free from the disciplinary authority of that church. I am aware that many excellent men are agreed with Mr. Mitchell in his views of these matters; and that the practice of some, at least, of the churches of Connecticut, with which Mr. M. was formerly connected, is in accordance with his views; nevertheless, I am constrained to regard this practice as a deviation from primitive Congregationalism, as uncalled for as it is unsafe. It seems to me to be one step towards those evils to which the plan of consociation, and the establishment of permanent and authoritative councils directly lead. I regret to say that this appears not to be the only particular in which the hearts of some of the children are turned *from* their fathers — in which some modern Congregationalists (so called) have deviated from those principles of which Cotton Mather speaks, when he says: "*I shall count my country lost, in the loss of the primitive principles, and the primitive practices, upon which it was at first established.*"

I will only add a single remark to this long note. The membership-relation of a pastor to his church has been considered too much in the light of a subjection of the pastor to "impertinent annoyances of weak, or officious and ill-disposed brethren." No pastor, let his relation to his church and people be what it may, can avoid these annoyances.

There is, however, another light in which I love to contemplate the relation of a pastor to his church, as a church member; and that is, in the light of a *privilege*. Is it not a privilege to be under the watch and care of a church, which, like the beasts seen by John, is "full of eyes before and behind," which may watch for our *safety*, and not merely for our *halting?* Has Jesus Christ condescended to make himself like one of us — to become our *elder brother* — that he might create a new bond of attachment, and encourage greater familiarity with him? and shall we, his servants, put ourselves upon our official dignity and claim exemption from that brotherly relation to our churches which, while it will exempt us from the discipline of these churches, will deprive us also of that fellowship and sympathy which should exist among all the members of the body? Surely, if it be a *privilege* for *any one* to be a church-member, it is for a pastor. And long may it be, ere it shall be regarded generally by our churches as "*the true doctrine*, that a minister by virtue of his ordination, ceases to be a church member *anywhere*." *

No. 14.

EXCOMMUNICATION AND WITHDRAWING FELLOWSHIP.

Note to page 208.

Two questions may be raised on the distinction intimated between excommunication and withdrawing fellowship: — First, Wherein does this act of withdrawing fellowship differ from excommunication? Secondly, Is it proper for a

---

* Mitchell, p. 240, note; Rutherford, the Presbyterian, makes a similar statement; T. Hooker, pp. 61, 81.

church to withdraw fellowship from a member, and leave him unconnected with any visible church? I will venture to answer both of these questions, and then leave the reader to form his own judgment.

First, Excommunication differs from the act of withdrawing fellowship in this: excommunication implies a forfeiture of *christian* standing; withdrawing fellowship, implies a forfeiture of *church* standing only. If one is excommunicated, he is "cut off," "put away," "purged out," "delivered unto Satan," — in a word, is dealt with as "a heathen man and a publican" — as one destitute of any claim to the character of a Christian. All this seems to be taught by the passages alluded to in the text. — See Matt. 18: 15–18. 1 Cor. 5: 1–5, 7, 13. Gal. 5: 12.

When Christ and his apostles use such language as that referred to, in describing the duty of a church towards offenders, they are speaking of persons who had committed *serious offences* — who had *sinned*, and continued obstinate in their sins. In the 18th chapter of Matt. our translators use the word *trespass* to designate the offence referred to by the Saviour — "If thy brother shall *trespass* against thee;" but the original word (ἁμαρτήσῃ) denotes a more serious offence than the English word trespass implies. It is the same word which is put into the mouth of the prodigal, Luke 15: 18, "*I have sinned* (ἥμαρτον) against heaven and before thee;" and it was used by Judas, when "he brought again the thirty pieces of silver to the chief priests and elders, Saying, *I have sinned* (ἥμαρτον) in that I have betrayed the innocent blood." — Matt. 27: 3, 4. So elsewhere it is used in the same sense, as Rom. 3: 23. Heb. 3: 17. 1 John 1: 10, *et al.*

The same view of excommunication is suggested by 1 Cor. v. and 2 Cor. 2: 4–11, where the Apostle gives directions respecting the treatment of an offender: he was to be delivered "unto Satan for the destruction of the flesh;" i. e.

he was to be cast out of the church, and abandoned to the god of this world. But, for what offence was this punishment to be "inflicted of many" — by the majority of the church? Not for a trifling irregularity, but for a serious offence — an open violation of the rules of christian conduct: it was for fornication; and "such fornication as is not so much as named among the Gentiles, that one should have his father's wife." — 1 Cor. 5: 1.

But what was the state of the case when the Apostle directed the Thessalonian church to "*withdraw* from every brother that walketh disorderly?" 2 Thess. 3: 6. The disorderly conduct to which he particularly referred, was idleness and gossiping: "We hear that there are some which walk among you disorderly, *working not at all*, but are *busy-bodies*."— 3: 11. These persons they were directed to "note" — take notice of, and withdraw from, and "have no company with." — 6, 14 vs. Yet, they were not to treat them as heathen men and publicans; for the apostle adds: "Yet count him not as *an enemy* but admonish him as *a brother*." — 15 v. This neglect of his lawful calling, and this meddling with what did not concern him, was irregular and disorderly; it was calculated to bring reproach upon the cause of Christ, and to injure the good name of the church: the church was therefore required to withdraw itself from all participation with the disorderly. Still, this disorderly conduct was not, necessarily, a proof that the offender was utterly destitute of the spirit of Christ. He might be acting under mistaken views of duty; he might conscientiously believe himself called to give up his secular employment, and to devote his time and efforts, well meant, though indiscreet — to doing good. We know that there are just such disorderly and busybodies in the churches now, — men, who by injudicious efforts to promote the cause of Christ, really injure it; and, by their ill-directed attempts to heal differences among brethren, or remove difficulties from families, become busybodies in other men's matters — meddlers with what does not concern them. Such persons, instead of being lights in the world, become a by-word and a hissing among the unbelieving, and spots upon the fair fame of the christian Church. Yet, they are the most difficult persons to convince and reclaim: for the simple reason, that, though perhaps truly pious, they are destitute of good-sense. Hence it might become necessary for the church, after due efforts to persuade such disorderly members to abandon their irregular proceedings, to withdraw from them; and thus let the world know, that the church did not approve of their irregularities, and would not sanction their disorderly conduct. At the same time, the church might, perhaps, count the disorderly as truly pious; and therefore, might admonish and treat them as *brethren* in Christ, and not as *heathen men and publicans*, as they would otherwise be required to do. If these views are correct, then, reasoning analogically, we are authorized in saying: That, whenever a church member, from mistaken views of duty, or other cause, persists in any course of conduct which, though not destructive of christian character, is yet plainly inconsistent with what the church of which he is a member, believe to be agreeable to the order which Christ requires — the church is bound to withdraw fellowship; and thus declare to the world, that they approve not of his peculiar notions or irregular doings. In so doing, they pass no judgment on the *christian* standing of the disorderly person; but they simply declare, that his sentiments and practices are so inconsistent with what they deem orderly, that they can no longer walk with him in church fellowship.

In thus drawing a distinction between excommunication and the withdrawal of fellowship, I can plead but few authorities. The Platform seems rather to contradict such a distinction, when it says: "The church cannot make a member no member, but by excommunication." — Ch. 13, § 7. But, as it speaks of the treatment of no other offences except such as are of a more serious nature, for the commission of which a person, remaining impenitent, should be cast out of the church as a heathen man and a publican; the passage quoted may not be so decisive as at first sight may be supposed. Further, in the passage quoted from the Platform, the term *excommunication* may be used in a generic sense, including both expulsion for unchristian sentiments or conduct, and withdrawing fellowship for disorderly notions and practices. Thus the term is used by some modern writers, who are careful to note a difference between the *treatment* of persons excommunicated for what is deemed *unchristian*, and what is deemed simply *irregular* and *disorderly*.* Thus Bloomfield calls the act of the church required in 2 Thess. 3 : 14, "*a sort* of excommunication." Neither Macknight nor Scott regard this act the same as that required in Matthew 18 : 15–18. Indeed, every man must feel that there should be a difference in the treatment of such as have forfeited their christian standing, and such as have, from conscientious, though mistaken views of truth and duty, or from inadvertency, fallen into conduct simply disorderly.

Cotton Mather, in the Magnalia, (Vol. II. p. 235) speaks of the matter now under consideration, and seems to authorize, fully, the view which I have presented. His words are: "It may sometimes come to pass, that a church member, not otherwise scandalous, may sinfully withdraw and divide himself from the communion of the church to which he belongeth: in which case, when *all due means* for the reducing him prove ineffectual, he having thereby cut himself off from the church's communion; the church may justly esteem and declare itself discharged of any further inspection over him." This is precisely what I mean by *with-*

---

* Mr. Mitchell, (*Guide to N. E. Chhs.* p. 115, 116) does; and he quotes from the Saybrook Platform to sustain his position.

drawing fellowship: — it is just giving up all care of a person, as a church member, and all responsibility for his conduct; leaving him to stand or fall to his own master.

If, however, in the treatment of a disorderly person, he should exhibit an unchristian spirit, and pursue an unchristian course — then the ground of action for the church would be changed, and the offender should be arraigned and *excommunicated* for disorderly and *unchristian* conduct.*

Isaac Chauncy, in his "*Divine Institution of Congregational Churches,*" etc. published in 1697, says: "Excommunication may be considered as *direct* or more *indirect;*" and after explaining "direct" excommunication as "the casting out of an impenitent or notorious sinner from communion of the church," he proceeds to say: "Besides this *direct* way of proceeding against an offending member, there is another much of the like nature, which we call *indirect,* because the church puts not the party out of its communion before the party hath secluded himself, and not by any regular way, but indirectly and contrary to all rules of order. For it is when a church member, by reason of some offence taken at the church, or some member thereof not discharging his own duty, withdraws himself, and separates from the communion of the church. A person having thus excommunicated himself, as it were, the church ought to consider what is their duty; and though a particular member (or more) hath usurped to himself the power of the keys, the

---

* The case of Mrs. Hutchinson, so famous in the early history of New England, may illustrate in some respects this point. She was tried by the church in Boston, for her erroneous opinions and irregular practices: for these, she made a confession and a sort of recantation; but, in the management of these, she was guilty of falsehood: and was finally cut off and cast out of the church, not for her erroneous notions and practices, but for "*gross lying.*" — *Magnalia,* Vol. II. p. 446–448; *Hutchinson's Hist. Mass. Bay,* Vol. I. p. 70–72 and note.

church ought not to acquiesce therein, but maintain the power which Christ hath committed to it; and though it cannot hinder the inordinateness of a brother's unruly passions and ungovernable temper, when God leaves him to it; but that he will run away from the church, rend himself off, breaking all order and covenant obligations, in opposition to all fraternal endeavors to stay him in the place that Christ hath set him in; the church is bound to show and assert the power of Christ, which he hath intrusted it with, and judicially shut the door, and turn the key upon so sinful and disorderly a departure from them; declaring that he having sinfully departed from the communion of that congregation [church] he is no longer under its care and watch, and is not to return to the communion of the church as before, till he hath given satisfaction to the church," — *Chapter* XIII. § 9, and 17.

The treatment of a disorderly member here pointed out by one of the fathers of New England, is substantially what I advocate in these pages.

Having thus answered the first question — Wherein does excommunication differ from the act of withdrawing fellowship? we are prepared to consider the second inquiry: — Can a church withdraw fellowship from one who has not connected himself with some other church? Very rarely will this act of church discipline be required, except when a member so far changes his sentiments as to feel constrained to connect himself with some other denomination, which either does not acknowledge our churches as scriptural in their organization, or embraces some doctrinal views which, though not so fundamental as entirely to destroy our christian confidence in him, are yet such as we cannot conscientiously approve, or by any act of ours sanction.

Still, I apprehend, that there may be instances in which a church would be justified in withdrawing from a brother, and leaving him disconnected with any christian body. If my construction of 2 Thess. 3: 6, 14 be correct, the apostle required this to be done by the Thessalonians; for, if that church withdrew from their disorderly brethren in the way suggested, they must have left them unconnected with any christian church, as there was no other in the city.

However these questions may be answered — and I but give my own judgment respecting them — all, it is believed, will agree in this, that whether or not we distinguish between excommunication and withdrawing fellowship, there should be a difference in our *treatment* of such as are separated from the church for *unchristian* opinions and conduct and such as from mistaken notions, or inconsiderateness, fall into what are deemed by us *disorderly* courses, not destructive of christian character.

No. 15.

MANUAL FOR CHURCH MEETINGS.

[The following Manual — which I have slightly altered — was kindly furnished for this work by an intelligent layman, who was familiar with parliamentary usages, and withal a very hearty Congregationalist — the late David Hale of N. Y.]

Those rules which have been found convenient in Legislative assemblies are equally applicable to all bodies convened for deliberation; the object being always the same; namely, the preservation of order, the security of the right of each member to speak his sentiments freely in debate, and the ascertainment of the opinion of the majority by their votes.

In Congregational churches the pastor is generally regarded as the standing moderator of the church. In case a church is destitute of a pastor, a standing moderator may be chosen, or one may be selected at each succeeding meeting. No brother should be allowed to hold the chair, who makes use of it to control the deliberations of the church, contrary to the common rules of order, or who claims the power to adjourn the meeting at his pleasure, to refuse to put to vote such questions as are disagreeable to himself, or in any way to embarrass the church in its deliberations or its decisions. The presiding brother, whoever he may be, derives all his power from the body over which he presides; and all his decisions are subject to its revision.

When the church is assembled, without a pastor, some member should rise and nominate a moderator and put the question upon his election. But before the question is put, any member may propose a different candidate, and he will be chosen who receives the majority of votes.

A clerk must next be chosen, unless the stated clerk be present. If the meeting be adjourned to another day, the same officers preside again, for an adjournment is but the continuance of the *same meeting*.

Every motion must be made in writing, *if required* by any member; and, when seconded, must be read by the moderator and submitted to the consideration of the church. Until this motion is disposed of, all subsequent propositions must be made by way of amendment to it. An amendment may go to the exclusion, addition, or substitution of words or sentences; indeed, a motion to amend by striking out all the words after the word *resolved*, and substituting an entirely new proposition upon the same subject, is in order. Until some vote has been taken on a resolution or an amendment to it, it may be withdrawn by the mover. There are certain motions which are termed "*privileged*," which may be made *at any time;* such is the motion to postpone indefinitely, to commit to a committee, to lay on the table, (which means to lay aside for the present,) to postpone to a future time fixed, and to adjourn. All these motions may be debated except the last. The motion to adjourn is always in order except when a member is speaking, and then no motion can be made but with the consent of the member who has the floor.

When any motion is before the church, every member has a right to express his views concerning it; and while doing so, the moderator is bound to confine him in his remarks to the point under consideration, and also to protect him against all interruption, except to call him to order if he violates the rules of courtesy, or the rules of debate: but after the matter of order is adjusted, he has a right to go on to the end of his remarks.

The proposition *last made* is always the proposition under consideration, and the first to be voted on; so that, when several amendments or propositions are before the meeting, the order in which they are to be voted upon is usually the *reverse* of the order in which they were made. If several *sums* are proposed, the *largest* is to be first put to vote; if several *times*, the *longest;* and as to numbers generally, the largest.

When a motion is put to vote, it should be first clearly stated from the chair, so that there may be no possible misunderstanding about it. Then the moderator says: As many as are in favor of this resolution, will please to say aye — or lift up their hands — or rise, as the custom of the church may be. Then:

As many as are against this resolution or — as are of a different opinion — will please to say no; or — lift up their hands — or rise. Then the moderator declares the result by saying — it is a vote, or it is *not* a vote, — as it seems to him.

If any member thinks the moderator in error, or that an accurate count would change the result, he has a right to demand it immediately: when the question must be put again, and the votes carefully counted. After the question is put to vote, there can be no debate, and no new proposition made, until the voting is finished. After the vote is taken, any member who voted in the *majority*, may, during the same meeting, move a reconsideration; which motion opens the subject again for debate: and, if the vote to reconsider is adopted, the whole matter stands just as it did before the reconsidered vote was taken.

Questions of *order* are to be decided by the moderator; but if any member thinks the decision incorrect, he can appeal to the meeting, whose decision is final.

When the report of a committee is presented, it will of course be put on file. A vote to accept and adopt, is an expression of concurrence with the views of the committee.

When a member has a motion to make, or wishes to speak on a pending motion, he must rise and address himself respectfully to the moderator.

A member who has a motion to make, may preface it with such remarks as explain his design; but with this exception, speaking is out of order, unless some definite proposition has been submitted and is under consideration.

These rules have been selected from "Jefferson's Manual of Parliamentary Practice," or supplied from the known practice of the most respectable bodies. Many churches have brought upon themselves great trouble by a want of system in their proceedings. In fact, the maintenance of business order, at all times, according to established rules, cannot be too highly estimated. Over-legislation is a fault of churches, whether Congregational or others, as it is of political bodies. Churches should pass very few votes, and never any, without careful deliberation.

No. 16.

REPORT ON THE INDUCTION OF DEACONS,

Submitted to the Union Church in Essex street, Boston, May 19, 1843.

[This Report, though not entirely accordant with views already expressed, on the ordination of deacons, yet presents those of many sound Congregationalists.]

"According to the most ancient Congregational usage, as described by the Cambridge Platform, every church should have three kinds of officers; Teaching Elders, or Pastors, Ruling Elders, and Deacons; and these, after election, should be set apart by prayer and the imposition of the hands of the elders of that church, or if the church had no elders, by "brethren orderly chosen by the church thereto;" or it was held to be *allowable* to invite Elders of other churches to impose hands at ordination. Since the adoption of the Platform, there have been several important changes in the practice of the churches. 1. The office of Ruling Elder has fallen into disuse, as not required in the Scriptures, and inconvenient in practice. 2. The ordination of Pastors by a committee of the church is deemed improper, inasmuch as it shows an unchristian spirit of self-sufficiency, and disregard of the neighboring churches and their Pastors. All now agree that in churches situated as ours are, a Christian spirit and sense of propriety require that in the ordination of a Pastor, a council be called, and hands be imposed by the Pastors of neighboring churches. 3. The ordination of Deacons has fallen into general disuse. Professor Upham, in his Ratio Disciplinæ, says that "this ceremony has been disused for many years;" and again, that it "is not practised at the present day, or at least but very seldom;" and yet again, that it "seems to be permanently abolished." He represents this change as the result of deliberate conviction, and not of mere neglect, saying that it has been "approved by the greater number."

In the Presbyterian church, Deacons are to be set apart to their office by prayer and exhortation, without the imposition of hands.

In all the Episcopalian churches, Deacons are regarded as a third order of the clergy, authorized to preach, and are therefore ordained by the imposition of the hands of a Bishop. As we do not consider a Deacon to be a preaching officer, their authority can weigh nothing with us.

The weight of modern authority, therefore, is decidedly against the induction of Deacons by the imposition of hands. It seems never to have been practised in the Presbyterian church, and has long been contrary to the general opinion and practice of Congregational churches. And it is worthy of remark, *that the imposition of hands recommended by the Cambridge Platform, is a ceremony which, it was understood, might be performed by a committee of the brethren with entire propriety.* The Platform gives no countenance to the idea, that they should be inducted by a ceremony in which the presence of an ordained minister is necessary.

But "to the law and the testimony." The opinions and practices of evangelical churches claim our respectful attention, but our obedience is due only to the word of God. What, then, do the Scriptures teach concerning the induction of Deacons?

The only passage which bears directly on this point, is the account of the appointment of the seven deacons, in the sixth chapter of the Acts of the Apostles.

It appears from the preceding chapters, that many of the Christians then at Jerusalem were in need of pecuniary assistance, and that rich believers contributed liberally to supply their wants. Some of them sold real estate to raise money for this purpose. And whatever money was given, was laid at the feet of the apostles. But as the number of believers increased, the labor of ascertaining and supplying the wants of the necessitous likewise increased, while the time of the apostles was more and more engrossed with spiritual labors. At length, "there arose a murmuring of the Grecians [that is, either Greeks by descent, or, more probably, Jews born in Greek cities, and speaking the Greek language] against the Hebrews, because their widows were neglected in the daily ministrations." Very possibly, there was some foundation for the complaint; not from any partiality in the apostles, but from the fact that they had not time to search out all the cases of want among obscure strangers, residing for a short time in the city. However that may have been, a suspicion of partiality was beginning to show itself. The apostles therefore called a meeting of the church, and said: "It is not reason that we should leave the word of God, and serve tables. Wherefore, brethren, look ye out among you seven men of honest report, full of the Holy Ghost and wisdom, whom we may appoint over this business. But we will give ourselves continually to prayer, and to the ministry of the word." That is, the Deacons were needed, not to assist the ministers in spiritual things, but to relieve them of all secular cares, that they might devote themselves wholly to the spiritual duties of their office. "And the saying pleased the whole multitude;" and they chose seven men, whom they set before the apostles; and when they had prayed, they laid their hands upon them.

To some, this appears conclusive in favor of the ordination of Deacons by the imposition of hands. To us, it appears otherwise. It is by no means certain that the apostles, by laying their hands on the seven, meant to perform what we call ordination.

It had been a custom from the earliest ages, to lay hands on any one for whom prayer was offered. Jacob, in Egypt, laid his hands on the heads of Ephraim and Manasseh, when he blessed them. Moses laid his hand on Joshua, at his public appointment as civil and military leader of the Israelites. Our Saviour laid his hands on the little children that were brought to him for his blessing, and often upon the sick, when he healed them. He mentions, among the signs which "shall follow them that believe," that "they shall lay hands on the sick, and they shall recover." Peter and John laid their hands on the believers at Samaria, and "they received the Holy Ghost." Ananias laid his hand on Saul at Damascus, before his baptism, "that he might receive his sight." The brethren at Antioch fasted and prayed and laid their hands on Saul and Barnabas, who had been several years in the ministry, when about to commence their first missionary excursion through Asia Minor. There are two instances in the First Epistle to Timothy, where the laying on of hands is mentioned as a part of the ceremonies of ordination; and these are the only instances of the kind in the New Testament.

We can draw no decisive inference, therefore, from the fact that the apostles laid their hands on the seven Deacons, when they prayed for them. It was merely a customary gesture, performed by any one, on any occasion, in praying for another. We are no more bound to imitate it, than we are to lay our hands on children, when we pray for their conversion; or on the sick, when we pray for their recovery; or on our friends, when we pray that God may be with them on a journey. Indeed, there is no reason to suppose that praying for Deacons with imposition of hands, then, meant any thing more than praying for them without it means now. The prayer, too, was offered immediately after their election and acceptance. To appoint a future day, after their election and acceptance, for their formal induction into office, and on that day to induct them by ceremonies not commonly used in praying for individuals, would be a plain departure from the only apostolic example.

The idea that Deacons ought to be inducted by special ordination services, probably grows out of a mistake concerning the nature of their office. As appears from what has already been said, they were not appointed for the sake of assisting the clergy in spiritual affairs; but for the sake of effecting a complete separation of the temporal affairs of the church from the spiritual, so that the clergy might give themselves wholly to the latter. Their office is correctly described in the Cambridge Platform, which says: "The office and work of a Deacon is, to receive the offerings of the church, gifts given to the church, and to keep the treasury of the church, and therewith to serve the tables which the church is to provide for; as the Lord's Table, the tables of the ministers, and of such as are in necessity, to whom they are to distribute in simplicity." "The office, therefore, being limited unto the care of the temporal good things of the church, it extends not to the attendance upon and administration of the spiritual things thereof, as the word and sacraments, or the like." The constitution of the Presbyterian church speaks to the same purpose. Its words are: "The Scriptures clearly point out Deacons as distinct officers in the church, whose business it is to take care of the poor, and to distribute among them the collections which may be raised for their use. To them also may be committed the management of the temporal affairs of the church." The Scriptural requisitions concerning their character correspond to this idea of their duty. Aptness to teach is not required of them. They must be "men of honest report, full of the Holy Ghost and wisdom;" that is, men of well-known integrity, piety, and business talents; men in whose capacity, faithfulness, and impartiality the brethren will feel entire confidence; sound in the faith, and of good example in all things, that, as their office will call them to be much among their brethren, their whole influence may be salutary; and as their office will cause them to be looked upon by the world as chosen samples of Christian character, they must be men who will command the respect of "those that are without."

It is, indeed, customary, that the Deacons should act as moderators of the church in the absence of the Pastor, and in many other ways take a leading part in the spiritual affairs of the church; and the custom is a good one, if we use it lawfully. Such services must be rendered by some of the brethren; and though they are no part of the Scriptural duties of a Deacon, yet the Deacons are usually the very men best qualified to perform them. Their appointment to an important office, authorizes them to take a leading part in such matters, without exposing themselves to the charge of arrogance; especially as it is now understood that the brethren expect it of them, and chose them to their office with that expectation. Still, it is perfectly proper for the church, whenever it is deemed expedient, to call on some other brother to perform these duties. It is the custom in some parts of New England, for a church, on losing its Pastor, to choose some neighboring Pastor as its moderator during the vacancy. On this point, we are anxious not to be misunderstood. We would by no means interfere with the present usage of the churches; a usage which extensive experience, for more than a century, has shown to be, in our circumstances, at once harmless and convenient. We only wish to set forth the grounds on which that usage rests, and to show that, as it is a mere usage, adopted in modern times for the sake of convenience, and which we are at liberty to lay aside if a change of circumstances should require it, and as it relates only to duties which any member may lawfully be called upon to perform, it can be no reason why Deacons should be inducted into office by imposition of hands.

Perhaps a few facts from history may throw light on some parts of the subject.

Originally, we know, there were but two kinds of church officers; the Pastors, who were also sometimes called bishops, and sometimes elders, and the Deacons. Not long after the death of the apostles, through the workings of pride, ambition, and worldly policy, some of the Pastors began to be exalted over others, as diocesan Bishops, and even went so far as to claim that they alone were Bishops, and the other Pastors were only Elders. More effectually to secure their own exaltation, they maintained that the Deacons were appointed as assistants to the Bishop, and not to the Elder. Having carried this point, they next labored to increase the power of the Deacons; and thus there sprung up a sort of alliance between the diocesan Bishops and the Deacons, both of whom strove to take power from the Pastors and divide it between themselves. The Bishops made new orders of Deacons. Some of them were Arch-Deacons, and governed many Pastors in the name of the Bishops. Others of them were called Cardinal Deacons, and afterwards, simply Cardinals, being members of the Roman conclave, whose business it is, when a Pope dies, to elect one of themselves as his successor.—See *Coleman's Chr. Ant.* p. 107–114.

For the successful execution of this plan, of breaking down the Pastors by means of the Deacons, it was necessary that the Deacons should be reckoned as a third order of the clergy, and for that purpose, should receive clerical ordination, and should be authorized to preach. So things went on till the Reformation. And even now, in the Protestant Episcopal churches, Deacons are ordained as preaching officers, while their appropriate duties are left to be performed by church-wardens, or other officers not considered as clerical. It is not strange that a mistake which prevailed almost universally for more than a thousand years, and still prevails in all Episcopal churches, whether Greek, Romish, or Protestant, should be slow in disappearing from any part of the world, and that an indefinite impression in favor of ordaining Deacons should frequently reappear. The notion, that the office of a Deacon relates to spiritual things, and that he is appointed to exercise spiritual authority, still lingers in some minds; and because they have such views of the office, they think it should be conferred by ordination. Let this error be thoroughly dispelled; let it be fully understood that the Deacon is appointed, not to unite temporal and spiritual cares in his own person, but to separate them, by taking the temporal wholly into his own hands, and leaving the Pastor free to attend to the spiritual; and then the seeming propriety of their ordination will disappear.

One thing more ought to be particularly mentioned, though it has already been implied. The imposition of hands in prayer has fallen into disuse, except at ordinations and installations. By use, it has acquired a fixed and definite meaning. It is understood to be a symbolical recognition of spiritual authority in him on whom hands are laid. The idea of conveying or recognizing spiritual authority is as clearly and unavoidably conveyed by that act, as it can be by the use of any words in our language. Its use, therefore, in the ordination of a Deacon, when no such authority is to be recognized, has become a decided impropriety, and can hardly fail to deceive some of those who witness it. Its universal use would naturally lead, at no distant day, to a general misunderstanding of the nature of the office, to the serious injury of the Deacons themselves, of the Pastors, and of the churches.

We conclude, therefore, that the Scriptural mode of inducting Deacons into office is the following:—

1. Let the minister, in church meeting, state the nature of the office, and the necessary qualifications.

2. Let the brethren elect a suitable number of men to fill the office.

3. Let the minister invoke the divine blessing upon the transaction; using the same attitude and gestures which are customary in prayer.

These exercises, in the only apostolic example on record, appear to have followed each other in the order above stated, at the same meeting of the church. Sometimes, however, they will unavoidably be interrupted by an adjournment. In that case, there can be no objecting to the offering of appropriate prayer, as often as the subject comes before the church."

No. 17.

A CHURCH COVENANT.

[It is a principle with our denomination, that every church, in order to be rightly constituted, must be united by solemn covenant, expressive of the principles on which their union is formed. This may be included in the Articles of Faith, or, as perhaps is most common among us — it may form a distinct instrument, following the Articles of Faith.

The Covenant here given from Cotton Mather's Ratio, appears to have been the common form used in 1726. It presents an excellent model for the substance of these important instruments.]

"*Covenant.*

"We whose names are hereunto subscribed, apprehending ourselves called of God into the church-state of the gospel, do first of all confess ourselves unworthy to be so highly favored of the Lord, and admire the free and rich grace of his which triumphs over so great unworthiness; and then with an humble reliance on the aids of grace therein promised for them, that, in a sense of their inability to do any good thing, do humbly wait on him for all, we now thankfully lay hold on his covenant; and would choose the things that please him.

"We declare our serious belief of the Christian Religion, as contained in the sacred Scriptures, and with such a view thereof as the Confession of Faith in our churches has exhibited; heartily resolving to conform our lives unto the rules of that holy religion as long as we live in the world.

"We give up ourselves unto the Lord Jehovah, who is the Father, and the Son, and the Holy Spirit, and avouch Him this day to be our God, our Father, our Saviour, and our Leader, and receive Him as our portion forever.

"We give up ourselves unto the Blessed Jesus, who is the Lord Jehovah, and adhere to him as the Head of his people in the covenant of grace, and rely on him as our priest, and our prophet, and our king, to bring us unto eternal blessedness.

"We acknowledge our everlasting and indispensable obligations, to glorify our God in all the duties of a godly, and a sober, and a righteous life; and very particularly in the Duties of a church-state, and a Body of people associated for an obedience to him, in all the ordinances of the gospel: and we thereupon depend upon his gracious assistances for our faithful discharge of the duties thus incumbent on us.

"We desire and intend, and (with dependence on his promised and powerful grace) we engage, to walk together as a church of the Lord Jesus Christ, in the Faith and Order of the gospel, so far as we shall have the same revealed unto us: conscientiously attending the public worship of God, the sacraments of his New Testament, the discipline of his kingdom, and all his holy institutions, in communion with one another; and watchfully avoiding sinful stumblingblocks and contentions, as becomes a people whom the Lord has bound up together in a bundle of life.

"At the same time, we do also present our offspring with us unto the Lord; purposing with his help, to do our part in the methods of a religious education, that they may be the Lord's.

"And all this we do, flying to the blood of the everlasting covenant, for the pardon of our many errors, and praying that the glorious Lord who is the great Shepherd, would prepare and strengthen us for every good work, to do his will, working in us that which will be well pleasing to him; to whom be glory forever and ever. Amen."

No. 18.

THE VETO POWER.

Does Congregationalism recognize the right of a pastor to *veto* the acts of his church? or to dissolve a church meeting, to prevent the church from acting contrary to his wishes? Intelligent Congregationalists may smile at such questions, and may almost deem an apology necessary for introducing them, even into the appendix of a work on Congregationalism. We should think so, did we not know that the claim alluded to has actually been set up by ministers calling themselves Congregationalists; and that two or more instances of this kind of assumption of power have recently occurred in this vicinity.

The assumption is substantially this:—By virtue of his ministerial office, and his pastoral relation to a particular church, the pastor of a church has the right to refuse to put motions which are offensive to him; to dissolve a church meeting, in order to prevent the passage of objectionable votes; or to interpose his *veto,* and thus annul the acts of the church.

More preposterous assumptions of ministerial power than these in a Congregationalist, cannot easily be conceived.

On Congregational principles, a pastor is, *ex officio*, the moderator of the church — its presiding officer; and as such, has all the power that a presiding officer in our best regulated legislative or deliberative bodies has; but nothing more. It is his duty to see, so far as in him lies, that the business of the church is conducted in an orderly manner; consistently with the general principles recognized in the Scriptures, and the approved practice of our churches. He may give his opinion as to the proper course to be pursued in a given case; he may protest against any action which he may believe to be wrong; he may, even, as a last resort, vacate the moderator's chair, and leave the church to go on, if they will, under the moderatorship of one of their own number, chosen for the purpose; — he may do all this, when he finds the church determined to act contrary to his settled convictions of what is proper, orderly, or right; but he cannot dictate to a church; he cannot annul their votes; nor dissolve their meetings: — in a word, he cannot "lord it over God's heritage."

If authorities are demanded for these assertions, the inquirer is referred to the dictates of common sense, as manifested in the rules of all popular, deliberative assemblies; to the essential principle of Congregationalism — that all church power on earth belongs to the individual church as a body; and to the entire spirit of the teachings of the New Testament on this subject. No standard writer on Congregationalism, so far as I remember, has ever thought it worth while to discuss this subject, or even to allude to this absurd, unscriptural, and dangerous assumption of ministerial veto power, — a power, which, if admitted by the churches, would at once destrcy them as independent, Congregational bodies, authorized to transact all church business.

INDEX.

A.

C.

E.

F.

G.

H.

L.

M.

P.

R.

T.

U.

V.

W.

THE

CONGREGATIONAL BOARD

OF

PUBLICATION.

The general Depository of the Congregational Board of Publication is kept at No 16 Tremont Temple.

BOOKS AND TRACTS PUBLISHED BY THE BOARD.

THE WORKS OF JOSEPH BELLAMY, D. D.

Two Volumes, Octavo. Price, $3.50.

Dr. Bellamy was one of the most distinguished writers of the last age. He is discriminating, and will aid his readers in detecting error, in understanding the pure doctrines of the gospel, and in directing inquirers in the way of life. His works are eminently doctrinal, and eminently practical. They are such as we would commend especially to students for the ministry, and also to ministers and members of the churches, for a careful perusal. The issue of this edition of Bellamy's Works will be regarded as a valuable service to the interests of theological literature in our country. — *Christian Observer, Philadelphia.*

There is a grandeur in the simplicity, spirituality, and deep earnestness of Bellamy. His theology is full of the glow and unction of practical religion. He reasons to convince and convert men, and every form of thought and reason becomes subordinate to the great end of enforcing the truth that saves. We hardly know of a work, since some of Baxter's, more searching in its spiritual analysis, and more powerful in the application of truth, than the True Religion Delineated. We are very glad to see it, and the other works of its pious and able author, presented in an attractive form, and at a cheap rate. If the Congregational Board shall go on as they have begun, they will not only deserve, but attain success, and lay the church under deep obligation. — *New York Evangelist.*

THE WORKS OF JONATHAN EDWARDS, D. D.

Two Volumes, Octavo. Price, $3.

Dr. Edwards was a very acute and able writer, who will be honored in succeeding ages for having given so much of its present excellency to the New England theology.

Besides the intrinsic value of the works of the younger Edwards, they are an almost indispensable part of a minister's library, for the light they throw upon the obscure and abstruse portions of the works of his father. — *New York Observer.*

THE WORKS OF JOHN ROBINSON,

Pastor of the Pilgrim Fathers. With a Memoir, and Annotations, by Rev. Robert Ashton, Secretary of the Congregational Board, London. Three Volumes. Price, $3.50.

John Robinson was privileged to have opened the head-springs of New England character. Aside from the intrinsic value of this book, as a book, it deserves a place in the family library of every true son of the Pilgrims. Robinson is in such a sense the father of us all, that we do honor to ourselves by cherishing his memory, and using his printed pages to impress it upon the rising generation. But this book asks not a place in our libraries merely as a relic or memento of departed greatness. It has intrinsic value. It is pervaded by living thought. Robinson, though an exile from his native country, and the pastor of a poor flock of exiles, had vast mental resources, and with all his disadvantages, won his way to the highest estimation in the University of Leyden. He stood in the first rank among theologians of that age. And one has to read only a few pages of his writings, to feel himself under the instruction of a master mind. — *Puritan Recorder.*

THE WORKS OF SAMUEL HOPKINS, D. D.

Three Volumes, Octavo. Price, $5.

This is the first complete edition of Dr. Hopkins's works. They must have an enduring interest, not merely on account of the high intellectual merit which they may justly claim, and the spirit of earnest piety by which they are pervaded, but as making an epoch in the history of theological opinion, at least in this country. There are few men who lived in this country during the same period whose history possesses so varied an interest as that of this distinguished man. He becomes legitimately incorporated with the ecclesiastical history of his country and age. He was one of the greatest philanthropists of his day. The first volume contains an original memoir of the author, by Professor Park, which is remarkably complete, interesting, and instructive. Nobody can doubt that Hopkins was at once a profound reasoner and an eminent Christian; and he stood before the world, through a long life, as one of the lights of his generation.

In speaking of the reproduction of the writings of the eminent men of former times, and of having their scattered productions brought together and sent out on a new mission of usefulness, the Recorder adds, — In this labor of love for posterity, the Congregational Board of Publication is taking a large share. It is only a short time since they gave us a fine edition of the works of the immortal Robinson, and at a little earlier period they published an equally good edition of Bellamy, who to this day must be reckoned a prince among New England preachers; and now they have rendered another important service to our Christian and theological literature, by giving us, in three large volumes, the works of Dr. Samuel Hopkins — volumes well worthy the society's publications. — *Puritan Recorder.*

The Memoir of Hopkins, by Professor Park, is a work of deep interest and great value. It is a perfect key to Hopkins as a man, a Christian, a divine, a pastor, and a reformer. We cannot here attempt a critique upon Hopkins's works. We will only say, that without them, no man can understand the theological history of New England; and that after the works of Edwards himself, no more important gift has been made to the churches of New England than these volumes of Hopkins. — *Congregationalist.*

We congratulate the theological public that the Congregational Board of Publication have commenced the republication of such standard books. Our national honor demands this enterprise. We have no right, as good patriots, to allow the productions of our divines to lie, some of them unpublished, some of them forgotten. They are valuable in their intrinsic character. They are useful as developing the history of theological opinion. They will instruct and gratify many private Christians, while they task the energies of clergymen and scholars.— *Bibliotheca Sacra.*

MEMOIR OF ASAHEL NETTLETON, D. D.

By Bennet Tyler, D. D. 12mo. Price, 60 cents.

Dr. Nettleton is too well known to need any commendation. Very few men have ever lived who have been the honored instruments of turning so many souls from darkness to light, and from the power of Satan unto God. This is a very faithful and instructive memoir of this uncommon man, and would be a very valuable book in every family.

A COMPENDIUM OF THE SYSTEM OF DIVINE TRUTH.

By Jacob Catlin, D. D. 12mo. Price, 60 cents.

This is a series of brief and connected essays on the various topics of theology. It is well adapted for Bible classes, and adult classes in Sabbath schools, and will be found particularly valuable to all families and individuals who cannot find time to read more extended discussions.

INSPIRATION OF THE SCRIPTURES.

By Robert Haldane, Esq., of Scotland. 18mo. Price, 25 cents.

A timely and important subject for this day of abounding scepticism and unbelief. From the importance of the subject, and the clearness with which it is treated, it possesses much value.

THE GOSPEL WORTHY OF ALL ACCEPTATION.

Or, The Duty of Sinners to believe in Jesus Christ. By Andrew Fuller. 18mo. Price, 20 cents.

The name of the writer, who was decidedly the best English theologian of his day, is a sufficient guaranty for this excellent little volume.

THE SCRIPTURE DOCTRINE OF REGENERATION.

By Charles Backus, D. D. 18mo. Price, 20 cents.

This is a brief and clear view of the doctrine under the following heads: 1. Nature of Regeneration. 2. Necessity of Regeneration. 3. Agency of the Holy Spirit in Regeneration. 4. Character of the Regenerate.

THE DOCTRINE OF ELECTION.

By Gardiner Spring, D. D.; and The Doctrine of the Perseverance of the Saints. By Bennet Tyler, D. D. 18mo. Price, 20 cents.

A most clear, scriptural, and convincing statement and defence of these important doctrines.

THE WORKS OF THOMAS SHEPARD,

Pastor of the First Church in Cambridge, with a Memoir. By J. A. Albro, D. D. Three Volumes. Price, $3.

A more rich and valuable contribution to the cause of evangelical truth and godliness has rarely, if ever, been made by the labors of man. Shepard was taught of the Spirit; he lived habitually at the foot of the throne.

It is a service of inappreciable value which the Congregational Board is rendering to the church and the world by the collection and republication of this and kindred works of the American fathers, in a style of neatness and elegance unsurpassed, and at a cost so reasonable that those of small means may without difficulty possess them. — *Congregationalist.*

These works have at once a doctrinal, practical, and experimental character. Though they are characterized by great simplicity and directness, there is in them a commanding power, and richness, and depth of thought, which could have been the product only of an extraordinary mind. But what seems to us their most striking feature, is the earnest and effective manner in which they expose a delusive experience, and the facility with which they probe the very depths of the heart. The exposition of the parable of the ten virgins, particularly, seems like a perpetual stream of light directed straight to the hypocrite's conscience. — *Puritan Recorder.*

DISTINGUISHING TRAITS OF RELIGIOUS CHARACTER.

By Gardiner Spring, D. D. Price, 50 cents.

This is a book of uncommon discrimination and excellence. It clearly distinguishes that hope which is as an anchor to the soul from that which is only as the spider's web. It should be read by every Christian, and especially by every young convert.

PARK STREET LECTURES.

By E. D. Griffin, D. D. Price, 60 cents.

This is a work of great merit. It is enough to say that it is one of Dr. Griffin's happiest efforts.

THE WORKS OF LEONARD WOODS, D. D.

Five Volumes.

These works are too well known to need any commendation.

SCOTT'S FORCE OF TRUTH.

Price, 30 cents.

This is a handsome edition of this very instructive and interesting narrative. Appended are John Newton's Letters to Dr. Scott, which were among the means which led to his conversion. This little volume should have a place in every family.

THE FAITHFUL STEWARD.

By Rev. S. D. Clarke. Price, 20 cents.

A Prize Essay. Discriminating, able, and faithful.

NEW ENGLAND'S MEMORIAL,

With Governor Bradford's History, and an Appendix containing the views of the Pilgrims and early settlers on the subject of Church Polity. Price, $2.

This volume contains the most reliable and interesting history of the Pilgrims from the time of their first organization in England to the year 1690. With great care and labor, new Notes have been collected from Bradford, Prince, Hutchinson, and others, and a long Appendix of great value has been added, making this edition more valuable than those that have preceded it. So much is now said, and justly said, of the Pilgrims and their influence upon New England character and institutions, that this edition of this valuable work, so long out of print, is well timed. It should be read and studied by all the descendants of the Pilgrims, that their origin and ancestors may be known and appreciated. Children and youth should read this volume. Nobody in New England, or out of New England, should be ignorant of the principles and character of the men who laid the foundations of all our good institutions.

THE LIFE AND TIMES OF JOHN PENRY,

Martyr of Southwark. By John Waddington. Price, 60 cents.

"In this volume, new light is thrown upon the primal movements of the Nonconformists of England, by the documents which the singular industry of Mr. Waddington has brought to light Penry, it seems, was the actual originator of the migration of the Pilgrim Fathers — a measure from which such important and world-wide results to liberty and religion have followed. It is earnestly hoped that the publication of such a Memoir, written with such simplicity, elegance, and brevity, will do not a little to vindicate the early Puritans from much of the obloquy thrown upon them by prejudiced or ignorant historians, and to exhibit the force, greatness, and worth of those principles for which they cheerfully suffered, many of them even unto death."

PRIMITIVE PIETY REVIVED,

Or, the Aggressive Power of the Christian Church; a premium Essay. By Henry C. Fish, Newark, N. J. Price, 50 cents.

This is a premium essay. The subject assigned was, The better exemplification of the doctrines of the Bible in Christian life, with a view to the conversion of sinners to Christ. It is eminently fitted to do a good work in reviving Christians, in bringing them back to a state of primitive, apostolic piety. It is truly a book for the times, and should be read by every minister and every professor of religion. It cannot be read without profit. It has in a few weeks passed to its fourth edition of 2000 copies each.

LIFE AND LETTERS OF REV. DANIEL TEMPLE,

For twenty-three years a Missionary of the American Board in Western Asia. By his son, Rev. Daniel H. Temple; with an Introductory Notice, by Rev. R. S. Storrs, D. D. Price, $1.

It is chiefly letters of this godly man and missionary, containing many happy illustrations of passages of Scripture and interesting incidents in missionary life.

THE CAMBRIDGE PLATFORM OF CHURCH DISCIPLINE,

Adopted in 1648, and the Confession of Faith adopted in 1680; to which is prefixed a Platform of Ecclesiastical Government, by Nathaniel Emmons, D. D. Price, 30 cents.

MEMOIR OF DR. HOPKINS.

By Professor Park. Price, 80 cents.

See notice under Hopkins's works.

A TREATISE ON THE MILLENNIUM.

By Dr. S. Hopkins. Price, 25 cents.

This is a scriptural and interesting view of this important subject, and well adapted to meet and confute the errors of many at this time.

A DIALOGUE, AND OTHER ARTICLES ON SLAVERY.

By Dr. Hopkins. Price, 12½ cents.

This is an able, scriptural, and common-sense view of the subject, exceedingly well timed, and all the more valuable for having been written during the last century. Its historical relations, as connected with the great men of the revolution, are interesting.

PARABLE OF THE VIRGINS.

By Rev. Thomas Shepard. Price, $1.

The admirable work to which President Edwards so often refers.

A PRACTICAL TREATISE ON PRAYER.

By Rev. Thomas Cobbett, Pastor of the Church in Lynn.

Mr. Cobbett was distinguished for his "rich experience in prayer." Cotton Mather passes high encomiums on him, and especially on this book. He says, that of all the books written by Cobbett, none deserves more to be read by the world, and to live till the general burning of the world, than that on prayer. He was himself eminently a man of prayer. "His thoughts come out, all warm and glowing, from a heart deeply moved by the Spirit of God." A recent writer says, "This book ought to be republished and placed in every Christian family."

PRACTICAL EVANGELISM,

Or, Bible Christianity enforced. By Rev. William M. Cheever, Terre Haute, Indiana.

This essay shows with great clearness and force the duty of Christians to come up to a higher standard of devotion to Christ, and to give themselves more unreservedly and unremittingly to the promotion of his kingdom. It is like "Primitive Piety Revived," a book for the times, greatly needed, and should be universally read.

HISTORICAL TEXT BOOK AND ATLAS OF BIBLICAL GEOGRAPHY.

By Lyman Coleman, D. D.

This is a work of laborious and extended research by its learned author. As the preface says, "It is the result of an humble effort and earnest desire to associate together the history and geography of the Scriptures, and to allure the young, and assist them in an interested and intelligent perusal of the Book of God. The subject of this book undeniably ought to have a place, not only in the Bible class and Sunday school, but in the primary and grammar school, the college and the theological seminary. By means of the chronological table, and general index, this book offers the advantages of a gazetteer for occasional reference, as well as of a manual for the consecutive reading and study of the Bible."

THE BOOK OF PSALMS.

Metrically arranged. Price, 25 cents.

THE NEW ENGLAND PRIMER.

Price, 4 cents.

A fac-simile of the original work, which, in former days, wrought such influence in the formation of New England character.

TWO VOLUMES OF TRACTS.

12mo. Price, $1. Or separately, forty-five Tracts, on the following subjects: —

No.	Subject	*Pages.*
No. 1.	Doctrinal Knowledge, the Foundation of Religion,	16
2.	Mankind utterly Depraved,	12
3.	Covenant of Redemption,	16
4.	Slanderous Reports refuted,	16
5.	Objections to Prayer Answered,	4
6.	Perseverance of the Saints,	28
7.	Decrees of God Consistent with Free Agency,	16
8.	Doctrine of Election,	28
9.	Purifying Influence of the Christian Hope,	16
10.	Personality and Offices of the Holy Spirit,	16
11.	Things Secret and Things Revealed,	16
12.	Disappointment in the Last Day,	16
13.	Nature and Influence of Faith,	24
14.	Plea of Sinners against Endless Punishment,	20
15.	Sinners Wilful and Perverse,	16
16.	Love Thyself and thy Neighbor,	16
17.	The Prayer of Faith,	16
18.	All for the Best,	16
19.	Renewal of Sinners the Work of Divine Power,	32
20.	The Bible the only sure Test of Religious Character,	20
21.	Duties of Parents,	24
22.	The Immutability of God,	16
23.	Necessity of the Holy Spirit to give Efficacy to Preaching,	16
24.	The Duty of Professing Religion,	20
25.	Importance of Believing the Truth,	16
26.	Man's Inability to Comply with the Gospel,	52
27.	Man's Activity and Dependence,	20

		Pages.
28.	Doctrine of the Trinity,	20
29.	Sovereignty of God in the Exercise of Mercy,	16
30.	Mode of Baptism,	28
31.	God glorified in the Work of Redemption,	16
32.	Importance of Scriptural Views of the Character, Offices, and Works of the Holy Spirit,	16
33.	Receiving the Atonement Necessary,	20
34.	Nature of Submission to God,	12
35.	Infant Baptism,	48
36.	Nature and Design of Infant Baptism,	16
37.	Close Communion,	20
38.	Prayer for the Holy Spirit,	20
39.	The Duty of Young Children,	36
40.	Rotation in the Pastoral Relation,	20
41.	The Divine Law,	20
42.	Future Judgment in Opposition to the Opinions of Universalists,	24
43.	Justice of God Displayed in the Endless Punishment of the Wicked,	28
44.	Doctrine of Divine Providence,	16
45.	Assurance of Hope,	16
46.	Scriptural Platform of Church Government,	24
	Amount,	936

FORM OF BEQUEST TO THE SOCIETY.

I give and bequeath to the Treasurer, for the time being, of the CONGREGATIONAL BOARD OF PUBLICATION, incorporated by the Legislature of Massachusetts in March A. D. 1850, with the name Doctrinal Tract and Book Society, which was changed in 1854 to the Congregational Board of Publication, the sum of
dollars for the purposes of said Society, and for which the receipt of said Treasurer shall be a sufficient discharge.

CORRESPONDENCE.

All communications relative to the concerns of the society, or the means of extending its usefulness, should be addressed to Rev. SEWALL HARDING, Secretary of the Congregational Board of Publication, No. 16 Tremont Temple.

www.ingramcontent.com/pod-product-compliance
Lightning Source LLC
LaVergne TN
LVHW020115110826
845151LV00001B/165

* 9 7 8 1 4 2 5 5 4 2 8 5 6 *